PRAISE FOR TH

"Vasilios' book *Ars Vercanus: Advanced Mag*
and detailed examination of magick by a master describing many sound
magickal principles and concepts. Well worth reading."
~ *Kerr Cuhulain, Kerr Cuhulain, award winning author of Magickal Self Defense,
Wiccan Warrior, and Full Contact Magick.*

"Ars Vercanus is a masterful work on an ephemeral subject. It clearly conveys
profound mystic and occult concepts in an easy-to-use, thoroughly accessible
format. Rediscover ancient wisdom with a modern, practical focus."
~ *Nancy Black, Astrologer and Columnist, Linda Black Horoscopes
(Chicago Tribune)*

"Vasilios Wennergren has produced a truly scholarly work in aggregating a
great variety of magickal technologies and techniques available across the
multi-cultural spectrum, world-wide. His work is presented in a user-friendly
format, accompanied by the ethereal and intuitively creative symbolic illustrations of Lynn Wennergren, magickal in their own way."
~ *Ness S. Carroll, PhD, Author, and President of The International University, School
Of Universal Learning*

ARS VERCANUS

ARS VERCANUS
ADVANCED MAGICKAL TECHNIQUES

Written and illustrated by
Vasilios Wennergren & Lynn Wennergren

Megalithica Books
Stafford England

Cover design, illustrations and layout: Vasilios Wennergren & Lynn Wennergren
Credit:
> *Alchemical Engraving, page 27, Photos.com/ThinkstockPhotos/GettyImages*
> *Talismanic Hand, page 152, Illustrated by V. & L. Wennergren, hand by Sergey Kandakov/Shutterstock*
> *Mandrake, page 338, ivan-96/iStockPhotos/GettyImages*

> *Photo of Lynn Wennergren by Isaac Hernandez*

Set in Adobe Caslon Pro and Minion Pro.

MB0171

ISBN 978-1-905713-97-4

A Megalithica Books Publication
An imprint of Immanion Press

info@immanion-press.com
www.immanion-press.com

Contents

Contents

Contents

Contents

Contents

Contents

Contents

Contents

Contents

List of Illustrations

List of Illustrations

Chapter 1

THE MAGICKAL PARADIGM

For as long as humanity has existed, there have been those skilled in the occult arts. Such individuals are capable of transforming the self, perceiving the subtle aspect of existence, and affecting reality via nonphysical means. In every culture, across every era, shamans, magi, mystics, and seers have refined their arts. This has produced a rich and varied collection of magickal techniques and rituals. While not always in the forefront, magick has been and remains a vital force in the world's mystic, philosophical and spiritual traditions. In the West, this ubiquitous undercurrent of magick may be found in the Greek Magical Papyri, Neoplatonic theurgy, goetia, and the various magico-religious practices of pagan Europe. In the East, it exists within magical traditions such as Tantra, Tibetan Bon, and magickal Taoism. Cross-culturally, magick is prominent within the ritual and shamanic practices of indigenous peoples and syncretic traditions such as Hoodoo. Core techniques distilled from the rich corpus of cross-cultural mystic and magickal practices form the foundation of Vercanus Magick. These powerful techniques have been combined into an eclectic, modular system. While drawing from traditional sources, Vercanus techniques are adapted for pragmatic use in the modern era.

The theories of Vercanus Magick impart a comprehensive understanding of how magick actually works. Vercanus techniques clearly delineate methods by which magick may be effectively performed. This style of magick entails a profound shifting of consciousness, facilitating an enhanced perception of reality. Through this expanded consciousness the practitioner perceives the deeper aspects of reality. It is at this numinous level of existence that magick occurs. The techniques of Vercanus Magick involve the mastering of consciousness and internal energies. Through regular training, this mastery induces a profound transformation in the magus. Thus transformed, the magus is capable of shaping reality at this deeper level.

1

Magick Defined

*Magick is the art of perceiving and affecting reality
at the subtle etheric level of existence.*

*The term magus refers to one who transforms the self
via esoteric disciplines, and uses the resulting abilities
to perceive and affect reality at the etheric level.*

Magick is the highest art. It is a quest for knowledge, power, and transformation. Through magick one may re-create the self, shift reality, and move beyond the reach of death. Practitioners of this great art are part of a rich and ancient tradition of those seeking to access unseen forces and explore the mysteries of existence. This path entails a complete transformation of the spirit. Such transformation shifts the awareness, facilitating perception of the subtle aspect of existence and unification with a larger ecology of consciousness and energy. Through this perception and unification, the practitioner may powerfully shift existence at the subtle etheric level to effect change at the material level.

The Etheric Aspect of Reality

The ultimate nature of reality has been explored within the mystic and philosophical traditions of various cultures. This ultimate reality has been described in various ways and by many names such as Brahman, ParamaShiva, the Tao, and the One. In attaining states of inner stillness and expanded awareness the magus may achieve a deeper more comprehensive understanding of the nature of reality in its entirety. Existence may be described as energy/consciousness in various states of being, a single continuum manifesting a spectrum of spirit to matter. This universal energy/consciousness manifests the material universe from itself. Material reality is the dense, physical aspect of existence. Etheric reality is the subtle, energetic aspect of existence. These realities are two sides of a single, nondual continuum. The dense corporeal aspects of this continuum manifest as the material world while the subtle etheric aspects are immanent within yet exist beyond material reality. Though unified, each aspect exists in a different state of being, distinct, yet part of a nondualistic whole. In shifting the consciousness through this continuum of matter to spirit the magus becomes aware of new realities. The scope of the continuum perceived is dependent upon the state of the observer's awareness. Reality extends far beyond that which is perceived by the physical senses. For ages, mystics, shamans and seers have described a "spirit world", an ethereal side of existence that typically goes unseen. During ordinary states of consciousness, humans perceive only a portion of reality. Ordinary awareness creates the illusion that the material aspect is all that exists. Expanded states of consciousness provide a deeper, more holistic perspective. As the etheric and material aspects of the continuum exist in different states of being, reality at the subtle etheric levels of the continuum behaves differently than at the familiar material level. At the subtle levels of existence, time, space, and causality are governed by non-physical mechanisms. As such, action at this level is not limited by the causal, spatial, temporal, or physical constraints of material existence. It is at this subtle level of existence that magickal, spiritual, and paranormal phenomena occur.

The continuum of existence is described differently by various esoteric systems. Within certain systems the subtle densities of the continuum are divided and named separately, such as the etheric plane, astral plane, mental plane, etc. These ethereal variations in density are not divided by hard borders. They are various gradations of the collective spirit world, each a phase within a spectrum. This lessens the significance of distinction as it pertains to the art of magick. As such, in the context of Vercanus, the term "etheric" refers to the entirety of nonphysical, energetic existence.

ETHERIC PHENOMENA

Magick entails skillfully affecting reality at the etheric level. The following etheric phenomena are of particular importance to the art of magick.

Pneuma / Subtle Energy

The continuum of existence may be described as a spectrum from subtle, ethereal phenomena to dense, material manifestations. Reality at the etheric level consists entirely of a numinous, subtle energy. This subtle element has been pondered by philosophers and mystics for millennia. It has been known by many names including Chi, Prana, Aether, and Pneuma. This ever present pneuma exists in various forms from vast energetic fields and currents to complex etheric patterns.

Pneuma may flow as a fluid, tactile force or emanate as a radiant, expansive energy. This subtle pneuma should not be confused with the familiar energy of physics. In the context of physics, energy refers to quantifiable, predictable phenomena such as electricity or heat. By contrast pneuma is an ethereal, subtle medium. This subtle energy interacts with and affects material phenomena, yet exists in a state of being outside the boundaries of material reality (See Etheric Convergence). Pneuma is a fundamental tool of magick. Three types of pneuma are of particular importance to the art of magick. Cognitive pneuma is the etheric energy of thought, awareness, and information. Emotive pneuma is the energetic essence of the various emotive states. Raw pneuma is undifferentiated, primal etheric energy. The subtle energetic nature of etheric reality is extremely sensitive to consciousness, emotion, and etheric energy. Through training, transformation and ritual the magus gains the ability to generate and summon these etheric energies in abnormally potent, large amounts. Through the magickal techniques these energies are merged together to create pneuma capable of directly affecting change at the etheric level. The magus uses this powerful blend of consciousness, emotion, and raw energy to alter reality at the etheric level in accordance with the magickal goal. The ancient Greeks spoke of such potent pneuma as Pyr Technikon or "creative fire". This pneuma technikon created during magickal acts is an extension of the self, a life-force that embodies the intention of the working.

The externalization of consciousness and energy is a feature of various magickal traditions, an example being found within the occult practices of Tibet. In such practices, powerful energy work and meditative states are employed to externalize consciousness and energy towards the creation of tulpas (thoughtforms), the vivification of ritual items such as phurbas (ritual daggers) and to effect change at a distance by etheric means.

Universal Etheric Field

The subtle etheric aspect of existence permeates, yet exists beyond material reality. It is an imminent life force connecting all things at the etheric level via a ubiquitous field of subtle energy. This ambient sea of pneuma forms vast patterns of energy and consciousness, unifying existence as a collective whole. All phenomena emanate etheric energies. As such, the consciousness, emotion, and energy of all things emanate into and become part of this Universal Etheric Field. All phenomena are part of and in direct contact with this ever present field of consciousness and energy. This creates an environment in which all things are affected by and connected to each other. This connection underlies many magickal processes. Awareness of this ever-present subtle medium/consciousness is reflected in the philosophical and mystic traditions of various cultures. Within ancient Greek philosophy terms such as pneuma and pyr technikon were used to describe a universal life force that permeates, interconnects, and shapes existence. Within Hindu Mysticism the terms Brahman and ParamaShiva describe an ever present unifying energy/consciousness as the immanent yet transcendent reality. Taoism speaks of a unifying principle or essence underlying the functioning of the universe, a Great Oneness that pervades and connects all things. Expanded states of consciousness confer the perception of the cosmos as a multifaceted monad tangibly unified by an imminent, ever present life force. Through such expanded states the magus may merge the spirit into union with the root of being to become one with existence in its entirety.

Etheric Entities

Etheric entities are infinite in type and number. They range from simple spirits, with animal level sentience, to deities of vast consciousness and power. Etheric entities are comprised of different types of pneuma. Those consisting of harmful or destructive energy are typically perceived as malevolent or evil. Beings comprised of beneficent or harmonious energy may be perceived as good. These entities have interacted with humanity throughout time. They are the gods, spirits, ghosts, fairies and demons of folklore. Magi have traditionally fostered relationships with these beings as magickal partners and teachers.

Etheric Environments

Natural variations in energetic tone, pattern, and complexity within the Universal Etheric Field result in vast tapestries of unique etheric environments throughout existence. Such etheric environments are rich ecosystems comprised of etheric beings, energies, form, and phenomena diverse in complexity. Etheric environments may be merged with the local material environment, or exist independently of material reality. When merged with a material environment, etheric environments include the etheric aspect of material surroundings as well as purely etheric phenomena. An example would be the etheric aspects of trees, animals, and humans existing together in an environment with etheric energy currents, power spots (naturally occurring upwellings or concentrations of etheric energy), and etheric entities. These etheric environments surround us and affect our daily lives. They range from commonplace etheric surroundings to the sacred spots, forest shrines, and holy mountains venerated by various cultures. Interacting with such environments is fundamental to the art of magick. In shifting perception to the etheric aspect of existence the magus becomes aware of the rich etheric environments that surround our daily lives. Such environments are present throughout the etheric aspect of reality and extend far beyond the immediate etheric surroundings. The Universal Etheric Field permeates, surrounds, and extends beyond material reality. As such, these etheric environments may be encountered above, below, within, or entirely beyond the material aspect of reality. Such environments are the Upper-Worlds, Lower-Worlds, Heavens, Hells, abodes of the Gods, higher realms of existence, etc. described in the religion, mysticism, and mythology of various cultures. The magus accesses and explores these etheric realms to obtain insight, acquire information, gather power, and forge relationships with beings residing therein. Certain environments may act as a gathering point for energy and entities possessing a similar energetic tone. The action of resonance / dissonance naturally draws these similar energies and entities together into complex collectives within the Universal Etheric Field. Such environments may be centered around a powerful deity, energy current, power spot, or energetic field.

Etheric environments, like all etheric phenomena, have a very real effect upon the material world. Shifts in etheric environments cause change to occur in material environments. These shifts may be caused by the actions of energy currents, power spots, or entities within the environment. Over time magi have developed methods for accessing and living in balance with etheric environments. Feng Shui, for example, is a Chinese art form involving the manipulation of etheric environments to protect and benefit the human inhabitants of a specific region. Another example may be found in the cross-cultural practice of leaving offerings to nature spirits at shrines and sacred sites.

THE ETHERIC ASPECT OF THE SELF

Understanding and mastering the etheric aspect of the self is integral to the art of magick. The subtle, energetic aspect of the body is often referred to as the "spirit", "energy body", "subtle body", or "spirit body". This etheric aspect is a complex system that works in unison with the material systems of the body. The etheric body is comprised of several etheric systems and structures, just as the material body is comprised of organs and flesh. The etheric components of primary interest to the magus include etheric centers, energy channels, and the etheric form.

Energy Channels

Streams of energy flow through established pathways within the etheric body. This system of energy channels interconnects the various components of the body. These channels are known as Jing Luo within Taoist mysticism and nadis within Hindu mysticism. All aspects of the body are nourished and sustained by this complex network of channels. The major channels circulate the body's core energies through the major etheric centers. Major channels also conduct core energy through the arms, legs, and to various regions within the body. Minor channels branch out from the major channels to form a complex web of energy throughout the body. The largest quantity of the body's energy flow circulates through the major channels. It's important to note that the major channels are not the thin veins and connected dots depicted two dimensionally in traditional acupuncture or medical diagrams, but are robust, larger streams of living energy flowing through the body's core. Such diagrams typically illustrate surface channels and access points associated with the deeper flow of internal core energies. The major channels focused upon during the circulation of energy vary based upon tradition. Taoist mysticism places greater emphasis upon a circuit consisting of a dorsal/spinal channel moving up the back of the body, and a ventral channel moving down the front of the body. Hindu mysticism primarily focuses upon a dorsal/spinal channel intertwined by two lateral channels. Mastering the flow of energy through the etheric body is essential to the practice of magick.

The Etheric Centers

The etheric centers are dynamic energy fields that exist at energetic nexus points within the etheric body. These spheroid fields of circulating energy emanate from the dorsal channel and manifest along the body's vertical axis. The centers are connected to the flow of internal energy via the body's network of etheric channels. They serve to generate, emit, receive, store, refine, and perceive various types of energy, emotion, and consciousness. Moving internal energy into these fields alters consciousness as the centers expand and increase in energetic intensity. Within Hindu mysticism these centers are known as the Chakras. Such chakras are poetically described and artistically depicted in Hindu literature and art as lotuses blooming out from the dorsal channel. Taoism and the internal martial arts refer to the centers as the upper, middle, and lower Tan Tiens or Elixir Fields. Various traditions describe three to seven major etheric centers within the body's energetic system. These major centers are situated along the body's central axis at the perineum, genitals, navel, chest, throat, head, and crown. The centers located at the head, chest and navel are of particular importance to the art of magick. These centers of Mind, Emotion, and Power are capable of generating the potent thoughts, emotions, and energies essential to magickal operations. Awakening and expanding these centers facilitates the altered states of consciousness and perception used in magick. In addition to the major etheric centers, there exist a great number of minor etheric centers in various locations throughout the body. The minor etheric centers in the palms, fingertips, and soles of the feet are of particular importance to the art of magick as these centers are frequently accessed to draw in and project energies.

The Center of Power is located just below the navel. It is described as an important power center within Taoist, Hindu, and Tibetan mysticism. Taoists refer to this center as the Lower Tan Tien, in Hindu mysticism this center is referred to as the Manipura Chakra. Within Tibetan practice this center is referred to as the Nirmana Chakra. The navel center is a powerful storehouse of core internal energies. This center plays a vital role in the generation, refining, and cultivation of internal and external energies. In accessing the Center of Power the magus may tap into core internal energies and generate the large amounts of raw pneuma necessary to power magickal acts. In its perceptive function, the Center of Power senses the energetic intensity of surrounding phenomena. This frequently accessed center is integral to magickal power.

The Center of Emotion is located within the chest. Taoist mysticism refers to this center as the Middle Tan Tien, within Hindu mysticism it is referred to as the Anahata Chakra. In its perceptive function, it allows the magus to discern the emotive tone of specific energies. In its generative function, this center is capable of producing the pneuma of emotion. This energy lends the emotive component to the magickal operation.

Located within the head at brow level, the Center of Mind is a focal point of consciousness, governing cognition and etheric vision. Taoist mysticism refers to this center as the Upper Tan Tien, within Hindu mysticism it is referred to as the Ajna Chakra. In the context of magick, the Center of Mind primarily serves to direct energies, perceive external consciousness and confer etheric sight. In its perceptive capacity, this center is the focal point of etheric vision. Functioning as the etheric organ of sight, this center perceives etheric emanations and interprets them visually. As such, this center is referred to as the "Third Eye" in various traditions. When transitioning into a receptive state, the Center of Mind is capable of directly perceiving external emanations of consciousness from other individuals, entities, and the larger universal collective. In its generative function, this center produces the pneuma of consciousness, which lends the cognitive component to magickal acts.

Energy may be emitted from the etheric centers to directly affect reality at the etheric level. Such energy is typically emitted from the etheric centers in the palms and fingertips. This practice is fundamental to many magickal operations. The ancient Chinese art of Chi Gong refers to such emitted energy as Wai Chi. During acts of magick, pneuma may be emitted as currents of energy, waves of force, radiant energy, or streams of energy. When emitted as streams, this projected pneuma functions as an extension of the etheric body. These streams of living energy serve as the etheric appendages of the magus. Such extended energies may be used to carry out a variety of practical functions. Extended energy streams are used to directly manipulate etheric phenomena, transfer energy, and enhance perception.

The Etheric Form
The etheric form is an energetic matrix of varying densities that constitutes the fundamental structure of the etheric body. The innermost layers of the etheric form typically conform to the shape of the material body, while the outer layers tend to be elliptical in shape. In normal states of being the innermost layers mirror the material body and extend up to several inches beyond it. The outermost, elliptical layers extend just beyond an outstretched arm. Certain esoteric systems divide and name the various layers of the etheric form separately, such as the etheric body, astral body, mental body, etc. These subtle layers function together as a unified whole. This lessens the significance of distinction as it pertains to the art of magick. The etheric form is often the subject of esoteric techniques and practices. It acts as a natural barrier to harmful etheric energies. Magickal techniques may be used to strengthen the form and enhance its protective qualities. Additionally, the polymorphic nature of the etheric form facilitates the practice of shape shifting.

Basic Diagram of the Etheric Body

The etheric body is perceived subjectively via the etheric centers, as such each individual clairvoyant will have a slightly different perception of the body's fundamental etheric structures. Additionally, the etheric body is protean in nature and to a degree, varies in form per each individual's state of being, development, and health. As such, the description of the etheric body varies among and within traditions such as Taoist, Hindu, and Tibetan mysticism, the basic description of the fundamental features however, is similar. The following diagrams are basic illustrations of the etheric form, the major etheric centers, and channels. A full understanding of the etheric body can only be obtained via clairvoyance and direct experience of the etheric self.

Layers of the Etheric Form

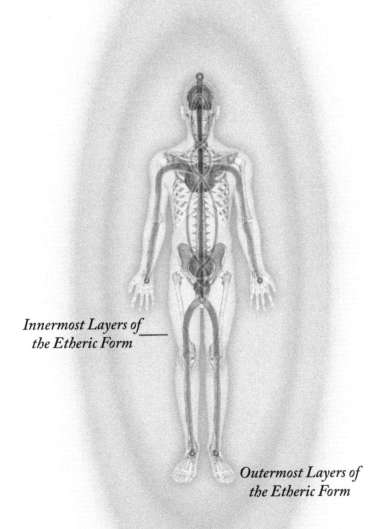

Innermost Layers of the Etheric Form

Outermost Layers of the Etheric Form

Basic Diagram of the Etheric Body
Front View

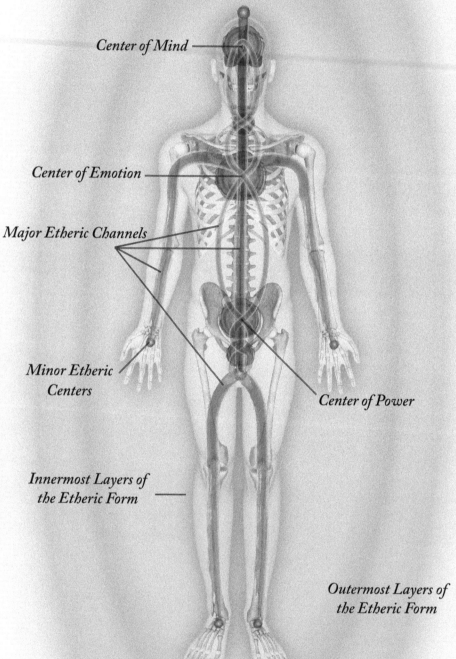

Center of Mind

Center of Emotion

Major Etheric Channels

Minor Etheric
Centers

Center of Power

Innermost Layers of
the Etheric Form

Outermost Layers of
the Etheric Form

Basic Diagram of the Etheric Body
Side View

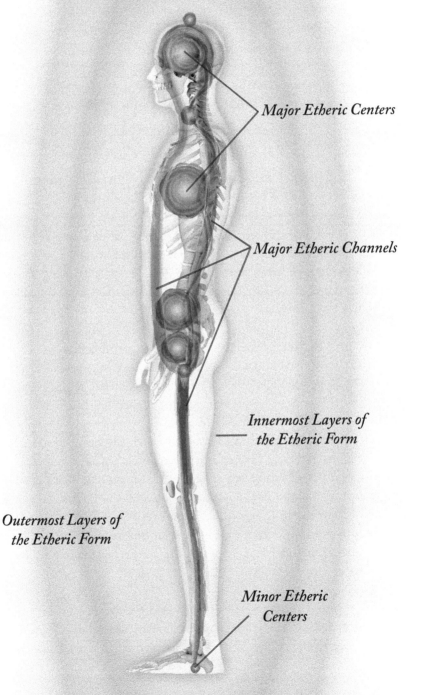

Major Etheric Centers

Major Etheric Channels

Innermost Layers of the Etheric Form

Outermost Layers of the Etheric Form

Minor Etheric Centers

The Etheric Aspect of Material Phenomena

Magick is often directed at the etheric aspect of material subjects. It is at the etheric level that material phenomena may be altered via the art of magick (see Etheric Convergence). Perception and understanding of a subject's etheric aspect is essential to effectively alter its material aspect.

FUNDAMENTAL PROPERTIES OF ETHERIC REALITY

Etheric Reality is not Subject to Physical Laws

Not subject to physical laws, etheric reality is unfettered by the limitations of material reality. The traditional understanding of space, time and concepts of causality must be entirely reinterpreted as they behave differently at the etheric level. Additionally, physical limitations presented by solid matter, gravity, weight, size, etc. are not an obstacle at the etheric level. This lack of conformity to physical laws allows the magus to achieve goals that would appear impossible by ordinary standards.

Etheric Reality and Temporal Ambiguity

Ordinary states of consciousness provide a limited perception of existence. As such, the perception of time itself is typically quite limited. Through expanded states of consciousness the magus may perceive time at the subtle etheric level. Time is the expansion of existence in an eternal state of becoming. The subtle aspects of existence extend further into the time stream than do denser aspects. This temporal extension facilitates the perception of potential futures. Events from the past leave an etheric trace. These traces may last indefinitely. Expanded consciousness may provide simultaneous perception of the past, present and future. Thus, phenomena perceived at the etheric level exist in a broader temporal context that extends beyond what is normally understood as the present. As such, perception of etheric reality is typically more complex and multi-layered than that of material reality.

All Things are Connected at the Etheric Level

At the etheric level all things are connected via the Universal Etheric Field. This interconnectivity forms the basis of a wide spectrum of magickal action including the ability to instantaneously affect distant phenomena, expand consciousness into perception of reality at large, communicate across vast distances, affect reality on a large scale, and attain various states of union.

Etheric Reality and Spatial Ambiguity

Traditional understanding of distance and location cannot be applied to etheric reality. All things are directly connected at the etheric level via the Universal Etheric Field. This interconnectivity creates an environment in which the magus may perceive and affect subjects regardless of distance. Additionally, the etheric body of the magus is capable of traveling great distances in brief periods. As such, the magus may travel to and directly interact with distant subjects as if physically present. This further minimizes the significance of physical distance and location.

Material Reality is Affected by Etheric Means via the Action of Etheric Convergence

All material phenomena possess an etheric aspect beyond their apparent physical attributes. The material and etheric aspects of any given subject are two sides of a single unified continuum. Thus, changes made to the etheric aspect of a subject are translated to its material aspect. When the etheric aspect of a subject is altered, the material aspect is shifted into conformity with the etheric change. This effect is typically subtle, yet profound. This Etheric Shift strongly affects the probability that the material aspect will conform to the etheric change. Through this Etheric Convergence, matter is altered in accordance with the willed change. This change, however, may not be immediately apparent and may manifest in unexpected ways. The etheric and material aspects of reality are two sides of a continuum, each aspect existing in a different state of being. Existence at the etheric level is not subject to spatial, temporal, or physical constraints. As such, results may be achieved at this level of reality that would appear magickal by ordinary standards. Action at the etheric level is not limited by physical location or distance. Free of this spatial limitation, distant subjects may be affected as if physically present. Additionally, action at the etheric level may shift events into alignment with the magickal goal across large, non-localized regions. As such, the magus may shift the entirety of a complex system into alignment upon a single goal. Via temporal extension at the etheric level of existence, the magus may perceive reality and the action of cause and effect as it extends forward in time. Therefore, etheric shifts may influence events beyond what is typically understood as the present. Free from the boundaries of physical existence, the magus may effect change at the etheric level unhindered by material constraints such as gravity and solid matter. The material results of action at the etheric level are at times immediate and profound. Typically, however, the subtle yet boundless effect of this action manifests at the material level as a complex series of events that are in accordance with the magickal goal, or a gradual conformity in the subject to the etheric change.

Etheric Reality is Affected by Consciousness, Emotion and Energy

Consciousness, emotion, and energy exert a profound effect upon the subtle, energetic nature of etheric reality.

Consciousness

Consciousness is capable of shaping and guiding etheric phenomena. This change is in accordance with the thoughts and information that comprise the consciousness.

Emotion

The various emotive states generate energies that exert distinct effects upon reality at the etheric level. For example, malign emotions such as anger and hate tend to exert a destructive, discordant effect upon etheric reality. Benign emotions exert a supportive, harmonious effect upon reality at the etheric level.

Energy

Large amounts of raw etheric energy affect etheric phenomena primarily via blunt force; the more powerful the energy, the greater its ability to affect etheric reality. Such raw energy is used to power magickal acts and directly affect reality at the etheric level.

ETHERIC MECHANISMS

There are certain fundamental mechanisms of etheric reality that underlie many magickal processes. Primary mechanisms include emanation, saturation, resonance / dissonance, and the behaviors of pneuma technikon. An understanding of these mechanisms is useful when determining which magickal operation is best suited to the task at hand.

Emanation

All phenomena emanate etheric energies. This radiant energy is generated by purely etheric phenomena and the etheric aspect of material phenomena. Such emanations exert a strong effect upon their surroundings.

Saturation

Saturation occurs when an object, area, being, or phenomenon is inundated with pneuma technikon. Saturating a subject with pneuma technikon dramatically alters the subject at the etheric level. This change is in accordance with the nature of the pneuma technikon. Saturation may occur as the direct result of a magickal act. In such instances the magus generates a large amount of pneuma technikon and projects it directly into the subject. Saturation may also occur indirectly. Indirect saturation occurs when an item or individual is in close proximity to a saturated object. Typically such an object is a talisman or enchanted item. Pneuma technikon emanating from such an object saturates surrounding phenomena. The more powerful the pneuma, the greater its range and effect.

Resonance / Dissonance

Resonance occurs when individual phenomena possess similar energetic tone. This induces a harmonious state in which the sympathetic cognitive, emotive, or energetic emanations of the phenomena resonate and intensify. Such resonance increases the intrinsic power of each individual phenomenon. This essential sympathy forms connections between individual phenomena via action of emanations through the Universal Etheric Field. Phenomena in resonance tend to attract like phenomena. Those in dissonance tend to repel. This mechanism is commonly employed in magick to draw phenomena in resonance with the magickal goal and deflect dissonant phenomena.

Behaviors of Pneuma Technikon

Through the magickal techniques, consciousness, emotion, and raw energy are merged into a single potent life force. This pneuma technikon generated during magickal acts is an extension of the self, a life force imbued with thoughts, emotions, and energies pertinent to the magickal goal. As such it may directly shape and alter reality at the etheric level in accordance with this goal. The unique composition of such pneuma allows it to act with a degree of autonomy. Once introduced into an area or subject, it behaves in accordance with its cognitive and emotive tone. This protean energy may affect surrounding phenomena by exerting waves of force, emitting radiant emanations, projecting streams of energy, and shifting existence at the etheric level. Such pneuma technikon exerts a powerful effect upon beings with whom it comes into contact. It may be introduced into the subject's etheric centers directly or enter the centers via saturation. The cognitive, emotive, and energetic components of such pneuma directly affect the subject's centers of Mind, Emotion, and Power. The thoughts, emotions, and feelings introduced into the subject are experienced as his or her own. This influences the subject to take action in accordance with the willed change. This influence is typically experienced at a semiconscious level.

Symbol for Magus

Magickal Aptitude

To effectively practice magick, the magus must possess natural talent and the Magickal Requisites. Natural Talent consists of a predilection towards mind control, energy control and etheric perception. Mind control refers to the general ability to control the flow of internal thoughts, emotions, and states of awareness. Energy control is the basic ability to guide etheric energy. In the context of natural talent, etheric perception refers to a general awareness of the subtle aspect of existence, surrounding etheric phenomena, and a tendency towards precognition. Natural talent is not present if these predilections do not exist or if the student is incapable of mastering the Preliminary Techniques. Through training and development of the etheric self, the magus attains the Magickal Requisites of power, perception and control. These three attributes are essential to affect etheric reality.

Natural Talent: A Predilection Towards Mind Control, Energy Control and Etheric Perception

In the context of natural talent, mind control refers to the general ability to control the flow of one's thoughts and expand the awareness. Energy control refers to the basic ability to guide etheric energy. Etheric perception refers to perceiving by use of faculties other than the physical senses. Once magickal training has begun, it will become apparent if the necessary abilities are present. Natural talent is not present if the student is incapable of mastering the Preliminary Techniques. As with any art, mastery of magick requires natural talent honed by extensive training.

The Magickal Requisites
Magica Requisita

The primary goal of training is to gain mastery of magickal techniques and practices. Training also produces the three essential qualities required to affect etheric reality: perception, power, and control. Attainment of the Magica Requisita produces a profound transformation in the magus.

Perception
Etheric Perception allows the magus to perceive etheric phenomena accessed during magickal operations. The magus who lacks this perception is working blind, unable to effectively interact with etheric reality.

Power
Power refers to the amount of etheric energy at the disposal of the magus. Acts of magick require large amounts of energy. The more power present, the greater the effect upon etheric reality. Cultivating internal energy and accessing external power sources is essential to the magickal arts.

Control

In the context of magick, control refers to the mastery the mind, internal energies and external forces. It is required at virtually all stages of the magickal process.

EXPECTATIONS

Through the art of magick one enters a world of mystery and wonder. The trained magus may transform the self, bend the course of events, control occult forces, and peer into the future. The magus develops the means to communicate with the great gods, spirits of the dead and those of nature. Perception is expanded as the magus learns to see without using the eyes and travel vast distances without moving the physical body. In the ways of magick, boundaries dissolve and doors to new paths open, including the ability to grow beyond the reach of death itself. Magick is an unending exploration of the great mysteries.

Magick allows one to transcend the boundaries of material existence, it is however important to understand its limitations. The traditional pagan and magickal practices of western culture have been largely suppressed by monotheistic religion. In the west, true magi, shamans and mystics are rarely encountered, therefore popular belief regarding magick is shaped by fictional tales which propagate unrealistic expectations. Magick affects material reality via etheric means. The etheric and material are two aspects within a continuum. These two aspects are unified yet exist in different states of being. As etheric phenomena exist at the most subtle end of the continuum, they rarely cause direct movement or transmutation of matter. As such, it is unlikely that the magus will gain the ability to levitate stones or disappear into thin air. These sorts of fanciful expectations are a product of folklore and do not accurately reflect magick in action. Action at the etheric level is capable of exerting a profound yet subtle effect upon material phenomena. The material manifestation of this action is at times immediate and miraculous. Typically however, the effect of etheric change is less grandiose but equally profound, manifesting as a complex series of events that are in accordance with the magickal goal, or a gradual conformity in the subject to the etheric change.

The disciplines of science confer understanding and mastery of the material aspect of existence. The disciplines of magick confer understanding and mastery of the etheric aspect of existence. The two disciplines are not incompatible, but rather may be used in tandem to confer a holistic world view. Unlike science, magick is an art and a mystery that lacks the comforts of predictability and precision. In order to fully understand the mechanics of magick the magus must set aside material expectations. Etheric reality does not conform to the laws of physics. The unique properties of etheric reality create an environment that is incomprehensible by material standards. Spatial and temporal ambiguity and non-linear causality are the norm at this end of the continuum of existence. Therefore, the results of magickal acts may be difficult to consistently reproduce, and may manifest in unexpected ways.

Though magick lacks the predictability and precision of science, its use does not require blind faith. Magickal knowledge is based upon observation, experimentation, and direct experience. The results of magickal operations are directly perceived and evaluated by the magus. The practice of magick profoundly alters the world view of the practitioner. This world view, however, is not based upon dogma or second hand information. It is based instead upon the expanded perception of reality conferred by the transformation attained via the art of magick.

WHEN DESIRED RESULTS ARE NOT ACHIEVED

Like any endeavor, magick sometimes fails to achieve the desired results. There are various reasons that a magickal operation may be unsuccessful:

Insufficient Power

The magus fails to summon enough energy to affect the desired change, or the pneuma technikon used was not potent enough to achieve the desired effect. Power is dependent upon the ability to cultivate internal energies and summon energy from external sources. The potency of the pneuma technikon generated is dependent upon the degree of focus achieved and the emotive intensity attained.

Incorrectly Performed

The technique or practice was performed incorrectly. This may be due to a loss of control or focus during the magickal operation, or a general lack of experience.

Unrealistic Goal

The goal of the operation simply cannot be attained via magick. Causality at the etheric level is often non-linear. The action of Etheric Convergence is often subtle and gradual, manifesting as a complex series of events that are in accordance with the magickal goal. As such the effect of Etheric Convergence cannot be relied upon to cause immediate, precise change to material reality. For instance, attempting to use magick to stop a speeding car would be unrealistic. Likewise, attempting precise control of an event or system may also prove unrealistic.

External Interference

Existence is in a constant state of flux. Events are set into motion by forces far greater than humanity. Terms such as Fate, Destiny, Dharma and Karma have been used to describe such forces. These forces manifest as large etheric currents, time streams, and powerful inertial flows. The magus should strive to work with the flow of events rather than against them. A magickal operation may fail if it is working against the flow of such forces. Etheric perception and Expanded Perception may be used to identify external interference.

It is unrealistic to expect to use magick alone to achieve all goals. Some goals are best achieved through magick, others are best achieved by action taken in the material world. The use of magick is often beneficial, but should not be solely relied upon to achieve goals. Through experience, the magus will gain the ability to discern when and how to use magick.

ETHICAL USE OF MAGICK

The transformation and expanded perception of the magickal path fosters an enhanced ethical paradigm. The perception that all things are connected typically engenders a deep empathy for other beings. This empathy generally fosters fellowship and compassion, which precludes the use of magick to cause harm. Through transformation, the magus evolves past petty traits such as hatred, jealousy, and the need for vengeance. Without such traits, the magus has little motive to harm others. Knowledge of the mechanism of resonance / dissonance awakens the magus to the inevitable ethical conclusion that one will have to live with and be surrounded by that which one has become. A malevolent individual will invariably be surrounded by other malevolent individuals, beings, and energies. Such individuals exist in a state of discord and isolation. Likewise, a beneficent individual will be surrounded by beneficent individuals, beings, and phenomena. Such individuals exist in a state of harmony and union. Like any tool magick may be used for good or ill. The art of magick possesses no commandments, book of taboos, or orthodox moral code. Ultimately, the magus must rely upon wisdom to guide the use and application of this great art.

CONCLUSION

The subtlest levels of existence are not perceived by the limited physical senses. Through altered states of consciousness and expanded perception these aspects of existence may be perceived via the etheric senses. This subtle aspect of existence is extremely sensitive to consciousness, emotion, and energy. The magus uses consciousness, emotion, energy, and the spirit body to directly affect reality at this level. The material and etheric aspects of existence are two sides of a single unified continuum. Thus, changes made to the etheric aspect of reality are translated to the material aspect. The two aspects exist in different states of being. Action at the subtle etheric level is boundless. This action typically translates to the material as gradual change or a series of events in alignment with the willed goal.

Chapter 2

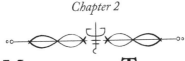

CORE MAGICKAL TECHNIQUES

Throughout the rich tapestry of cross-cultural mystic and magickal practices, those proficient in the esoteric arts use various techniques to perceive and affect reality at the subtle etheric level of existence. Within Eastern mysticism, adepts employ rigorous disciplines to master the etheric aspect of the self. Such disciplines entail controlling the mind and emotions, awakening and cultivating core internal energies, and awakening the etheric centers. These practices allow adepts to perceive subtle realities, control etheric energies and unify the consciousness/energy with existence on a larger scale. Such skills confer siddhis or magickal powers. Shamans from indigenous cultures project the spirit body beyond the material aspect of the self to effect change at the etheric level and travel to various material and etheric locations. Cross-culturally, sorcerers, magi and shamans use ritual, spells, and enchantments to focus the mind, direct subtle forces, and inflame emotive power. Through these rituals and enchantments cognitive and emotive energies are powerfully generated and focused. This infuses the life force of the practitioner into the ritual act or enchantment.

The techniques of Vercanus Magick are a powerful means to affect reality at the etheric level through the skilled and disciplined used of consciousness, emotion, energy, and the spirit. Through the Arts of Perception, the magus may perceive and interact with etheric reality. The Preliminary Techniques prepare the magus to perform acts of magick. Through these techniques the mind, energies, and emotions are controlled, stilled, and focused. The etheric centers are awakened, facilitating the generation of powerful energies and perception of reality at the etheric level. Internal core energies are awakened, blended with powerful external energies, and circulated throughout the channels and etheric centers of the body. The awakened etheric centers are used to generate powerful thoughts and emotions. These cognitive and emotive energies are merged with the circulating energies to create a potent life force possessing consciousness and energetic tone specific to the working at hand. Upon completion of the Preliminary Techniques the mind is focused, the perception is altered, and the body is inflamed with powerful pneuma technikon. From this altered state of being, the magus draws upon three core techniques to accomplish the magickal goal. These Three Great Techniques are fundamental methods by which the magus affects reality at the etheric level. Having affected the desired change, the Closing Techniques transition the magus to normal awareness. Vercanus techniques are general and may be expanded upon. The methods delineated are modular and may be combined, modified, adapted or abbreviated as needed to achieve various magickal goals.

Breath, Movement, and Gesture

Many of the techniques presented in this chapter may be enhanced by the use of controlled breath, gesture, and movement. The mind guides etheric energies. The breath, gestures and movement may be used in concert with the mind to guide both internal and external energies. The arts of Tai Chi, Chi Gong, and Yoga provide excellent examples of mind, breath, and movement guiding energy. The yogic practices of mudra, asana, and bandha may also be used to direct, focus and concentrate the energy and awareness.

THE ARTS OF PERCEPTION
Artes Perceptionis

The Arts of Perception are a class of intuitive magicks. These techniques involve the shifting of consciousness and the perception of etheric phenomena. The Artes Perceptionis do not require the generation of large amounts of energy and therefore do not typically require the use of Preliminary Techniques. The arts of perception include Etheric Perception, Etheric Communication, Etheric Reading, and Expanded Perception.

ETHERIC PERCEPTION
Perceptio Aetherica

Etheric Perception entails Centering, Banishing, Awakening and Expanding the Etheric Centers, Stillness, and Perception.

Centering

During the normal functioning of daily life, the thoughts emotions and energies are somewhat scattered and fragmented as they focus upon and interact with surrounding phenomena. Through the practice of Centering, the cognitive, emotive, and energetic awareness is aligned within the self and rooted in the moment at hand. In setting the awareness properly within the etheric centers, the self becomes fully present. Such centering is the initial step in the transition from mundane states of consciousness to the altered states necessary to perform magick. The practice of Centering is also used upon completion of the magickal working to transition consciousness back to normal states of being.

Symbol Formula for Etheric Perception

Banishing

Banishing is used to remove unwanted thoughts, emotions and energies from the etheric body. In the context of Etheric Perception, the technique of banishing removes internal phenomena that could interfere with the perception of external etheric phenomena.

Awakening and Expanding the Etheric Centers

Etheric perception entails the shifting of the etheric centers from a normal state of narrow focus to an expanded, receptive state. This shift produces the altered states necessary to perceive the etheric aspect of reality. During normal awareness, the centers typically remain in an unexpanded state. In this unexpanded state the centers provide minimal perception of etheric reality as awareness is focused upon material reality. During etheric perception, the centers of Power, Emotion and Mind awaken and expand. Awakening entails increased energy circulation within the center. This increase in energy facilitates the expansion of the center from a normal size of approximately three to four inches in diameter to an expanded size of seven to ten inches. The size of the expanded center varies by both the individual person and the particular center. As the centers awaken and expand they become receptive to etheric reality. Smaller etheric centers throughout the etheric body may also be used to perceive etheric phenomena. Those in the palms of the hands and fingertips are particularly well suited for this task. Similar to the five senses, the major etheric centers work synergistically to provide a comprehensive experience of etheric surroundings.

Center of Mind

The awakening and expansion of the Center of Mind induces a profound shift in consciousness. As this center expands, the awareness shifts focus from material reality to the etheric aspect of reality. In expanding the Center of Mind, the magus becomes acutely receptive to etheric emanations. This receptive state fosters an awareness of etheric surroundings. Additionally, this receptive state allows the magus to directly perceive emanations of consciousness. This enables the magus to perceive the thoughts of other beings.

The awakening and expansion of this center induces a light, visionary trance which is conducive to the perception of etheric phenomena. Functioning as the etheric organ of sight, the Center of Mind perceives etheric emanations and interprets them visually. The resulting visionary experience is a range from simple imagery to complex scenes. Initially, only glimpses of etheric reality may be perceived. With experience, these visions will become more complete. As the magus masters the technique, etheric imagery may be simultaneously overlaid upon the view of material reality producing a deeper, more complete perception of surrounding phenomena.

The Center of Mind interprets etheric emanations of both external and internal phenomena. Internal visions may be produced by fantasy or visualization. When practiced correctly, Etheric Perception minimizes the generative function of the mind and enhances receptive ability. This reduces internally generated imagery allowing the magus to focus upon perception of etheric reality. The Center of Mind offers the power of magickal sight. The magus must, however, distinguish between elements generated by the mind and actual etheric phenomena. Familiarity with both enables the magus to make this important distinction.

Center of Emotion

During Etheric Perception, the center of emotion directly perceives the energetic tone of etheric phenomena. This energetic tone is experienced as emotion.

For example, phenomena malign in nature may elicit feelings of loathing and revulsion. Phenomena benevolent in nature may elicit feelings of attraction or affection. Initially, only the basic differentiations of positive or negative reactions may be made. Eventually a wider range of emotions will be perceived. During Etheric Perception the generative function of this center is minimized to facilitate accurate interpretation of external phenomena.

Center of Power

In the context of etheric perception, this center is responsible for sensing energetic intensity. It is used by the magus to gauge the power of surrounding phenomena.

Stillness

Stillness is the complete cessation of thought. During ordinary awareness, the mind is busy processing sensory information, words, images, and thoughts. This process creates constant mental chatter. Through stillness the magus maintains a state of clarity that is free of internal distraction. This state allows the magus to experience pure awareness, unobscured by mental chatter. A still mind heightens sensitivity to etheric emanations and facilitates clear perception of external etheric phenomena.

Perception

Awakening and expanding the etheric centers and entering stillness induces a receptive, visionary state. In this state the magus is extremely sensitive to etheric emanations. This is typically experienced as intense visceral perception of the energetic tone of surrounding phenomena paired with a light visionary trance. This altered state is conducive to the perception of etheric surroundings. Etheric Perception is subjective. Etheric phenomena are directly perceived and visually interpreted by the Center of Mind. As such, visual perception of external phenomena will differ depending on the internal symbol system, culture and predisposition of the magus. Interpretation of consciousness and emotive tone will also vary, depending upon nature of the magus. Therefore two magi may perceive a single etheric phenomenon completely differently. Perceptual subjectivity is further compounded by the spatial and temporal ambiguity of etheric reality. As a result of spatial ambiguity, phenomena that are actually at a distance may be perceived locally. Due to temporal ambiguity, phenomena perceived may originate in the past, present or future.

TECHNIQUE Etheric Perception

	PROCEDURES	ANNOTATION
1	**Centering** Gather and focus the cognitive, emotive, and energetic awareness into the centers of Mind, Emotion, and Power. Feel the awareness become centered within these axial, etheric nexuses. Become acutely aware of the moment at hand perceived via these etheric centers.	*Beginning at the Center of Power and moving up to the center of Mind, gather and focus the awareness within the etheric centers.*
2	**Banish** Beginning at the Center of Power, use the mind, breath, and energy to remove unwanted thoughts, emotions, and energies from the body. Upon inhale, circulate energy within this center. Upon exhale, radiate energy out from the center. Use this energy to push unwanted elements out of and away from the body. Raise internal energy from the Center of Power up the dorsal channel and repeat this process of purification for all of the etheric centers. Once all centers have been purified, move energy from the Center of Mind down the ventral channel back to the Center of Power. Circulate purified undifferentiated internal energy up the dorsal channel and down the ventral channel for one to two rounds, returning it to the Center of Power.	*Use the mind and breath to draw internal energy up the dorsal channel into each etheric center. Upon the inhale, circulate energy within the center. Upon exhale, radiate energy out from the center. Use this energy to push unwanted elements out of and away from the body.*

3	**Awaken and Expand the Center of Power** Use the mind and breath to awaken and expand the Center of Power. Employ the inhalation and exhalation of the breath to circulate and intensify energy within this center. Upon the exhale, gradually expand the center to a size of seven to ten inches in diameter.	*Awakening and expanding the centers may be performed using several breaths or a single, deep inhalation and exhalation.* *As this center expands it becomes receptive to the energetic intensity of surrounding phenomena.*
4	**Awaken and Expand the Center of Emotion** Use the mind and breath to move the energy awakened at the Center of Power upward along the dorsal channel to awaken the Center of Emotion. Use the inhalation and exhalation of the breath to circulate and intensify energy within this center. Upon the exhale, gradually expand the center to a size of seven to ten inches in diameter.	*As this center expands it becomes receptive to the emotive tone of surrounding phenomena.*
5	**Awaken and Expand the Center of Mind** Use the mind and breath to move energy awakened at the Center of Emotion upward along the dorsal channel to awaken the Center of Mind. Use the inhalation and exhalation of the breath to circulate and intensify energy within this center. Upon the exhale, gradually expand the center to a size of seven to ten inches in diameter.	*As the center of Mind expands allow your awareness to shift from the tight, hard focus upon material reality to a softer, expanded focus upon the etheric aspect of reality. Allow the expanded Center of Mind to induce a receptive, light trance.* *Upon expanding, the Center of Mind becomes receptive to surrounding emanations of consciousness and induces clairvoyance.*

6	**Stillness** Become aware of the breath.	
7	Upon inhale, feel the mind become still.	
8	Upon exhale, use the energy within the Center of Mind to radially push emerging thoughts out of and away from the body.	*Push the thoughts away from the body until completely dissipated.*
9	Continue this process to hold the mind in a still state free of all thought.	
10	Immerse the mind in this state of Stillness.	
11	**Perceive** Use the Center of Mind to visually perceive etheric phenomena. This center may also be used to perceive emanations of consciousness. Use the Center of Emotion to discern emotive tone and the Center of Power to sense the energetic intensity of surrounding phenomena.	*Upon expanding, the Center of Mind induces a receptive, visionary state. Use this light trance to become immersed in your etheric surroundings. Move the eyes into a soft focus. It may also be helpful to begin Etheric Perception with the eyes closed or half open. This limits perception of material reality, shifting perception to the Center of Mind. The eyes are then slowly opened, facilitating simultaneous perception of both etheric and material phenomena.* *Use your entire body to perceive surrounding phenomena. Smaller etheric centers throughout the body may be used to perceive etheric phenomena. The centers in the palms of the hands and fingertips are particularly useful.*

| 12 | **Center and Return to Normal Consciousness** Become aware of the internal energy raised to awaken the etheric centers. Use the mind and breath to draw this energy down the body from the Centers of Mind and Emotion, collecting it in the Center of Power. As the energy leaves these centers, contract them sequentially. Upon the inhale, gather and circulate energy within the center. Upon the exhale, contract the center as energy is drawn down the ventral channel. As the energy reaches the Center of Power, contract the center to its normal size and cultivate internal energy for future use. | *As the centers contract, shift the awareness back to material reality. Set the awareness within the etheric centers and become acutely aware of the moment at hand.* |

ETHERIC COMMUNICATION
Communicatio Aetherica

Etheric Communication entails the sending and receiving of thoughts and emotions through the Universal Etheric Field. This technique may be applied to both short range and long range communication. Such communication entails a direct transfer of thoughts and emotions between two beings. It may be used to interact with humans, animals, and etheric entities. Communication may be entirely silent or combined with spoken dialog. Projected thoughts may be verbal in nature or consist of images, scenes, or powerful emotions. The efficacy of the communication is dependent upon the power, focus, and receptivity of the magus. It is also dependent upon the receptivity of the subject. Communication at a distance is typically achieved by combining this technique with Expanded Perception to locate and perceive the distant subject.

TECHNIQUE Etheric Communication

	PROCEDURES	ANNOTATION
1	**Centering** Gather and focus the cognitive, emotive, and energetic awareness into the centers of Mind, Emotion, and Power. Feel the awareness become centered within these axial, etheric nexuses. Become acutely aware of the moment at hand perceived via these etheric centers.	*Beginning at the Center of Power and moving up to the center of Mind, gather and focus the awareness within the etheric centers.*
2	**Banish** Beginning at the Center of Power, use the mind, breath, and energy to remove unwanted thoughts, emotions, and energies from the body. Upon inhale, circulate energy within this center. Upon exhale, radiate energy out from the center. Use this energy to push unwanted elements out of and away from the body. Raise internal energy from the Center of Power up the dorsal channel and repeat this process of purification for all of the etheric centers. Once all centers have been purified, move energy from the Center of Mind down the ventral channel back to the Center of Power. Circulate purified undifferentiated internal energy up the dorsal channel and down the ventral channel for one to two rounds, returning it to the Center of Power.	*Use the mind and breath to draw internal energy up the dorsal channel into each etheric center. Upon the inhale, circulate energy within the center. Upon exhale, radiate energy out from the center. Use this energy to push unwanted elements out of and away from the body.*

3	**Awaken and Expand the Center of Power** Use the mind and breath to awaken and expand the Center of Power. Employ the inhalation and exhalation of the breath to circulate and intensify energy within this center. Upon the exhale, gradually expand the center to a size of seven to ten inches in diameter.	*Awakening and expanding the centers may be performed using several breaths or a single, deep inhalation and exhalation.* *As this center expands it becomes receptive to the energetic intensity of surrounding phenomena.*
4	**Awaken and Expand the Center of Emotion** Use the mind and breath to move the energy awakened at the Center of Power upward along the dorsal channel to awaken the Center of Emotion. Use the inhalation and exhalation of the breath to circulate and intensify energy within this center. Upon the exhale, gradually expand the center to a size of seven to ten inches in diameter.	*As this center expands it becomes receptive to the emotive tone of surrounding phenomena.*
5	**Awaken and Expand the Center of Mind** Use the mind and breath to move energy awakened at the Center of Emotion upward along the dorsal channel to awaken the Center of Mind. Use the inhalation and exhalation of the breath to circulate and intensify energy within this center. Upon the exhale, gradually expand the center to a size of seven to ten inches in diameter.	*As the center of Mind expands allow your awareness to shift from the tight, hard focus upon material reality to a softer, expanded focus upon the etheric aspect of reality. Allow the expanded Center of Mind to induce a receptive, light trance.* *Upon expanding, the Center of Mind becomes receptive to surrounding emanations of consciousness and induces clairvoyance.*

6	**Stillness** Become aware of the breath.	
7	Upon inhale, feel the mind become still.	
8	Upon exhale, use the energy within the Center of Mind to radially push emerging thoughts out of and away from the body.	*Push the thoughts away from the body until completely dissipated.*
9	Continue this process to hold the mind in a still state free of all thought.	
10	Immerse the mind in this state of Stillness.	
11	**Send** Use the mind and breath to powerfully project thoughts and emotions to the subject.	*This communication may be entirely silent or may be combined with spoken dialog.*
12	**Receive** Cease the generation of thought and emotion. Return to a state of Stillness. Listen for the mental and emotive response from the subject.	*This response is typically experienced as sudden powerful thoughts, emotions, or imagery, that originate from outside the psyche of the magus.*
13	**Communicate** Continue to send and receive until the communication is complete.	*This communication may take the form of verbal dialog, visions, or powerful emotions.*

14	**Center and Return to Normal Consciousness** Become aware of the internal energy raised to awaken the etheric centers. Use the mind and breath to draw this energy down the body from the Centers of Mind and Emotion, collecting it in the Center of Power. As the energy leaves these centers, contract them sequentially. Upon the inhale, gather and circulate energy within the center. Upon the exhale, contract the center as energy is drawn down the ventral channel. As the energy reaches the Center of Power, contract the center to its normal size and cultivate internal energy for future use.	*As the centers contract, shift the awareness back to material reality. Set the awareness within the etheric centers and become acutely aware of the moment at hand.*

ETHERIC READING
Lectio Aetherica

Etheric Reading entails the perception of a subject's thoughts, emotions and energy. The ambient thoughts, emotions, and energies, of the subject are read by awakening and expanding the etheric centers and entering a state of Stillness. In expanding the etheric centers the magus becomes acutely receptive to the etheric emanations of the subject. It is important that the etheric centers of the magus are kept in a still, receptive state. This prevents the generation of thought and emotion, ensuring that the emanations being perceived are those of the subject. This technique does not by any means grant the magus complete access to the subject's mind. Rather, it provides the magus a glimpse of the consciousness, emotions, and basic nature of the subject.

TECHNIQUE Etheric Reading

	PROCEDURES	ANNOTATION
1	**Centering** Gather and focus the cognitive, emotive, and energetic awareness into the centers of Mind, Emotion, and Power. Feel the awareness become centered within these axial, etheric nexuses. Become acutely aware of the moment at hand perceived via these etheric centers.	*Beginning at the Center of Power and moving up to the center of Mind, gather and focus the awareness within the etheric centers.*

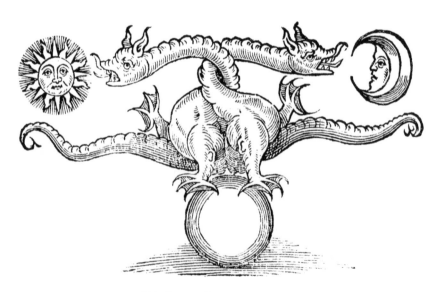

17th Century Alchemical Engraving

2	**Banish** Beginning at the Center of Power, use the mind, breath, and energy to remove unwanted thoughts, emotions, and energies from the body. Upon inhale, circulate energy within this center. Upon exhale, radiate energy out from the center. Use this energy to push unwanted elements out of and away from the body. Raise internal energy from the Center of Power up the dorsal channel and repeat this process of purification for all of the etheric centers. Once all centers have been purified, move energy from the Center of Mind down the ventral channel back to the Center of Power. Circulate purified undifferentiated internal energy up the dorsal channel and down the ventral channel for one to two rounds, returning it to the Center of Power.	*Use the mind and breath to draw internal energy up the dorsal channel into each etheric center. Upon the inhale, circulate energy within the center. Upon exhale, radiate energy out from the center. Use this energy to push unwanted elements out of and away from the body.*
3	**Awaken and Expand the Center of Power** Use the mind and breath to awaken and expand the Center of Power. Employ the inhalation and exhalation of the breath to circulate and intensify energy within this center. Upon the exhale, gradually expand the center to a size of seven to ten inches in diameter.	*Awakening and expanding the centers may be performed using several breaths or a single, deep inhalation and exhalation.* *As this center expands it becomes receptive to the energetic intensity of surrounding phenomena.*

4	**Awaken and Expand the Center of Emotion** Use the mind and breath to move the energy awakened at the Center of Power upward along the dorsal channel to awaken the Center of Emotion. Use the inhalation and exhalation of the breath to circulate and intensify energy within this center. Upon the exhale, gradually expand the center to a size of seven to ten inches in diameter.	*As this center expands it becomes receptive to the emotive tone of surrounding phenomena.*
5	**Awaken and Expand the Center of Mind** Use the mind and breath to move energy awakened at the Center of Emotion upward along the dorsal channel to awaken the Center of Mind. Use the inhalation and exhalation of the breath to circulate and intensify energy within this center. Upon the exhale, gradually expand the center to a size of seven to ten inches in diameter.	*As the center of Mind expands allow your awareness to shift from the tight, hard focus upon material reality to a softer, expanded focus upon the etheric aspect of reality. Allow the expanded Center of Mind to induce a receptive, light trance.* *Upon expanding, the Center of Mind becomes receptive to surrounding emanations of consciousness and induces clairvoyance.*
6	**Stillness** Become aware of the breath.	
7	Upon inhale, feel the mind become still.	
8	Upon exhale, use the energy within the Center of Mind to radially push emerging thoughts out of and away from the body.	*Push the thoughts away from the body until completely dissipated.*

9	Continue this process to hold the mind in a still state free of all thought.	
10	Immerse the mind in this state of Stillness.	
11	**Read** Use the expanded centers to perceive the subject's ambient emanations of thought, emotion and energy.	*Perception of the subject's thoughts, emotions and energy may be experienced as a sudden flash of insight, disjointed images, speech, or powerful emotions.*
12	**Center and Return to Normal Consciousness** Become aware of the internal energy raised to awaken the etheric centers. Use the mind and breath to draw this energy down the body from the Centers of Mind and Emotion, collecting it in the Center of Power. As the energy leaves these centers, contract them sequentially. Upon the inhale, gather and circulate energy within the center. Upon the exhale, contract the center as energy is drawn down the ventral channel. As the energy reaches the Center of Power, contract the center to its normal size and cultivate internal energy for future use.	*As the centers contract, shift the awareness back to material reality. Set the awareness within the etheric centers and become acutely aware of the moment at hand.*

EXPANDED PERCEPTION
Perceptio Expansa

Expanded Perception entails shifting the awareness into the Universal Etheric Field. This shift allows the magus to perceive existence on a large scale. Through the medium of the Universal Etheric Field the awareness may freely move, expand

and project. Expanded Perception is used to perceive distant phenomena, comprehend the flow of surrounding events, perceive surrounding phenomena and project awareness through time. A variety of practices make use of this technique.

The omnipresence of the Universal Etheric Field creates an environment in which all things are affected by and in contact with each other. Through this interconnection the magus may directly perceive and affect distant phenomena. All phenomena emanate etheric energies which become part of the Universal Etheric Field. Using the technique of Expanded Perception the magus may scan the awareness through the Universal Etheric Field to perceive specific subjects. Perception of the precise physical location of the subject is not required to affect the subject via magick. Perceiving the etheric aspect of the subject is sufficient to affect it via action through the Universal Etheric Field. A distant subject is typically perceived in proximity to the magus regardless of actual location.

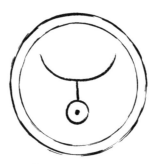

Symbol for Perception

TECHNIQUE Expanded Perception

	PROCEDURES	*ANNOTATION*
1	**Centering** Gather and focus the cognitive, emotive, and energetic awareness into the centers of Mind, Emotion, and Power. Feel the awareness become centered within these axial, etheric nexuses. Become acutely aware of the moment at hand perceived via these etheric centers.	*Beginning at the Center of Power and moving up to the center of Mind, gather and focus the awareness within the etheric centers.*

2	**Banish** Beginning at the Center of Power, use the mind, breath, and energy to remove unwanted thoughts, emotions, and energies from the body. Upon inhale, circulate energy within this center. Upon exhale, radiate energy out from the center. Use this energy to push unwanted elements out of and away from the body. Raise internal energy from the Center of Power up the dorsal channel and repeat this process of purification for all of the etheric centers. Once all centers have been purified, move energy from the Center of Mind down the ventral channel back to the Center of Power. Circulate purified undifferentiated internal energy up the dorsal channel and down the ventral channel for one to two rounds, returning it to the Center of Power.	*Use the mind and breath to draw internal energy up the dorsal channel into each etheric center. Upon the inhale, circulate energy within the center. Upon exhale, radiate energy out from the center. Use this energy to push unwanted elements out of and away from the body.*
3	**Awaken and Expand the Center of Power** Use the mind and breath to awaken and expand the Center of Power. Employ the inhalation and exhalation of the breath to circulate and intensify energy within this center. Upon the exhale, gradually expand the center to a size of seven to ten inches in diameter.	*Awakening and expanding the centers may be performed using several breaths or a single, deep inhalation and exhalation.* *As this center expands it becomes receptive to the energetic intensity of surrounding phenomena.*

4	**Awaken and Expand the Center of Emotion** Use the mind and breath to move the energy awakened at the Center of Power upward along the dorsal channel to awaken the Center of Emotion. Use the inhalation and exhalation of the breath to circulate and intensify energy within this center. Upon the exhale, gradually expand the center to a size of seven to ten inches in diameter.	*As this center expands it becomes receptive to the emotive tone of surrounding phenomena.*
5	**Awaken and Expand the Center of Mind** Use the mind and breath to move energy awakened at the Center of Emotion upward along the dorsal channel to awaken the Center of Mind. Use the inhalation and exhalation of the breath to circulate and intensify energy within this center. Upon the exhale, gradually expand the center to a size of seven to ten inches in diameter.	*As the center of Mind expands allow your awareness to shift from the tight, hard focus upon material reality to a softer, expanded focus upon the etheric aspect of reality. Allow the expanded Center of Mind to induce a receptive, light trance.* *Upon expanding, the Center of Mind becomes receptive to surrounding emanations of consciousness and induces clairvoyance.*
6	**Stillness** Become aware of the breath.	
7	Upon inhale, feel the mind become still.	
8	Upon exhale, use the energy within the Center of Mind to radially push emerging thoughts out of and away from the body.	*Push the thoughts away from the body until completely dissipated.*
9	Continue this process to hold the mind in a still state free of all thought.	

10	Immerse the mind in this state of Stillness.	
11	**Shift Awareness into the Universal Etheric Field** Become aware of the interconnectedness of all things. Shift the awareness into the Universal Etheric Field.	*Shift awareness beyond the self and into perception of existence on a larger scale.*
12	**Perceive Relevant Phenomena** Perceive phenomena relevant to the working at hand. This perception may be experienced as a sudden flash of insight, disjointed images, powerful emotions, or a fully immersive visionary experience.	*Move the awareness through the Universal Etheric Field to perceive the subject. This may entail scanning the awareness through the field to locate the subject, expanding the awareness to perceive surrounding phenomena or projecting the awareness through time.*
13	**Center and Return to Normal** Become aware of the internal energy raised to awaken the etheric centers. Use the mind and breath to draw this energy down the body from the Centers of Mind and Emotion, collecting it in the Center of Power. As the energy leaves these centers, contract them sequentially. Upon the inhale, gather and circulate energy within the center. Upon the exhale, contract the center as energy is drawn down the ventral channel. As the energy reaches the Center of Power, contract the center to its normal size and cultivate internal energy for future use.	*As the centers contract, shift the awareness back to material reality. Set the awareness within the etheric centers and become acutely aware of the moment at hand.*

COMBINING THE ARTS OF PERCEPTION WITH OTHER TECHNIQUES

The Arts of Perception are presented as stand-alone techniques. Occasionally, they may be used in conjunction with each other, or the Preliminary and Closing Techniques. In such instances, certain steps in the techniques may be redundant. For example, both the Arts of Perception and the Preliminary Techniques include steps to expand the etheric centers and attain stillness. Redundant steps need not be repeated. Only the core steps of the Arts of Perception are necessary when combining with other techniques.

PRELIMINARY TECHNIQUES
Artes Praeviae

The Artes Praeviae prepare the magus to perform acts of magick. These techniques serve to clear the mind and emotions, shift perception to etheric reality, focus the awareness and generate potent pneuma technikon. They are invaluable in the transition from ordinary cognitive, emotive and energetic states to the altered states necessary to perform magick. Use of these techniques profoundly alters consciousness and fills the magus with power. The Artes Praeviae are typically performed before using any of the Three Great Techniques.

The Preliminary Techniques consist of the following steps:
- ~ Centering
- ~ Banishing
- ~ Etheric Perception
- ~ Stillness
- ~ Energy Summoning
- ~ Circulation
- ~ Focused Awareness
- ~ Emotive Generation
- ~ Culmination

Centering

During the normal functioning of daily life, the thoughts, emotions and energies are somewhat scattered and fragmented as they focus upon and interact with surrounding phenomena. Through the practice of Centering, cognitive, emotive, and energetic awareness is aligned within the self and rooted in the moment at hand. In setting the awareness properly within the etheric centers, the self becomes fully present. Such Centering is the initial step in the transition from mundane states of consciousness to the altered states necessary to perform magick. The practice of Centering is also used upon completion of the magickal working to transition consciousness back to normal states of being.

Banishing

In the context of the Preliminary Techniques, banishing serves three primary purposes: purification of the magus, cleansing of the magickal space, and construction of a protective barrier. Purification of the self entails a cleansing of the mind, emotions and energy. This removes all thoughts, energies and emotions that may interfere with the working at hand. Without such a cleansing, the multitude of cognitive, emotional and energetic debris constantly present within the self would taint and disrupt the magickal operation. Construction of a protective barrier blocks any unwanted entities or forces from entering the magickal space or interfering with the working at hand. Additionally, the barrier clears the working space of unwanted energies and renders it energetically pure. This allows the magus to create a space within the barrier that is energetically beneficial to the working at hand.

An alternate banishing technique is given at the bottom of the Artes Praeviae. This technique, free of gestures, may be used if discretion is preferred.

Etheric Perception

Etheric Perception entails awakening and expanding the centers of Power, Emotion, and Mind. Upon expanding the major etheric centers, awareness and perception is shifted from material reality to the etheric aspect of reality. The state of Stillness is then employed to heighten sensitivity to etheric emanations and facilitate clear perception of external etheric phenomena. This process induces the altered states of consciousness and perception necessary to interact with and affect realty at the etheric level during magickal operations. This shift in consciousness facilitates perception of etheric phenomena and deeper realities beyond and within material manifestations. Without such perception, the magus is working blind.

Stillness

Through the practice of Stillness the magus temporarily suspends all thought. This still state of being facilitates the perception of external etheric phenomena and is a key component of Etheric Perception. Additionally, in the context of the Preliminary Techniques, this state facilitates clear, powerful focus upon a single magickal goal. It is from the stilled mind that the magus summons a solitary thought powerfully directed upon the working at hand. Stillness is integral to the meditative and trance states found in the magickal practices of various cultures.

Energy Summoning

Accessing powerful energies is vital to the art of magick. During this stage the magus projects internal energies to reach out and draw in powerful external energies. The greater the amount of internal energy, the greater the ability to access external energy. Internal energy is increased through magickal training and the practice of Energy Cultivation. This internal store of energy is sufficient to power magickal acts alone. However, accessing and channeling powerful external energies greatly increases the amount of energy at the disposal of the magus. The source accessed is typically a naturally occurring pool or current of raw pneuma. Such external energies sources may include power from within the earth, celestial energies such as those from the moon, sun, and skies, energies drawn from the elements of nature, and those from naturally occurring energy currents and power spots. The magus accesses external energy sources by projecting streams of energy from the etheric centers into the external power source. Energy from the external source is drawn back to the body as the magus retracts the extended energy. This creates an energy current which flows into the magus. This connection may be maintained throughout the magickal working or allowed to subside at will.

Energy summoning induces a euphoric, ecstatic state. This ecstatic state intensifies and augments the subsequent altered states of consciousness employed within magick. Use of such ecstatic states is prevalent throughout various cultures. The !Kung San shamans of the Kalahari, for example, employ rhythmic movement and dance when summoning "Num" energy to induce an ecstatic trance state known as "Kia". Such Num energy is said to reside in the belly or base of the spine. As this energy "boils" and is raised to the head, the altered state of Kia is induced.

Circulation

The energy summoned in the previous step is circulated throughout the etheric body. As this energy moves through the channels and centers, the magus is filled with raw power. This circulation continues throughout the remaining steps of the Preliminary Techniques.

Focused Awareness

Moving from the clarity previously attained through Stillness, the magus summons a solitary thought and focuses intently upon it. This thought may be a vision, chant, image, symbol, or combination thereof which represents the goal of the magickal working. Simple, direct thoughts tend to produce the best results. Focused Awareness may also entail intensely focusing upon the goal of the magickal operation to the exclusion of all else. All random thoughts are kept at bay as the magus focuses upon the magickal goal with extreme intensity. Focused Awareness is used during the magickal working to powerfully direct the consciousness and etheric phenomena toward a single objective. If focus falters during the working, the magus may lose control of the magickal operation, limiting effectiveness and accuracy. This intense focus generates abnormally potent cognitive energy. This energy is imbued with the consciousness and information relevant to the magickal goal. Focus is held as this cognitive pneuma joins the raw energy circulating through the body. A similar state of profound focus is described within Hindu mysticism as Dharana.

Emotive Generation

During emotive generation the magus becomes inflamed with emotive energy. This pneuma of emotion exerts a powerful effect upon reality at the etheric level. The emotion evoked corresponds to the working at hand. Envisioning the goal or subject of the working may assist in the production of the proper emotion or feeling. In generating powerful emotions the magus greatly increases the potency of the magickal act. The emotion generated sets the energetic tone of the working. Simple emotions may be more effective than complex emotions. The magus focuses upon the magickal goal to generate specific feelings or emotions that the goal evokes. Each particular goal may elicit a unique emotive response. It is at this stage that emotive pneuma joins the circulating energies. Occasionally, the magickal operation does not require the generation of emotive pneuma. In such instances, the step of emotive generation may be omitted.

Culmination

During the final step of culmination, the magus continues to draw in raw external energy while generating cognitive and emotive pneuma. These energies are combined via circulation to form potent pneuma technikon specifically crafted to affect reality in accordance with the magickal goal. Circulation is maintained until the magus is inflamed with this powerful life-force. The inflamed, focused, state and enhanced perception attained via the Preliminary Techniques is held while moving into the magickal operation.

TECHNIQUE Preliminary Techniques

	PROCEDURES	ANNOTATION
1	**Centering** Gather and focus the cognitive, emotive, and energetic awareness into the centers of Mind, Emotion, and Power. Feel the awareness become centered within these axial, etheric nexuses. Become acutely aware of the moment at hand perceived via these etheric centers.	*Beginning at the Center of Power and moving up to the center of Mind, gather and focus the awareness within the etheric centers.*
2	**Banishing** Use the mind and breath to extend streams of energy from the etheric centers in the palms of the hands and the fingertips.	
3	Starting just above the head slowly move the hands down the length of the body. As the hands move, extend these streams of energy into the body to collect all unwanted thoughts, energies and emotions. Draw these unwanted elements down the body.	

4	When the arms are fully extended downward, turn palms to face the ground. Use the mind and breath to project the unwanted elements deep into the Earth.	*The alternate Banishing technique, free of gestures, may be used if discretion is preferred.*
5	**Protective Barrier** Become aware of the Center of Power and the energy stored therein. Use the mind and breath to circulate and intensify the energy stored within this center.	*Use the inhalation and exhalation of the breath to circulate and intensify the energy within this center.*
6	Take a single deep breath. Upon exhale expand a sphere of protective energy outward from this center to include the entire magickal space. As the sphere expands, envision the area being cleared of unwanted energies while retaining any desired energies that may be present.	*The barrier is an extension of the self, a sphere of pneuma technikon directly controlled by the magus. This renders the barrier semi-permeable in nature. The magus may selectively allow energies and entities to pass through the barrier while maintaining defense against hostile phenomena.*
	If the operation requires that you be physically mobile, a smaller barrier may be extended just beyond the material body. In this case, the barrier merges with the outer layers of the body's etheric form. Through this merging, the barrier is attached to the body of the magus and moves with it.	*The barrier may be strengthened by fortifying the sphere with additional energy. This is accomplished by extending streams of energy from the etheric centers in the palms of the hands and fingertips into the sphere. Use these extended streams as a conduit to send energy into the shield. Fortifying of the magickal barrier is typically only necessary if the magus is under attack or exposed to particularly harmful emanations.*

7	**Etheric Perception** Use the mind and breath to awaken and expand the Center of Power. Employ the inhalation and exhalation of the breath to circulate and intensify energy within this center. Upon the exhale gradually expand the center to a size of seven to ten inches in diameter.	*Awakening and expanding the centers may be performed using several breaths or a single deep inhalation and exhalation.* *As this center expands it becomes receptive to the energetic intensity of surrounding phenomena.*
8	Use the mind and breath to move the energy awakened at the Center of Power upward along the dorsal channel to awaken the Center of Emotion. Use the inhalation and exhalation of the breath to circulate and intensify energy within this center. Upon the exhale gradually expand the center to a size of seven to ten inches in diameter.	*As this center expands it becomes receptive to the emotive tone of surrounding phenomena.*
9	Use the mind and breath to move energy awakened at the Center of Emotion upward along the dorsal channel to awaken the Center of Mind. Use the inhalation and exhalation of the breath to circulate and intensify energy within this center. Upon the exhale gradually expand the center to a size of seven to ten inches in diameter.	*As the center of Mind expands allow your awareness to shift from the tight, hard focus upon material reality to a softer, expanded focus upon the etheric aspect of reality. Allow the expanded Center of Mind to induce a receptive, light trance. Upon expanding, the Center of Mind becomes receptive to surrounding emanations of consciousness and induces clairvoyance.*
10	**Stillness** Become aware of the breath. Upon inhale, feel the mind become still.	

11	Upon exhale, use the energy within the Center of Mind to radially push emerging thoughts out of and away from the body.	*Push the thoughts away from the body until completely dissipated.*
12	Continue this process to hold the mind in a still state free of all thought.	
13	Immerse the mind in this state of Stillness.	
14	Use Etheric Perception to perceive the vast ecology of energy and consciousness that surrounds you and to become aware of external energy sources.	
15	**Energy Summoning** Remaining in a state of Stillness, move energy from the Center of Mind down the ventral channel back to the Center of Power.	
16	Use the mind and breath to circulate and intensify the powerful energy stored within this center.	*Use the inhalation and exhalation of the breath to circulate and inflame the energy within this center.*

17	Move this powerful internal energy through the body's etheric channels and out through one or more etheric center.	Centers commonly used to project energy from and draw energy into the body include: ~ The palms of the hands ~ Soles of the feet ~ The Center of Mind at the brow ~ Crown Center at the top of the head Commonly used paths to project internal energy from the body include: ~ Up the dorsal channel, then through the arms and out through the etheric centers in the palms. ~ Down the legs and out through the etheric centers in the soles of the feet. ~ Up the dorsal channel, and out through the etheric center in the crown.
18	Use the mind and breath to powerfully project streams of this energy into an external energy source.	Use the altered states of Etheric Perception and Stillness to directly perceive external energy sources. External energies sources may include power from within the earth, celestial energies such as those from the moon, sun, and skies, energies drawn from the elements of nature, and those from naturally occurring energy currents and power spots.
19	Retract this extended energy back in through the etheric centers, bringing with it a current of energy from the external source. Use the mind and breath to draw this energy into the body.	As the extended energy is retracted, feel the external energy flow into the body. This energy may be absorbed through any of the etheric centers. It may also be drawn into the body with the breath. This powerful current of energy may be maintained throughout the working or allowed to subside at will.

20	**Circulation** Circulate the external energy through the body's energy channels and etheric centers. Move energy up the dorsal/spinal channel and down the ventral channel. With each circulation draw additional external energy into the body. Maintain circulation as you move through the remaining steps of the Preliminary Techniques.	*Alternatively, any number of esoteric systems may be studied and implemented for the purpose of circulation. The arts of Chi Gong, Tibetan Tummo, Yogic Pranayama, and Kundalini Yoga provide excellent examples of energy circulation. In lieu of an orthodox system, energy may also be circulated through the body in whichever manner feels intuitive and natural.*
21	**Focused Awareness** Moving from the clarity previously attained through Stillness, focus intensely upon the goal of the working. Become completely immersed in this thought.	*This thought may be a vision, chant, image, symbol, or combination thereof which represents the goal of the magickal working.*
22	Maintain this focus while circulating and intensifying energies.	*It is at this stage in the Preliminary Techniques that cognitive pneuma is produced and joins the raw energy circulating through the body.*
23	**Emotive Generation** Become aware of the Center of Emotion. Powerfully generate the emotion or feeling evoked by focus upon the magickal goal, or generate the emotion appropriate to the magick at hand.	*Occasionally, the magickal operation does not require the generation of emotive pneuma. In such instances, the step of emotive generation may be omitted.*
24	Use the mind and breath to become inflamed with this emotion.	*It is at this stage in the Preliminary Techniques that emotive pneuma is produced and joins the raw energy circulating through the body.*

25	**Culmination** Continue to draw in external energy and circulate it throughout the body. As this energy circulates, merge it with the cognitive and emotive pneuma being generated via Focused Awareness and Emotive Generation. Maintain this circulation until you become inflamed with potent pneuma technikon.	
26	Hold this inflamed, focused state as you move into the magickal operation.	

Sigil of Sanctification

TECHNIQUE
Alternate Banishing Technique for use with Preliminary Techniques

	PROCEDURES	ANNOTATION
1	**Banish** Beginning at the Center of Power, use the mind, breath, and energy to remove unwanted thoughts, emotions, and energies from the body. Upon inhale, circulate energy within this center. Upon exhale, radiate energy out from the center. Use this energy to push unwanted elements out of and away from the body. Raise internal energy from the Center of Power up the dorsal channel and repeat this process of purification for all of the etheric centers. Once all centers have been purified, move energy from the Center of Mind down the ventral channel back to the Center of Power. Circulate purified undifferentiated internal energy up the dorsal channel and down the ventral channel for one to two rounds, returning it to the Center of Power.	*Use the mind and breath to draw internal energy up the dorsal channel into each etheric center. Upon the inhale, circulate energy within the center. Upon exhale, radiate energy out from the center. Use this energy to push unwanted elements out of and away from the body.*

THE THREE GREAT TECHNIQUES
Tres Magnae Artes

The Three Great Techniques are fundamental methods by which the magus affects reality at the etheric level. Each technique is unique in the way that it affects etheric change. The Tres Magnae Artes may be used alone or in sequence. The Great Techniques include Virium Emissio (Energy Casting), Proiectio Spiritus (Spirit Projection) and Communio Expansa (Expansive Union).

ENERGY CASTING
Virium Emissio

Integral to many operations, the technique of Virium Emissio entails the projection of pneuma to directly affect or manipulate etheric surroundings. Saturating a subject with pneuma technikon dramatically alters its etheric nature. Additionally, saturation changes the way that surrounding phenomena react to the subject. Similar practices have been used throughout human history, particularly in Eastern cultures. Excellent examples are found in the arts of Chi Gong, Tai Chi, and internal alchemy. These ancient arts project etheric energy, or Wai Chi, from the body for the purpose of healing and self defense.

Five energy casting techniques are presented below: a Primary Energy Casting technique, Impromptu Casting, Tactile Casting, Distance Casting, and Radiant Casting. When using these techniques, it is important that the magus does not become depleted of energy. Primary Energy Casting, Distance Casting, and Radiant Casting draw upon external energy sources to generate large amounts of pneuma technikon. When properly performed, these practices will not deplete internal energy stores. Impromptu Casting and Tactile Casting rely upon energy that the magus has previously stored within the Center of Power. This stored energy should be replaced on a regular basis to prevent depletion. Such energy is replenished through training and Energy Cultivation.

PRIMARY ENERGY CASTING
Virium Emissio Principalis

The Primary Energy Casting technique generates large amounts of pneuma technikon, which is then projected from the magus into the subject of the working. This technique is used in conjunction with the Preliminary and Closing Techniques. Primary Energy Casting is the most powerful of the energy casting techniques. It is used when the situation allows time for the prolonged summoning of energy and generation of pneuma technikon.

TECHNIQUE Primary Energy Casting

	PROCEDURES	*ANNOTATION*
1	**Preliminary Techniques** Perform the Artes Praeviae.	*When performing the Artes Praeviae generate thoughts and emotions in accordance with the goal of the working.*
2	Performing the last step in the Preliminary Techniques, continue to draw in external energy while generating cognitive and emotive pneuma. Circulate these energies until the body is filled to the point of overflowing with potent pneuma technikon.	
3	**Emit Pneuma From the Body** Select an etheric center or centers from which to project this pneuma.	*Commonly used centers include those within the palms of the hands and fingertips, and the major etheric centers.*
4	Use the mind, breath and gestures to project pneuma into the subject.	*Pneuma may be emitted as currents of energy, waves of force, or radiant emanations.*

| 5 | **Saturate the Subject**
Saturate the subject of the working with pneuma technikon. | *Use the mind and breath to concentrate and condense pneuma into the subject of the working. Continue to pour your thoughts, emotions, and energies into the subject until it is completely saturated. This pneuma technikon is an extension of the self. When saturating the subject, envision this life force powerfully affecting reality in accordance with the goal of the working.* |
| 6 | **Closing Techniques**
Perform the Artes Concludendi. | |

IMPROMPTU CASTING
Emissio Extemporalis

Impromptu Casting is used in situations that require immediate action or when prolonged energy summoning is not an option. This technique makes use of the energy stored within the body, along with the cognitive and emotive energies generated in reaction to the situation at hand to quickly produce potent pneuma technikon. This powerful pneuma technikon is briefly intensified and circulated through the body, then projected to affect reality at the etheric level. Impromptu Casting does not require use of the Preliminary or Closing Techniques. The optional step of banishing may be used if desired and if the situation permits. If necessary, banishing may be performed at a later time.

TECHNIQUE Impromptu Casting

	PROCEDURES	*ANNOTATION*
1	**Focused Awareness** Focus with intensity upon the magickal goal.	

2	**Produce Cognitive and Emotive Pneuma** Intensely generate the thoughts and emotions appropriate to the magickal goal.	*Impromptu Casting is typically used when a situation arises that requires immediate action. Allow the situation at hand to intensify the thoughts and emotions being generated.* *Chants or words of power may be used to summon specific thoughts, emotions and energies.*
3	**Energy Summoning** Become aware of the Center of Power and the energy stored therein. Use the mind and breath to circulate and intensify the energy stored within this center.	
4	**Circulation** Briefly circulate this energy though the body.	*Briefly circulate this energy through the body's energy channels and etheric centers. Move energy up the dorsal/ spinal channel and down the ventral channel*
5	As this energy circulates, feel it merge with the cognitive and emotive pneuma generated in the previous steps.	
6	Become inflamed with potent pneuma technikon.	
7	**Emit Pneuma From the Body** Select an etheric center or centers from which to project this pneuma.	*Commonly used centers include those within the palms of the hands and fingertips, and the major etheric centers.*
8	Use the mind, breath, and gesture to project pneuma into the subject.	*Pneuma may be emitted as currents of energy, waves of force, or radiant emanations.*

9	**Saturate the Subject** Saturate the subject of the working with pneuma.	*Use the mind and breath to concentrate and condense pneuma technikon into the subject. Continue to pour your thoughts, emotions, and energies into the subject until it is completely saturated. When saturating the subject, envision this life force powerfully affecting reality in accordance with the goal of the working.*
10	**Banishing (Optional)** Beginning at the Center of Power, use the mind, breath, and energy to remove unwanted thoughts, emotions, and energies from the body. Upon inhale, circulate energy within this center. Upon exhale, radiate energy out from the center. Use this energy to push unwanted elements out of and away from the body. Raise internal energy from the Center of Power up the dorsal channel and repeat this process of purification for all of the etheric centers. Once all centers have been purified, move energy from the Center of Mind down the ventral channel back to the Center of Power. Circulate purified undifferentiated internal energy up the dorsal channel and down the ventral channel for one to two rounds, returning it to the Center of Power.	*Use the mind and breath to draw internal energy up the dorsal channel into each etheric center. Upon the inhale, circulate energy within the center. Upon exhale, radiate energy out from the center. Use this energy to push unwanted elements out of and away from the body.*

TACTILE CASTING
Emissio Tactilis

The technique of Tactile Casting makes use of energy stored within the Center of Power. Cognitive and emotive energies are not essential to this practice, instead raw energy is extended from the body to directly effect change at the etheric level. Pneuma may be emitted as streams of energy or waves of force. This extended energy serves as the etheric appendages of the magus. Emissio Tactilis affords the magus a direct tactile experience of etheric surroundings. Tactile Casting does not require use of the Preliminary or Closing Techniques.

TECHNIQUE Tactile Casting

	PROCEDURES	ANNOTATION
1	**Energy Summoning** Become aware of the Center of Power and the energy stored therein. Use the mind and breath to circulate and intensify the energy stored within this center.	
2	**Circulation** Briefly circulate this energy though the body.	*Briefly circulate this energy through the body's energy channels and etheric centers. Move energy up the dorsal/spinal channel and down the ventral channel*
3	**Select Etheric Center** Select a center or centers from which to emit this pneuma.	*Commonly used centers include those within the palms of the hands and fingertips, and the major etheric centers.*
4	**Extend Pneuma** Use the mind, breath and gestures to direct the pneuma to the selected center or centers and out of the body.	*Pneuma may be extended as streams or currents of energy to interact with etheric surroundings. Waves of force may also be emitted to forcibly repel phenomena at the etheric level.*

5	**Interact with Phenomena** Use this projected pneuma to interact with surrounding phenomena.	
6	**Retract Extended Streams** Retract any extended energy streams back into the body.	

DISTANCE CASTING
Emissio Remota

Distance Casting employs the technique of Expanded Perception to affect a distant subject. The state of Expanded Perception allows the magus to directly perceive a distant subject via the Universal Etheric Field. The omnipresence of the Universal Etheric Field creates an environment in which all things are affected by and in contact with each other. The magus may instantaneously affect a distant subject by projecting pneuma through the Universal Etheric Field. The technique of Distance Casting makes use of this interconnectivity to saturate the distant subject with pneuma technikon. This technique is typically used in conjunction with the Preliminary and Closing Techniques.

TECHNIQUE Distance Casting

	PROCEDURES	ANNOTATION
1	**Preliminary Techniques** Perform the Artes Praeviae.	*When performing the Artes Praeviae generate thoughts and emotions in accordance with the goal of the working.*
2	Performing the last step in the Preliminary Techniques, continue to draw in external energy while generating cognitive and emotive pneuma. Circulate these energies until the body is filled to the point of overflowing with potent pneuma technikon.	

3	**Expanded Perception** Use Expanded Perception to perceive the distant subject.	*Shift awareness into the Universal Etheric Field to perceive the distant subject.*
4	**Emit Pneuma From the Body** Select an etheric center or centers from which to project pneuma.	*Commonly used centers include those within the palms of the hands and fingertips, and the major etheric centers.*
5	Use the mind, breath and gestures to project pneuma through the Universal Etheric Field and into the subject.	*The sensation of projecting energy across the Universal Etheric Field is unique due to the spatial ambiguity of etheric reality. The distant subject is typically perceived to be in proximity to the magus. There is however, a distinct sensation of distance as energies are projected across the Universal Etheric Field and into the subject.* *Pneuma may be emitted as currents of energy, waves of force, or radiant emanations.*
6	**Saturate the Subject** Saturate the subject of the working with pneuma.	*Use the mind and breath to concentrate and condense pneuma into the subject. Continue to pour your thoughts, emotions, and energies into the subject until it is completely saturated. When saturating the subject, envision this life force powerfully affecting reality in accordance with the goal of the working.*
7	**Closing Techniques** Perform the Artes Concludendi.	

RADIANT CASTING
Emissio Radians

Radiant Casting is used to alter the etheric nature of a large area. During this technique the magus emits a radial pulse of pneuma technikon outward from the Center of Power. The expanding pulse saturates the entire area. This saturation shifts all phenomena within the area into alignment with the magickal goal. The technique is typically used with both the Preliminary and Closing Techniques.

TECHNIQUE Radiant Casting

	PROCEDURES	*ANNOTATION*
1	**Preliminary Techniques** Perform the Artes Praeviae.	*When performing the Artes Praeviae generate thoughts and emotions in accordance with the goal of the working.*
2	Performing the last step in the Preliminary Techniques, continue to draw in external energy while generating cognitive and emotive pneuma. Circulate these energies until the body is filled to the point of overflowing with potent pneuma technikon.	
3	**Concentrate Pneuma Technikon into the Center of Power** Use the mind and breath to concentrate this circulating pneuma technikon into the Center of Power.	*As the energy is concentrated into the Center of Power, feel the energy circulate and intensify.*
4	Continue to concentrate pneuma technikon into this center until it is inflamed with power.	

5	**Saturate the Area** Use the mind and breath to powerfully expand a radial pulse of this pneuma technikon outward from the Center of Power.	*Take a single deep breath. Upon inhale, feel the pneuma technikon concentrated in the Center of Power become powerful to the point of growing beyond containment. Upon exhale expand a radial pulse of pneuma technikon to encompass the entire area of enchantment. This area may encompass immediate surroundings or a large geographic region. When saturating the region, envision this life force powerfully affecting reality in accordance with the goal of the working.*
6	**Closing Techniques** Perform the Artes Concludendi.	

Spirit Projection
Proiectio Spiritus

Proiectio Spiritus is the projection of the etheric body beyond the physical body. Free from material confines, the etheric body may travel at will to various etheric realms or geographic locations. Unlike its material counterpart, the etheric body may shift form, travel vast distances in a short period of time, or penetrate solid matter. During normal states of being, the consciousness spans the material and etheric aspects of the human body, both aspects working synergistically. Upon separating from the material body, the magus shifts consciousness to the etheric body. The magus then uses the etheric body to directly affect reality at the etheric level. Though they are separate, the etheric and material bodies remain linked via resonance through the Universal Etheric Field. As such, the degree of disassociation from the material body may vary. During Spirit Projection the consciousness may span from the material to the etheric body resulting in full or partial bilocation. The consciousness may also be completely shifted to the etheric body resulting in a total disassociation from the material body. Rhythmic drumming, drones and chants may be used to shift consciousness and assist in the projection of the spirit from the body. Consciousness altering plants are traditionally used in conjunction with this technique to facilitate projection from the body. While this augmentation is quite effective, it may be impractical in that it impairs the focused awareness necessary to carry out magickal operations, and may come to be relied upon when performing this technique. Perhaps the oldest magickal technique, Spirit Projection has been used by Shamans of various cultures for millennia.

Spirit projection is typically used in conjunction with the Preliminary and Closing techniques. The focus achieved during the Preliminary Techniques prevents disorientation and distraction while in a disembodied state. The etheric perception and clarity attained prior to projection facilitates shifting consciousness from the material body to the etheric body. The energies summoned and generated during the Preliminary Techniques render the spirit of the magus powerful prior to projection. This affords the magus greater ability to affect reality at the etheric level. During Spirit Projection, the material body is left somewhat vulnerable. The protective barrier formed during the Preliminary Techniques provides protection from unwanted etheric energies and entities, safeguarding the material body when the spirit is elsewhere. The Shifted Awareness step in the Closing Techniques assists in the reorientation to material reality.

TECHNIQUE Spirit Projection

	PROCEDURES	ANNOTATION
1	**Preliminary Techniques** Perform the Artes Praeviae.	*When performing the Artes Praeviae generate thoughts and emotions in accordance with the goal of the working.*
2	Feel your internal energy (previously summoned during the Preliminary Techniques) surging through and strengthening your etheric body. Gather this energy to the Center of Power.	

3	**Become Aware of the Etheric Body** The receptive state of Etheric Perception was initiated during the Preliminary Techniques. Use the heightened state of Etheric Perception to feel your etheric body within your material body.	*The technique of Spirit Projection may be performed from a sitting, standing, or lying position.*
4	**Separate Etheric from the Material Body** Focus upon the energy within the Center of Power. The energy with this center may be used to impel the etheric body in any given direction. Use the energy within this center to lift the etheric body out of the material body, through the sea of surrounding pneuma.	*The Center of Power impels the etheric body through the ambient sea of pneuma. The sensation of moving the etheric body via the Center of Power eludes verbal description. The experience may be likened to lifting, pushing, and pulling at the same time.* *Continue to raise your etheric body, stopping four to fifty feet above your material body.*
5	**Shift Consciousness to the Etheric Body** As the as the spirit leaves the physical body strongly shift your consciousness to the vantage point of your ascending etheric body.	
6	Observe your surroundings from the perspective of your etheric body.	
7	Experience the tactile sensation of your immediate surroundings in this disembodied state.	
8	**Select Form** Select a form in which to project, this may be an exact duplicate of your physical body, an animal, a protean field of energy, or a therianthrope (animal/human fusion).	*Experience the fluidity of the etheric body and the ease with which it may shift its form.*

9	**Focus Upon Destination** Focus upon the location to which you wish to travel, this may be a material location or an etheric environment.	
10	**Project the Spirit** Become aware of the Center of Power. Use the energy within this center to project the spirit to your destination.	*Travel is typically perceived as flight. The energy within the Center of Power is used to impel the etheric body towards the destination. This may be experienced as lifting, pushing and pulling at the same time. If in a theriomorphic form, travel may be augmented by the type of locomotion native to the selected animal.*
11	**Explore Surroundings** Upon arriving at the destination, explore your surroundings.	
12	Gather information or directly affect reality at the etheric level in accordance with the goal of the magickal operation.	
13	**Return to Material Body** Travel back to the material body.	
14	**Re-integrate with the Material Body** Slowly re-integrate the etheric body with the material body.	*This typically entails merging the etheric and material bodies together. Consciousness is then shifted back into the material self.*
15	**Closing Techniques** Perform the Artes Concludendi.	

EXPANSIVE UNION
Communio Expansa

Through Communio Expansa, the magus may expand the consciousness, energy and entirety of the etheric self into a state of union with all things in a particular region. This profound absorption into surrounding phenomena allows the magus to powerfully affect the entirety of a complex system. In becoming one with a region, the magus may affect a region. This is accomplished by using the consciousness, energy and expanded etheric body to shift surrounding phenomena into alignment with the magical goal. Within Hindu mysticism the term Samadhi is used to describe states of union akin to Cummunio Expansa. The Yoga Sutras of Patanjali indicate that various siddhis, or magickal abilities are attained via the state of Samadhi. Such siddhis include supersensory perception, omniscience, and mastery of the primal cause of matter and the elements.

In becoming one with a region, the magus may shift relevant phenomena into alignment with the magickal goal. During the state of Expansive Union, phenomena within the region move as one with the mind and energy of the magus. This allows the magus to directly shape and alter reality on a large scale. Components of a specific region may be bent towards the willed change, resulting in an etheric shift. Primary components affected include the etheric aspects of material phenomena, energy currents, and the minds of others. These components are shifted into alignment with the magickal goal. This typically entails drawing desired or beneficial phenomena while deflecting harmful or unwanted phenomena. Shifting may also entail reconfiguring the complex interaction of components within a large system. Perception of the inertial flow of causal events is essential to effectively shift such components into alignment with the magickal goal. The inertial flow of events is driven by the action of cause and effect upon the components of a complex system. Events set in motion possess momentum and follow a specific course. Perceiving and moving with this flow of causality allows the magus to work with inertial currents rather than fight against them. Towards this end, the magus artfully bends the existing flow of events into alignment with the willed change. Inertial currents may also be created and set into motion via the willed action of the magus.

Communio Expansa is well suited for affecting a large area, obtaining a goal that requires a complex series of events to occur, or using the entirety of a region to affect a single subject. This technique shifts reality at the etheric level and affects the inertial flow of causal events within the selected region. As such, the material outcome often manifests via a complex series of events that are in accordance with the magickal goal, or a gradual conformity within the region to the etheric change. The magickal action set in motion by Expansive Union does not cease when the magus returns to normal consciousness. During the Preliminary

Techniques the etheric body is filled with pneuma technikon. Expanding the etheric body saturates the entire region with this energy. This pneuma continues to shift the region towards the willed change after the completion of the magickal working. Expansion into a local region such as the immediate surroundings, a neighborhood, or city is typically sufficient for most workings. The experienced magus may however expand further to effect change on a global scale.

The technique presented below includes the individual steps of the Preliminary Techniques as they pertain to the use of Expansive Union. These steps are presented to fully illustrate the use of the Preliminary Techniques in conjunction with the Three Great Techniques. In the example below the external power source of earth energy is used.

TECHNIQUE Expansive Union

	PROCEDURES	ANNOTATION
	PRELIMINARY TECHNIQUES (Detailed Instruction)	
1	**Centering** Gather and focus the cognitive, emotive, and energetic awareness into the centers of Mind, Emotion, and Power.	
2	**Banishing** Banish unwanted thoughts, energies and emotions.	
3	**Protective Barrier** Expand a sphere of protective energy to encompass the entire magickal space.	
4	**Etheric Perception** Use the mind and breath to awaken and expand the centers of Power, Emotion and Mind. Shift awareness to the etheric aspect of existence.	

5	**Stillness** Use the mind and breath to dispel unwanted thoughts, becoming immersed in a state of Stillness.	
	From this state of Stillness, use Etheric Perception to perceive the vast ecology of energy and consciousness that surrounds you and to become aware of external energy sources.	
6	**Energy Summoning** Remaining in a state of Stillness, move energy from the Center of Mind down the ventral channel back to the Center of Power.	
7	Use the mind and breath to circulate and intensify the powerful energy stored within this center.	
8	Move this powerful internal energy up the dorsal channel, through the arms, and to the palms.	
9	Use the mind and breath to powerfully project streams of this energy through the etheric centers in the palms to connect to external energies deep within the earth.	*This step is typically performed in a standing position with the palms facing down*
10	Retract this extended energy, bringing with it a current of energy from the earth. Use the mind and breath to draw this energy through the body.	

11	**Circulation** Circulate the earth energy up the dorsal channel and down the ventral channel. With each circulation draw additional external energy into the body.	
12	**Focused Awareness** Moving from the clarity previously attained through Stillness, focus intensely upon the goal of the working. Become completely immersed in this thought.	
13	Maintain this focus while circulating and intensifying energies.	
14	**Emotive Generation** Powerfully generate the emotion or feeling evoked by focus upon the magickal goal.	
15	**Culmination** Continue to draw in and circulate external energy through the body. The clear, unwavering focus is directed upon goal of the working. The enhanced perception facilitates an awareness of the self within a vast etheric ecology, drawing upon powerful external forces. The emotions generated are in accordance with the working. Maintain this circulation, focus, and clarity as you become inflamed with potent pneuma.	

16	**Expand into Union with Region** Upon each inhale draw earth energy into the core, feel this energy build and intensify as the spirit body is filled with power. Upon each exhale use the intensified internal energy to expand the entirety of the etheric self through the Universal Etheric Field into ever widening union with surrounding phenomena. As the etheric self expands into union with the larger region, shift awareness beyond individuated consciousness into direct perception of surrounding phenomena. Allow this expanded, unified state to dissolve the separation between yourself and surrounding phenomena within the larger region.	*Use the mind, breath, and energy to expand the entirety of the etheric self into union with surrounding phenomena. This union may be experienced as expanding to great size, perception from a great height, or omnipresence throughout the region. As the etheric body expands it becomes a protean field of living energy merging into the Universal Etheric Field, becoming one with surrounding phenomena. Gestures and movement may be used in concert with the mind, breath, and energy to guide the expansion of the etheric self.*
17	Continue this expansion until you have achieved union with the entire region to be affected.	*Expansion into a local region is typically sufficient for most workings. This region may include the local surroundings, a neighborhood or city. However, the experienced magus may expand further to effect change on a global scale.*

18	**Become Aware of Relevant Phenomena** Focus upon the magickal goal. Become aware of phenomena within the region that are relevant to the magickal goal.	*Focus upon the intent of the magickal working and all interrelated phenomena that could potentially affect its successful attainment.* *Expansive Union typically entails working at the etheric level to attract, repel, or reconfigure phenomena that directly affect or surround the subject of the magickal goal. Primary elements affected include the etheric aspects of material phenomena, energy currents, and the minds of others.*
19	**Become Aware of Inertial Flow of Events** Become aware of the inertial flow of causal events as they surround and affect these relevant phenomena.	*Inertial currents are typically perceived as a visceral sensation of motion. This momentum may be felt as it shifts and pulls phenomena along trajectories and paths set in motion by the action of cause and effect.*
20	**Shift Relevant Phenomena** Having become one with the region, use the mind, energy, and protean nature of the expanded etheric body to shift phenomena within the region into alignment with the magickal goal.	*Become deeply aware of your union with relevant phenomena and the inertial flow of events in which they exist. Use the mind, energy, gestures and entirety of your being to shift all relevant phenomena and inertial currents into alignment with the magickal goal. This may entail drawing phenomena toward or deflecting phenomena away from yourself or another subject. It may also entail reconfiguring the complex interaction of components within the region into accordance with the magickal goal.*

| 21 | **Contract the Etheric Body** Use the mind and breath to contract the etheric self back into the material body.

Upon each inhale, contract the etheric body back into the material body. Upon each exhale, further condense the expanded etheric body. As the etheric body contracts into the material body, shift consciousness away from the expanded unified state, and return to individuated awareness. | |
| 22 | **Closing Techniques** Perform the Artes Concludendi. | |

CLOSING TECHNIQUES
Artes Concludendi

The Closing Techniques are typically used in conjunction with the Preliminary Techniques. The Preliminary Techniques induce an altered state of consciousness and leave the magus inflamed with pneuma technikon specifically crafted to the magickal goal. The Closing Techniques return consciousness and internal energies to normal states. They entail Banishing, Circulation, Centering and Cultivation. The act of banishing removes any unwanted remaining thoughts, energies, emotions, or entities that may be present. Circulation entails moving internal energies through the etheric channels and centers. This disperses and balances energy within the body and normalizes energetic flow. During this circulation, excess energies may be vented from the body and projected into the earth. Depleted energies may be augmented by drawing in energy from the external power source accessed during the Preliminary Techniques. In the context of the Closing Techniques, Centering returns the magus to normal consciousness and shifts focus back to the material aspect of reality. This entails sequentially contracting the etheric centers as energies accessed during the magickal working are drawn down the body to the Center of Power and vital energy. This sets the consciousness within the etheric centers and roots awareness in the moment at hand. Cultivation increases the amount of stored energy within the body. During Cultivation excess energies called upon during the working are gathered and stored within the Center of Power. Additionally, Cultivation reabsorbs the protective barrier generated during the Preliminary Techniques.

Sigil of Perception

TECHNIQUE Closing Techniques

	PROCEDURES	ANNOTATION
1	**Banishing** Banish yourself of any remaining unwanted thoughts, energies, and emotions. (See banishing in the Preliminary Technique section.)	*Do not banish any energies that you wish to retain.*
2	**Circulation** Become aware of the body's internal flow of energy. Use the mind and breath to circulate the energies awakened and accessed during the magickal working through the etheric channels and centers. If the flow of energy feels too powerful, vent energy deep into the earth from the etheric center in the palms and the soles of the feet. If internal energies feel depleted, draw energy in from the external power source and circulate it through the body. Continue circulation until the flow normalizes and internal energies feel balanced, strong, and flow freely.	*Perceive the flow of energy within the etheric body. After the magickal working, the energies awakened, generated, and summoned are typically still flowing strongly through the body. Unwanted thoughts, energies and emotions have been banished. The resulting flow of raw undifferentiated pneuma may be used to balance and strengthen the etheric self. Depleted energies may be replenished via the external power source accessed during the Preliminary techniques.* *The step of Circulation typically entails briefly moving energy through the body to establish a natural, balanced flow of energy throughout the body. Circulate energy up the dorsal channel and down the ventral channel. Alternately, any traditional paths of energy circulation may be used or energy may be circulated through the body in a manner that feels intuitive.*

3	**Centering** Use the mind and breath to draw these circulating energies down the body from the Centers of Mind and Emotion, collecting them in the Center of Power. As the energy leaves these centers, contract them sequentially. Upon the inhale, gather and circulate energy within the center. Upon the exhale, contract the center as energy is drawn down the ventral channel. As these energies reach the Center of Power, contract the center to its normal size.	*As the centers contract, shift the awareness back to material reality. Set the awareness within the etheric centers and become aware of the moment at hand.*
4	**Cultivation** Upon contracting the center of Power, cultivate internal energies within this center for future use.	*Use the mind and breath to condense internal energies into the Center of Power. Feel this energy intensify as it is concentrated into the center.*
5	Use the mind and breath to reabsorb the protective barrier generated during the Preliminary Techniques back into the Center of Power.	*Upon inhale draw the sphere into the Center of Power. Upon exhale condense the sphere into the Center of Power.*

Banishing the magickal space may occasionally be necessary if unwanted energies or entities remain. The magus uses Energy Casting to emit a radial pulse of energy outward to cleanse the magickal space. This step is performed prior to reabsorbing the protective barrier.

TECHNIQUE Banish the Immediate Surroundings (Optional)

	PROCEDURES	ANNOTATION
1	**Radiate Energy** Upon inhale feel the Center of Power become filled with energy. Upon exhale powerfully emit a radial pulse of pneuma to clear the area of unwanted energies and entities.	
2	**Repeat as Necessary** Repeat as necessary to cleanse the area of unwanted phenomena.	

The following technique may be used to banish objects that have become saturated with unwanted energies. This step of the Closing Techniques is typically required only in instances when specific objects are exposed to unwanted energies during the magickal operation.

TECHNIQUE Banish Specific Objects (Optional)

	PROCEDURES	ANNOTATION
1	**Emit Energy** Use the mind and breath to emit streams of energy from the etheric centers in the palms and fingertips. Extend this energy into the object.	
2	**Scan for Unwanted Energies** Use this energy to scan for unwanted energies within the object.	

3	**Draw out Unwanted Energies** If unwanted energy is detected, use the energy extended from the hands to collect and pull it from the object.	
4	**Discard Unwanted Energies** Push this energy from your hands deep into the Earth.	*Use the mind and breath to dispose of the unwanted energy. Upon inhale direct energy into the hands. Upon exhale strongly project the unwanted energy deep into the Earth.*
5	**Repeat as Necessary** Repeat this process until all unwanted energies have been extracted.	

Chapter 3

MAGICKAL PRACTICES

The practices presented in this chapter are a selection of magickal endeavors traditionally employed to transform and enhance the lives of practitioners and the communities they serve. These practices make use of core magickal techniques to perform a specific type of magickal action. The techniques provided are general and may be modified or adapted as needed. The magickal practices are typically performed within the framework of ritual. For further details regarding ritual see chapter four.

Commonly used magickal practices include:
- ~ Divination
- ~ Interacting with Etheric Entities
- ~ Healing
- ~ The Work of the Psychopomp
- ~ Magickal Influence
- ~ Blessing
- ~ Love Magick
- ~ Sex Magick
- ~ Cursing
- ~ Defensive Magick
- ~ Protection Magick
- ~ Dream Magick
- ~ Working with Magickal Substances
- ~ Working with Symbols
- ~ Chants and Words of Power
- ~ Working with Magickal Tools
- ~ Group Magick
- ~ Etheric Exploration
- ~ Training
- ~ Transformation

DIVINATION
Divinatio

Divination is the practice of acquiring information via magickal means. Temporal divination allows the magus to perceive the future and the past. Divination of the present is used to perceive the complex web of causality and underlying etheric phenomena that shape events in the now. Remote viewing is the perception of distant locations, people or events.

The Nature of Time

To understand temporal divination, one must understand the nature of time. Time is a process of movement and becoming. It is the expansion of the continuum of existence as it is coming into being. This expansion is experienced as the linear forward progression of time. The current relative point in this expansion is perceived as the present. Perception of material reality provides a limited perspective of this temporal "now". The subtle aspects of existence extend beyond the material aspects as the continuum of existence is coming into being. Via this temporal extension the magus may expand the awareness and perceive the inertial flow of events as they extend forward in time beyond what is typically perceived as the present. Such awareness facilitates the perception of potential futures as they are shaped by action in the present. All phenomena emanate etheric energies. Additionally, every action, event, and thought sends energetic waves, currents, and emanations into the Universal Etheric Field. This energetic interaction creates complex, ever changing patterns of etheric energy that move throughout the Universal Etheric Field like ripples in a pond. These patterns of energy and motion reflect the inertial momentum, trajectories, and energetic imprints of actions and events in the present. As these emanations move forward through the time stream they interact and shift configuration. These shifting configurations reflect potential futures as they develop along the time stream. Through expanded states of consciousness the magus may project the awareness through the Universal Etheric Field and forward in time to perceive the ever shifting configurations and movements of these emanations and the potential futures they reflect. Such perceptions are typically experienced as a sudden flash of insight, disjointed images, premonitory intuition, powerful emotions, or a fully immersive visionary experience. The future perceived is probable rather than finite due to the fact that events in the present are in a constant state of flux. Futures perceived during divination are ever-changing as they are continually

Symbol for the Future

re-shaped by action in the present. As such, divination of the future is the art of foreseeing probable outcomes rather than predicting certain fates.

TECHNIQUE Divination of the Future

	PROCEDURES	ANNOTATION
1	**Expanded Perception** Use the technique of Expanded Perception to perceive the subject within its larger environment. Become aware of phenomena that interact with and affect the subject. Expanded Perception may be used to perceive both distant subjects and those in close proximity.	*Center and banish, sequentially awaken and expand the centers of Power, Emotion and Mind. Enter Stillness and shift the awareness into the Universal Etheric Field to perceive reality on a large scale. Feel and perceive the flow of events that surround the subject.*
2	**Project Awareness Forward in Time** Project the awareness forward in time.	*Project the awareness forward in the time stream along with the flow of events that surround the subject.*

3	**Perceive Subject's Future** Perceive the energy currents, emanations, and waves of force sent forward in the time stream by subject's actions in the present. Become aware of the movement, interaction, and configuration of these emanations as they move forward in time. Use this perception to comprehend the future outcome of circumstances and events surrounding and affecting the subject in the present. Perception of this future may be experienced as a sudden flash of insight, disjointed images, premonitory intuition, powerful emotions, or a fully immersive visionary experience. The future is in a constant state of flux due to action and change in the present. Visions of the future fade and change as events in the present shift course. The visions perceived reflect the outcome of the current flow of events.	*Become immersed in the inertial flow of events as they interact and move forward in time. Perceive potential futures as they take shape.*

| 4 | **Center and Return to Normal Consciousness** Become aware of the internal energy raised to awaken the etheric centers. Use the mind and breath to draw this energy down the body from the Centers of Mind and Emotion, collecting it in the Center of Power. As the energy leaves these centers, contract them sequentially. Upon the inhale, gather and circulate energy within the center. Upon the exhale, contract the center as energy is drawn down the ventral channel. As the energy reaches the Center of Power, contract the center to its normal size and cultivate internal energy for future use. | *As the centers contract, shift the awareness back to material reality. Set the awareness within the etheric centers and become acutely aware of the moment at hand.* |

DIVINATION OF THE PAST

Divining the past entails perception of events that have already occurred. As time moves forward, past events leave an etheric trace. At the etheric level all things emanate energies, leaving trace emanations in surrounding phenomena and the Universal Etheric Field. Such traces may last indefinitely. Through enhanced perception the magus may experience echoes of past events contained within these traces. Traces may be perceived as images, emotions, or vivid visions of past events.

DIVINATION OF THE PAST VIA ETHERIC PERCEPTION

Etheric Perception may be used to perceive the traces of the past within the immediate surroundings.

TECHNIQUE Divination of the Past via Etheric Perception

	PROCEDURES	ANNOTATION
1	**Etheric Perception** Center and banish, sequentially awaken and expand the centers of Power, Emotion and Mind. Enter Stillness and shift consciousness to the etheric aspect of existence.	*Etheric traces are primarily perceived by the etheric centers of Mind, Emotion, and Power. Smaller etheric centers throughout the etheric body may also be used to perceive etheric traces. Those in the palms of the hands and fingertips are particularly well suited for this task.*
2	**Identify Traces of Past Events** Shift perception away from the foremost etheric phenomena and towards deeper background emanations. These emanations may be embedded in material objects or imprinted upon the Universal Etheric Field.	
3	Isolate etheric emanations that appear to originate in the past.	*When perceived, emanations of the past induce a sensation of being drawn backwards in time. This odd sensation may be used to identify past emanations.*
4	**Read Traces of the Past** Allow the awareness to be drawn into these echoes of the past. Traces may be perceived as images, emotions, or vivid visions of past events.	*The sensation of reading etheric traces may be likened to becoming immersed in a holographic recording of past events.*

5	Center and Return to Normal Consciousness	As the centers contract, shift the awareness back to material reality. Set the awareness within the etheric centers and become acutely aware of the moment at hand.
	Become aware of the internal energy raised to awaken the etheric centers. Use the mind and breath to draw this energy down the body from the Centers of Mind and Emotion, collecting it in the Center of Power. As the energy leaves these centers, contract them sequentially. Upon the inhale, gather and circulate energy within the center. Upon the exhale, contract the center as energy is drawn down the ventral channel. As the energy reaches the Center of Power, contract the center to its normal size and cultivate internal energy for future use.	

DIVINATION OF THE PAST VIA EXPANDED PERCEPTION

Divination of the past via Expanded Perception involves scanning the Universal Etheric Field to perceive traces of the past. This allows the magus to perceive traces regardless of their point of origin. By moving the awareness deeper into these traces, the magus perceives further into the past. This technique facilitates viewing the past of an individual or distant subject. When perceiving an individual's past, the magus becomes aware of the traces that the individual has left upon the Universal Etheric Field.

TECHNIQUE Divination of the Past via Expanded Perception

	PROCEDURES	ANNOTATION
1	**Perceive Traces of the Past** Use the technique of Expanded Perception to scan the Universal Etheric Field for traces of the subject's past.	*When perceived, emanations of the past induce a sensation of being drawn backwards in time. This odd sensation may be used to identify past emanations.*
2	**Read Traces of the Past** Allow the awareness to be drawn into these echoes of the past. Traces may be perceived as images, emotions, or vivid visions of past events.	*The sensation of reading etheric traces may be likened to becoming immersed in a holographic recording of past events.*
3	**Center and Return to Normal Consciousness** Become aware of the internal energy raised to awaken the etheric centers. Use the mind and breath to draw this energy down the body from the Centers of Mind and Emotion, collecting it in the Center of Power. As the energy leaves these centers, contract them sequentially. Upon the inhale, gather and circulate energy within the center. Upon the exhale, contract the center as energy is drawn down the ventral channel. As the energy reaches the Center of Power, contract the center to its normal size and cultivate internal energy for future use.	*As the centers contract, shift the awareness back to material reality. Set the awareness within the etheric centers and become acutely aware of the moment at hand.*

DIVINATION OF THE PRESENT

Divination of the present makes use of Expanded Perception and Etheric Perception to achieve an enhanced understanding of reality. The technique of Expanded Perception is used to perceive causality on a large scale as surrounding phenomena move in a constant flow of cause and effect. Such perception allows the magus to comprehend the interplay of components in a complex system. Etheric Perception is used to directly perceive the underlying etheric phenomena that often shape events.

Symbol for the Present

TECHNIQUE Divination of the Present via Expanded Perception

	PROCEDURES	ANNOTATION
1	**Expanded Perception**	*Shift the awareness into the Universal Etheric Field to perceive reality on a large scale.*
2	**Perceive Relevant Phenomena** Perceive relevant phenomena that interact with and affect the subject, and the inertial flow of causal events in which they exist.	*This perception may be experienced as a sudden flash of insight, disjointed images, powerful emotions, or a fully immersive visionary experience.*
3	**Comprehend Interaction** Become aware of the way in which the relevant phenomena and the flow of events affect the subject of divination.	*Such perception allows the magus to comprehend the way in which reality at large affects and interacts with the subject.*

| 4 | **Center and Return to Normal Consciousness**
Become aware of the internal energy raised to awaken the etheric centers. Use the mind and breath to draw this energy down the body from the Centers of Mind and Emotion, collecting it in the Center of Power. As the energy leaves these centers, contract them sequentially. Upon the inhale, gather and circulate energy within the center. Upon the exhale, contract the center as energy is drawn down the ventral channel. As the energy reaches the Center of Power, contract the center to its normal size and cultivate internal energy for future use. | *As the centers contract, shift the awareness back to material reality. Set the awareness within the etheric centers and become acutely aware of the moment at hand.* |

TECHNIQUE Divination of the Present via Etheric Perception

	PROCEDURES	*ANNOTATION*
1	**Etheric Perception** Use Etheric Perception to observe the subject matter of divination at the etheric level. Center and banish, sequentially awaken and expand the centers of Power, Emotion and Mind. Enter Stillness and shift consciousness to the etheric aspect of existence.	*Identify etheric phenomena that may be affecting the subject of divination. Phenomena that exert a particularly powerful effect upon reality include etheric entities, energy currents, positive or negative power spots, and potent etheric traces. This technique is also used to determine if a person, place or thing has been enchanted.*

| 2 | **Comprehend Interaction**
Comprehend the interaction of etheric phenomena with the subject. | *Perceive the way the in which etheric phenomena interact with the subject of divination. If an etheric entity is observed, it is important to determine its nature and intent and if it is interacting with the subject of divination. The mere presence of an entity does not necessarily imply that it is affecting the subject.*
Energy currents are ever present and are often observed moving through and around the subject. It is important to ascertain the energetic tone of these currents in order to determine their effect upon the subject.

Power spots are naturally occurring upwellings of etheric energy. The energetic tone of power spots may range from malign to beneficent. Proximity to such spots can exert a profound effect upon the subject of divination.

The energetic traces of powerful past events can continue to affect the present. If an energetic trace is perceived, determine its tone and intensity to ascertain the potential effect upon the subject.

The energetic traces of powerful past events can continue to affect the present. If an energetic trace is perceived, determine its tone and intensity to ascertain the potential effect upon the subject. |

	Comprehend Interaction *(continued)*	*To determine if an enchantment has been cast, scan the subject for unusually potent pneuma exhibiting cognitive and emotive properties. Such potent pneuma technikon may be recognized by its distinctive semi-sentient and reactive behavior. It may also appear to be out-of-place with surrounding energies and phenomena. Direct perception of this pneuma technikon allows the magus to "read" the intent of the enchantment. This is accomplished by observing the behavior of the pneuma technikon and perceiving its conscious objective and emotive tone. This perception may be experienced as a sudden flash of insight, disjointed images, powerful emotions, or a fully immersive visionary experience.*
3	**Center and Return to Normal Consciousness** Become aware of the internal energy raised to awaken the etheric centers. Use the mind and breath to draw this energy down the body from the Centers of Mind and Emotion, collecting it in the Center of Power. As the energy leaves these centers, contract them sequentially.	*As the centers contract, shift the awareness back to material reality. Set the awareness within the etheric centers and become acutely aware of the moment at hand.*

| 4 | Upon the inhale, gather and circulate energy within the center. Upon the exhale, contract the center as energy is drawn down the ventral channel. As the energy reaches the Center of Power, contract the center to its normal size and cultivate internal energy for future use. | |

Remote Viewing

Remote Viewing is used to locate and observe distant subjects and regions. This practice employs the techniques of Expanded Perception and Spirit Projection. Expanded Perception is used to view the subject or area from broad, somewhat detached perspective. Spirit Projection is used to transport the etheric body of the magus to the desired location. Upon projecting to the location the magus may view the scene as if physically present.

TECHNIQUE Remote Viewing via Expanded Perception

	PROCEDURES	ANNOTATION
1	**Locate the Subject** Use the technique of Expanded Perception to locate the subject.	*Scan the awareness through the Universal Etheric Field to locate and perceive the subject.*
2	**Perceive the Subject** Use state of Expanded Perception to perceive the subject.	*During Expanded Perception the subject is viewed from a somewhat detached perspective.*

| 3 | **Center and Return to Normal Consciousness** Become aware of the internal energy raised to awaken the etheric centers. Use the mind and breath to draw this energy down the body from the Centers of Mind and Emotion, collecting it in the Center of Power. As the energy leaves these centers, contract them sequentially. Upon the inhale, gather and circulate energy within the center. Upon the exhale, contract the center as energy is drawn down the ventral channel. As the energy reaches the Center of Power, contract the center to its normal size and cultivate internal energy for future use. | *As the centers contract, shift the awareness back to material reality. Set the awareness within the etheric centers and become acutely aware of the moment at hand.* |

TECHNIQUE Remote Viewing via Spirit Projection

	PROCEDURES	ANNOTATION
1	**Preliminary Techniques** Perform the Artes Praeviae.	*When performing the Preliminary Techniques, strongly focus upon the intent to travel to the desired location. Such focus prevents disorientation and assists in locating the desired subject or destination. Additionally, the clarity attained via the Preliminary Techniques facilitates accurate perception of remote phenomena.*
2	**Spirit Projection** Use the technique of Spirit Projection to leave the material body.	

3	**Project to the Subject** Using the technique of Spirit Projection, travel to the subject's location.	
4	**Observe Subject** The etheric body is now free to observe the subject from a first person perspective.	*Spirit Projection allows the magus to perceive the subject as if physically present at the subject's location.*
5	**Return to the Material Body** Return to the material body and normal consciousness.	
6	**Closing Techniques** Perform the Artes Concludendi.	

EXPECTATIONS

Shifting perception towards the etheric aspect of reality confers an expanded, holistic experience of existence. As such, the art of divination is subject to interference from various sources. Phenomena perceived may originate from the past, portend potential futures, or reflect distant spatial locations. Interference may also be generated from the thoughts of individuals as they emanate into the Universal Etheric Field. Therefore precise divination is not always possible. Precise divination of the future may be illusive due to an ever changing present. Divination of the past entails identifying and reading overlapping traces of past events spanning ages of history. When looking into the traces of the past, the magus is looking through multiple layers of time and the traces of multiple individuals. Divination via Remote Viewing may be subject to the temporal and spatial ambiguity of etheric reality, and interference from random emanations within the Universal Etheric Field. Due to the complex and incorporeal nature of etheric reality, the art of divination lacks the precision and predictability of ordinary perception. Divinatory perception is typically experienced as a sudden flash of insight, disjointed images, premonitory intuition, powerful emotions, or a fully immersive visionary experience.

ETHERIC ENTITIES
Entia Aetherica

The art of magick often involves working with etheric entities. The term etheric entity refers to a nonmaterial energetic being. At the etheric level, pneuma has evolved into complex energetic patterns. As these patterns increase in complexity they manifest the typical behaviors associated with living beings. A sufficiently complex etheric being possesses volition, emotion, and consciousness. Etheric entities vary greatly in form, power, and sentience. The greater the complexity of the etheric pattern, the greater the sentience of the being. Similarly, the greater the energy of the being, the greater its power to affect reality at the etheric level. There are several types of entities with which the magus may interact. Those commonly encountered include simple spirits, cultivated spirits, complex spirits, disembodied humans, and deities. All such entities are aspects of the multifaceted monad that is the cosmos. Deities are large fields of consciousness and power within the Universal Etheric Field. These intelligent energies are capable of manifesting themselves to humans in forms that can be apprehended by human consciousness. Spirits are smaller, more localized energetic complexes within the Universal Etheric Field. Such beings may change their form at will and are typically perceived subjectively. Human spirits, both incarnate and disincarnate are also aspects of the greater universal collective. In interacting with such entities, the magus draws upon and reconnects to a larger collective of consciousness and power.

Simple Spirits
Simple spirits are beings of limited sentience and power, such as elementals and rudimentary nature spirits. Commonly encountered in etheric environments, these spirits exert a relatively weak effect upon reality at the etheric level.

Cultivated Entities
Cultivated entities, also known as servitors, thoughtforms, or artificial elementals are simple creatures produced by specialized Energy Casting techniques. This process involves generating and emitting pneuma that is relevant to the intended function of the entity. This pneuma is then cultivated and shaped to the degree that it grows in complexity and power. When sufficiently developed, this externalized life force is capable of carrying out the basic functions of an etheric entity. For practical reasons, the cultivated entity may be attached to a material form. The material form typically consists of a statuette, wax or clay

figure, painting, sigil, talisman or crystal. The material basis may also consist of a sealed vial, flask, or bottle containing various materiae magicae possessing properties in resonance with the intended function of the entity. Such material is typically suspended within an oil or alcohol preparation. Attaching a cultivated entity to a material form saturates the material with the pneuma of the entity. This links the entity to the material form via action of resonance. When attached to a material form an entity is more easily summoned and sustained. Typically, cultivated entities serve as magickal assistants charged with carrying out simple tasks. Cultivated entities are of great practical use due to the fact that they are created by the magus for the sole purpose of service. These entities are an extension of the self, an externalized portion of consciousness and life force. If sustained, they will work tirelessly in service of their creator. Within Tibetan occultism, the term Tulpa is applied to similar externalized manifestations of consciousness and life force.

Complex Spirits

Complex spirits possess human level sentience and the power to significantly affect reality at the etheric level. Such spirits are described in folklore as elves, fairies, daemons etc. The magus may foster relationships with these beings as magickal allies.

Disembodied Humans

Disembodied humans are the spirits of the deceased. In certain circumstances the etheric body of an individual remains intact after the death of the material body. This postmortem survival is sometimes intentional, in other cases it is more or less an accident. The disembodied humans most relevant to magick are ghosts and immortals.

Disembodied Humans - Ghosts

The term ghost typically refers to the spirit of a deceased person who is attached to a particular location, object, or individual. This link to material reality may be formed by powerful obsession. Strong attachment in life can be carried over into death. In a state of obsession, an individual's consciousness, emotion and energy are focused upon a single subject. Occasionally this focus is strong enough to prevent postmortem dissipation and bind the spirit indefinitely to the subject of obsession. Due to their obsessive nature and accidental postmortem survival, ghosts may only be dimly aware of their surroundings and the fact that they are deceased. In some instances however, ghosts are fully aware and may interact with

---

the living. The magus may contact ghosts to obtain information or collaborate on magickal projects. The magus may also act as a psychopomp to free ghosts from obsession and assist them in moving to the next level of their existence.

Disembodied Humans - Immortals

Immortals are the spirits of individuals who have intentionally transformed their etheric bodies to the degree that they have survived death. Examples would include, ascended masters, mystics, and magi that have mastered the disciplines of immortality. The magus may foster relationships with immortals as magickal partners, guides, and teachers.

Deities

Deities are ancient, powerful etheric entities that have interacted with humanity for millennia. Such entities are the Gods and Goddesses described in mythology, religion and folklore. Deities exist as vast, complex fields of consciousness and power within the Universal Etheric Field. They manifest to humans in forms that can be apprehended by the human mind. The relationship between deities and mankind is mutually beneficial. In becoming one with a deity, the magus becomes one with the consciousness and power of a larger aspect of the universal collective. Human thought, emotion, and energy serve to nourish and strengthen deities. Traditionally, deities obtain these energies via human devotion, offerings and interaction. In turn, deities provide wisdom, power and general aid to humans with whom they are in resonance. These ancient spirits are a source of power and transformation.

INTERACTING WITH ETHERIC ENTITIES
Collaboratio cum Entia Aetherica

In order to work effectively with etheric entities the magus must develop the skills necessary to perceive and communicate with such beings. Etheric Perception is used to become aware of the presence of etheric entities. Etheric Communication is then employed to interact with entities. The nature of this interaction is typically dependent upon the type of entity being addressed, the relationship between the magus and the entity, and nature of the magickal goal. Perception of etheric entities is subjective. Etheric reality is interpreted by the mind of the magus. The Center of Mind interprets external etheric phenomena based upon the internal symbolism, thoughts and expectations of the magus. Therefore perception of etheric entities may vary between magi. This subjectivity is compounded by the polymorphic nature of etheric entities. Complex entities and deities, in particular, are able to manifest in forms that can be apprehended by human consciousness.

The magus relates to etheric entities in a variety of ways. This interaction is often mutually beneficial. The two primary factors that motivate an etheric entity to work with a magus are resonance and offertory. Resonance occurs when an entity and the magus possess a similar energetic tone. This induces a state of union in which the sympathetic cognitive, emotive, and energetic emanations of the two beings resonate and intensify. Such resonance increases the power of both the entity and the magus. Additionally, this essential sympathy forms a strong bond of fellowship between the two beings. The term offertory refers to an energetic offering given by the magus to an etheric entity. Etheric entities are both nourished and made powerful by offertory. This energetic offering may consist of pneuma directly projected into the entity or a material substance that is rich in or has been saturated with pneuma. Traditionally used offertory substances include wine, beer, bread, grain, incense, and flowers. Any material that is naturally rich in life force may serve as a material basis for offertory. Etheric entities absorb the pneuma within such material offerings. When generating pneuma technikon for offertory the magus produces energies specifically crafted to nourish and increase the power of the entity. Providing offertory to an etheric entity in exchange for services is an ancient, cross cultural practice. Detailed references to such practices are found in the Papyri Graecae Magicae (Greek Magical Papyri).

The basis of the relationship between the magus and an entity varies depending upon the type of entity. Deities are vast, powerful beings. These entities are strengthened by the thoughts, emotions and energies of those with whom they are in resonance. This resonance increases a deity's power. While deities also benefit from offertory, these ancient beings are primarily strengthened by entering a state of resonance with a large number of humans. Such resonance forges deep and meaningful bonds between both deity and human. Simple spirits, complex spirits and ghosts may greatly benefit from offertory and establishing a close, personal relationship with the magus. The power of such beings is lesser than that of deities. Such spirits typically require energy sources to sustain their existence, therefore offertories given by the magus are greatly valued. They seldom interact with humans, and can be quite fond of the companionship and resonance experienced when working with a magus. Cultivated spirits are an extension of the self, created to serve a specific purpose. Therefore, they require little motivation to serve the magus, but may weaken if not provided with regular offertory. Immortals interact with humans in accordance with their own personal missions. Such relationships may be based upon a deep resonance. Immortals do not typically seek offertory but appreciate and benefit from it none the less.

EVOCATION

Evocation is used to powerfully draw an entity to the magus. The term evocation typically refers to the calling of an entity to manifest outside the self. Entities may be evoked to obtain information, forge relationships, and collaborate on magickal goals. During evocation the magus uses potent thoughts, emotions, and energies to reach out to an entity and powerfully influence it to appear. This cognitive and emotive pneuma is generated by intensely focusing upon calling forth the spirit. Such focus typically entails strongly envisioning the entity while intoning simple chants such as "spirit come to me". This focus is maintained until the magus is inflamed with potent pneuma. Etheric Communication is then used to strongly project this pneuma out through the Universal Etheric Field. The potent cognitive and emotive energies within such pneuma are capable of directly communicating with and influencing etheric entities. The greater the raw power of the pneuma, the greater the ability of the magus to call upon an entity. Subtle and energetic in nature, etheric entities are sensitive to powerful cognitive and emotive energies. When correctly performed, such evocation induces in the entity a strong desire to respond to the call of the magus. The nature of evocation varies depending upon the entity being evoked. Evocation may entail reaching out to an entity and using the power of influence to graciously request its presence. It may also entail using such influence to powerfully summon an entity.

Possessing specific information about an entity enhances the ability of the magus to focus upon and contact the entity. Prior to evoking an entity, the magus gathers information regarding its nature. Typically this information consists of the entity's emotive temperament, intelligence, and behavioral traits. Additional information may include the entity's true name, preferred form, abode, sigil, or evoking incantation. This information is focused upon during the generation of pneuma. Occasionally the magus may choose to evoke an entity of which little is known. In such instances the magus simply focuses upon contacting and drawing the entity known to reside in a specific location.

ENLISTING THE AID OF SPIRITS

When enlisting the aid of a spirit the magus may call upon one with whom a relationship has already been formed. Entities cataloged in the corpus of existing grimoires and traditional lore may also be evoked. Such entities are selected in accordance with the goal of the magickal working. Evocation is used to call the entity to the location of the magus. The magus then informs the entity that an energetic offering will be provided in exchange for a service. This offertory is typically provided after completion of the task. This arrangement may be continued on an ongoing basis to achieve various goals. The nature of this interaction may range from simple quid pro quo arrangement to a close friendship. It is important to be specific in communicating the details of the task. Simple, clearly defined tasks may be better suited for entities of limited sentience. Those of higher sentience are capable of more complex tasks. If the task is to be performed at a distant location, Expanded Perception may be used to direct the spirit to the correct location. Working with spirits in this manner is mutually beneficial for both parties. The grimoires of old are filled with incantations to threaten and compel spirits. Forcibly compelling spirits to serve is both unethical and inadvisable, often resulting in rebellion and betrayal.

INVOCATION

A deity may be invoked to bring a particular type of energy to the magickal operation. Invocation is also used to imbue the magus with the attributes and powers of a specific deity. The term invocation typically refers to calling the power or consciousness of an entity into the self. When invoking a deity the magus first generates pneuma that is in resonance with the cognitive and emotive nature of the deity. This may be accomplished by strongly envisioning the attributes associated with the specific deity. Expanded Perception is then used to perceive the deity. The magus then calls upon the entity using Etheric Communication. This call is typically a formal request to the deity to bestow its power upon the magus. The call may be combined with chant, words of power and recitation to increase its power. If the request is granted, the magus and deity enter a state of resonance. In this state of union, the magus becomes inflamed with the deity's power, consciousness, and emotions. The deity in turn benefits from the powerful energetic resonance produced by the pneuma generated during Preliminary Techniques. The magus may redirect the deity's energy to any desired magickal goal.

TECHNIQUE Perceive and Communicate with an Etheric Entity

	PROCEDURES	ANNOTATION
	Etheric Perception	
1	**Etheric Perception** Center and banish, sequentially awaken and expand the centers of Power, Emotion and Mind. Enter Stillness and shift consciousness to the etheric aspect of existence.	
2	**Locate and Perceive the Entity** Use the expanded, receptive centers to perceive emanations from surrounding etheric phenomena. Use the Center of Mind to visually perceive the entity. This center may also be used to perceive emanations of consciousness. Use the Center of Emotion to discern the entity's emotive tone. Use the Center of Power to sense the energetic intensity of the entity.	*Attune the centers of Mind, Emotion, and Power to locate and perceive the entity.* *Use the Center of Mind to visually perceive the form of the entity. The Center of Mind may also be used to "listen" for the entity's thoughts or communications. The Center of Emotion may be used to identify the presence of strong emotions emanating from the entity. The Center of Power may be used to sense the integral power of the entity. The etheric centers in the palms of the hands may also be used to perceive emanations from the entity. Together, these expanded receptive centers provide a comprehensive perception of the etheric entity.*

Etheric Communication		
3	**Send Communication** Use the mind and breath to strongly project thoughts and emotions to the entity.	*Project thoughts and emotions to contact and greet the entity. Communicate the intent of your interaction. This communication may be entirely silent or may be combined with spoken dialog.*
4	**Receive Communication** Cease the generation of thought and emotion. Return to a state of Stillness. Listen for the mental and emotive response from the subject.	*This response is typically experienced as sudden powerful thoughts, emotions, or imagery, that originate from outside the psyche of the magus.*
5	**Continue Communication** Continue to send and receive until the communication is complete.	*This communication may take the form of verbal dialog, visions, or powerful emotions.*
6	**Center and Return to Normal Consciousness** Become aware of the internal energy raised to awaken the etheric centers. Use the mind and breath to draw this energy down the body from the Centers of Mind and Emotion, collecting it in the Center of Power. As the energy leaves these centers, contract them sequentially. Upon the inhale, gather and circulate energy within the center. Upon the exhale, contract the center as energy is drawn down the ventral channel. As the energy reaches the Center of Power, contract the center to its normal size and cultivate internal energy for future use.	*As the centers contract, shift the awareness back to material reality. Set the awareness within the etheric centers and become acutely aware of the moment at hand.*

TECHNIQUE Evoke and Communicate with an Etheric Entity

	PROCEDURES	ANNOTATION
1	**Preliminary Techniques** Perform the Artes Praeviae.	*When performing the Artes Praeviae, generate thoughts and emotions to call forth the entity. This is typically accomplished by strongly envisioning the entity while silently intoning simple chants such as "spirit come to me". Additional information such as the entity's name, form, abode, sigil, or evoking incantation may also be focused upon.*
2	**Call the Entity** Use Etheric Communication to call the entity.	*Project a powerful flow of thoughts and emotions across the Universal Etheric Field to call the entity. Feel the potent pneuma technikon generated during the Preliminary Techniques radiate out with this call. This pneuma may be emitted out with the breath and the etheric centers in the palms. It may also be radiated into the Universal Etheric Field from major etheric centers such as the Center of Power or the Center of Mind. The entity may be called from any distance. The call may combined with an evocation chant or recitation.*
		Entities are typically evoked to manifest outside the protective barrier or magickal circle.
3	**Perceive the Entity** Use Etheric Perception to perceive the entity.	*The receptive state of Etheric Perception was initiated during the Preliminary Techniques. Attune the centers of mind, emotion, and power to directly perceive the entity as it manifests.*

4	**Communicate with the Entity** Use Etheric Communication to interact with the entity.	
5	**Dismiss the Entity** Use Etheric Communication to inform the entity that the interaction is complete and ask it to leave.	*Dismissal varies depending upon the type of entity and the nature of the interaction. It typically consists of thanking the entity and asking it to leave. In the rare instance that the entity refuses to leave or becomes hostile, Magickal Influence or Defensive Techniques may be used.*
6	**Closing Techniques** Perform the Artes Concludendi.	

TECHNIQUE Invoke the Power of a Deity

	PROCEDURES	ANNOTATION
1	**Preliminary Techniques** Perform the Artes Praeviae.	*When performing the Artes Praeviae, generate thoughts and emotions that are in resonance with those of the deity to be invoked. This may be accomplished by strongly envisioning the attributes associated with the specific deity.*
2	**Become Aware of the Deity** Use Expanded Perception to become aware of the deity.	*Shift awareness into the Universal Etheric Field to perceive the deity.*

3	**Call Upon the Deity** Use Etheric Communication to powerfully send a call out to the deity.	*This entails strongly projecting thoughts and emotions through the Universal Etheric Field. Typically a formal request is made of the deity to bestow its power upon the magus. If the request is granted, the magus and entity enter into a state of resonance. Typically, this resonance is experienced as an overpowering wave of the deity's power, consciousness, and emotion. If this resonance is not felt, the magus should thank the deity and cease the communication. Deities rarely interact with humans with whom they do not resonate.*
4	**Resonate With the Deity** Merge into a state of union with the deity. Become completely immersed in the consciousness and power of the deity.	
5	**Become filled with the Deity's Power** Feel the deity's energy flow into you and circulate through the energy channels and centers of your body.	*In resonating with the deity, the magus becomes saturated with its power. This experience can be quite euphoric, deity energy is incredibly potent.*
6	**Direct Invoked Energy toward Goal** Use Energy Casting techniques to apply this energy to the magickal goal.	*This energy may be used to imbue the magus with the traits and powers of the deity. The energy may also be redirected towards a specific magickal goal. Additionally, power may be directed into a talisman or some form of materia magica.*
7	**Thank the Deity** Use Etheric Communication to thank the deity.	

| 8 | **Closing Techniques**
Perform the Artes Concludendi. | *Do not banish deity energies that you wish to retain.* |

TECHNIQUE Creation of a Cultivated Entity

PROCEDURES	*ANNOTATION*
Stage One of the Working (Optional), Banish the Material Form	
1 **Select Material Form** The material form is typically a statuette, small painting, sigil, talisman, or crystal.	*The material form should be in resonance with the intended nature of the entity. Statues and paintings typically reflect the intended etheric form of the entity. Sigils and talismans symbolically reflect the nature of the entity. Crystals are selected that possess etheric properties in resonance with the entity.* *The material form is typically anointed or implanted with Materiae Magicae that is in resonance with the intended nature of the entity.*
2 **Etheric Perception** Etheric Perception is used to determine if the material basis contains unwanted energies.	*Center and banish, sequentially awaken and expand the centers of Power, Emotion and Mind. Enter Stillness and shift consciousness to the etheric aspect of existence.*
3 **Banish the Material Basis (Optional)** If necessary, use the Banish Specific Object technique at the end of chapter two to cleanse the material basis of any unwanted energies.	*Statues, paintings, and material objects that have been purchased or that have an unknown history may contain energies antithetic to the intended nature of the entity. Banishing may be used to cleanse the material basis of any unwanted energies. Crystals should be carefully banished before use. When banishing a crystal it is important to remove only the unwanted energies perceived within the stone, all energies native to the crystal must be left intact.*

4	**Center and Return to Normal Consciousness** Become aware of the internal energy raised to awaken the etheric centers. Use the mind and breath to draw this energy down the body from the Centers of Mind and Emotion, collecting it in the Center of Power. As the energy leaves these centers, contract them sequentially. Upon the inhale, gather and circulate energy within the center. Upon the exhale, contract the center as energy is drawn down the ventral channel. As the energy reaches the Center of Power, contract the center to its normal size and cultivate internal energy for future use.	*As the centers contract, shift the awareness back to material reality. Set the awareness within the etheric centers and become acutely aware of the moment at hand.*

Stage Two of the Working, Create The Entity

1	**Preliminary Techniques** Perform the Artes Praeviae.	*When performing the Artes Praeviae, intensely focus upon the intended function of the entity. This is typically accomplished by strongly envisioning the entity carrying out its task. This focus may be enhanced by silently or verbally intoning a simple chant that delineates the entities task. An example would be "protect this house".*

2	Performing the last step in the Preliminary Techniques, continue to draw in external energy while generating cognitive and emotive pneuma. Circulate these energies until the body is filled to the point of overflowing with potent pneuma technikon.	
3	**Create a Sphere of Pneuma** Use the technique of Primary Energy Casting to direct this pneuma to the etheric centers in the palms and fingertips.	
4	Emit this energy to form a sphere of potent pneuma between the palms. Pour the entirety of your thoughts, emotions, and expectations of the entity into this sphere	
5	**Cultivate the Entity** Continue to project pneuma into the sphere while strongly envisioning the form, attributes, and function of the fully developed entity.	*Feel the sphere become vibrant and powerful. This pneuma technikon is an extension of the self, envision this life force embodying the essence and purpose of the entity.*
6	**Shape the Entity** Use the mind, breath, and energy to guide the development of the pneuma into the desired form of the entity.	*Upon inhale feel the pneuma circulate through your body. Upon exhale feel this life force move through your hands and into the sphere. As the pneuma moves into the sphere, use the mind and energy to guide its transformation into the desired form of the entity.*

7	**Release the Entity or Attach it to a Material Form** When the entity is fully developed and has begun to move on its own accord it may either be released from the hands or placed upon its material form.	*If a material basis is not used, release the entity from the hands and allow it to remain before you.* *If using a material basis, use the energy filled hands to place the entity within, around, or upon its material basis. Allow the entity to merge into the material basis.*
8	**Task the Entity** Use Etheric Communication to delineate the details of the task.	*The entity may be set upon its task immediately, or be summoned at a later time. It may remain in its material form or move about freely.*
9	**Closing Techniques** Perform the Artes Concludendi.	*Do not banish the cultivated entity.*
10	**Sustain the Entity** When properly sustained, a cultivated entity will remain powerful, capable, and loyal. This typically entails regularly summoning the entity and presenting it an offertory of pneuma. If the entity has been provided with a material form, offertory pneuma may be projected directly into the form.	*Pneuma may be directly projected into the entity or provided via saturated material offerings. Regular offertories provide sustenance and maintain bonds of fellowship.*

TECHNIQUE Creation of a Material Offertory

	PROCEDURES	*ANNOTATION*
1	**Select the Material Offering** Traditional offerings include wine, beer, bread, grain, incense, and flowers. Any material that is naturally rich in life force may serve a material basis for offertory.	

2	**Preliminary Techniques** Perform the Artes Praeviae.	*When performing the Artes Praeviae, generate thoughts and emotions that are in resonance with those of the entity. Pneuma generated during the Preliminary Techniques is used as an energetic offertory to the entity. A general purpose offertory may be produced by generating thoughts, emotions, and energies of bliss and pleasure.*
3	Performing the last step in the Preliminary Techniques, continue to draw in external energy while generating cognitive and emotive pneuma. Circulate these energies until the body is filled to the point of overflowing with potent pneuma technikon.	
4	**Saturate the Offering with Pneuma** Use the technique of Primary Energy Casting to saturate the offering with this pneuma. Holding the offering with both hands, use the mind and breath to direct pneuma into the offering. Continue to pour pneuma into the offering until it is completely saturated.	
5	**Closing Techniques** Perform the Artes Concludendi.	*During the closing techniques banish only yourself, do not banish the offering.*

6	**Use of Material Offerings** Material offerings may be placed upon deity shrines or altars, presented to an entity, or left at a sacred spot or location known to be frequented by an entity.	

TECHNIQUE Creation and Use of an Energetic Offertory

	PROCEDURES	*ANNOTATION*
1	**Preliminary Techniques** Perform the Artes Praeviae.	*When performing the Artes Praeviae, generate thoughts and emotions that are in resonance with those of the entity. Pneuma generated during the Preliminary Techniques is used as an energetic offertory to the entity. A general purpose offertory may be produced by generating thoughts, emotions, and energies of bliss and pleasure.*
2	Performing the last step in the Preliminary Techniques, continue to draw in external energy while generating cognitive and emotive pneuma. Circulate these energies until the body is filled to the point of overflowing with potent pneuma technikon.	
3	**Call the Entity** Use Etheric Communication to call the entity.	*This entails projecting thoughts and emotions across the Universal Etheric Field to call the entity. This communication may be accomplished at any distance. As you call the entity, communicate your intent to bestow an offering.*

4	**Perceive the Entity** Use Etheric Perception to perceive the entity.	*The receptive state of Etheric Perception was initiated during the Preliminary Techniques. Attune the centers of mind, emotion, and power to directly perceive the entity as it manifests.*
5	**Communicate with the Entity** Use Etheric Communication to greet the entity and inform it of your intention to bestow an energetic offertory. If the entity agrees, proceed to the offertory. If the entity declines, dismiss it and end the operation.	
6	**Offertory** Become aware of the powerful pneuma generated during the Preliminary Techniques. Use the technique of Primary Energy Casting to project this offertory energy into the entity.	*Gently project this nourishing energy into the entity. Pneuma may be emitted from any desired etheric center. Commonly used centers include those within the palms of the hands and fingertips, and the major etheric centers.* *It may be emitted as currents of energy, or radiant emanations. Care should be taken to offer only the pneuma generated during the current working. Tapping into stored energy may leave the magus depleted.*
7	**Dismiss the Entity** Use Etheric Communication to inform the entity that the interaction is complete and ask it to leave.	*Depending upon the type of entity and the nature of the interaction, this may include thanking the entity and asking it to leave, using Magical Influence, or defensive techniques in the rare instance that the situation becomes hostile.*
8	**Closing Techniques** Perform the Artes Concludendi.	

THE WORK OF THE PSYCHOPOMP
Opus Psychopompi

The psychopomp provides counseling, guidance and healing to the deceased. This work can greatly ease transition of the spirit into the next phase of existence, particularly in instances of unexpected death or situations in which the deceased has unresolved issues. The departed may be called upon via the technique of Evocation. Etheric Communication is used to interact with the spirit. A dialog may be established to address needs or concerns. Common issues addressed include afterlife paths and means of communicating with the living.

Spirits of the deceased are often initially encountered in a state of confusion, fear, or denial. Discussing the deceased's transition to a new state can allay some confusion. Presenting various afterlife paths may alleviate fear and provide comfort. A spirit in denial refuses to accept death, sometimes refusing to leave the material body. The spirit may be overwhelmed by anger or sadness or be deeply concerned about remaining family members or loved ones. Discussion of afterlife paths is often welcome. Commonly selected afterlife paths include reincarnation, remaining a disembodied spirit, entering a blissful etheric environment or that of a specific deity, or expanding into union with the cosmos at large. The psychopomp works to guide the spirit to its preferred afterlife. Through the technique of Spirit Projection, the magus leaves the body and accompanies the spirit upon the initial steps into the afterlife, leading the way and providing comfort.

It is important to convey to the deceased that communication with the living is still possible. By focusing thoughts, emotions and energy a spirit is able to directly communicate with a living person. This communication is typically perceived by the individual at a semiconscious level. Living individuals are more susceptible to communication from spirits while dreaming. As such, spirits may be directed to contact friends and loved ones through dreams.

It may be determined that the etheric body of the deceased requires healing. The etheric body of the spirit may have been damaged by the circumstance of death, illness during life, or other maladies. Often the techniques of extracting harmful energy and adding healing energy will suffice, but occasionally more comprehensive measures are needed to heal the spirit. This allows the spirit to move into the next phase of existence with a healthy, undamaged etheric body.

HEALING
Curatio

Etheric healing treats disease and injury by affecting the etheric body of the patient. The healer identifies the etheric aspect of a given illness then uses magickal techniques to treat the illness at the etheric level. The material and etheric aspect of the body are two sides of a single unified continuum. By treating the etheric aspect of an illness the magus may greatly improve physical recovery. This occurs via the action of Etheric Convergence. Etheric healing should be used in addition to a patient's existing medical treatment. It should not be attempted by the untrained. Intimate knowledge of the body's etheric systems and mastery of Etheric Perception and Energy Casting is necessary to safely treat the etheric body.

Numerous techniques are employed in etheric healing to treat the etheric body. Some techniques focus upon altering the etheric aspect of the material body, others treat purely etheric body systems. Commonly used healing techniques include the extraction of harmful energy, etheric regeneration, addition of healing energy, and energy circulation. These techniques are modular and may be combined as needed to treat a variety of ailments. Typically, they are used in succession, in the order listed. When the healer does not have the benefit of physical proximity to the patient, remote healing may be used.

In addition to the energetic healing techniques listed above, materiae magicae may also be used to heal, this typically entails the use of talismans, potions, washes, oils and incenses. Healing talismans are worn close to the body or bound to the sick or injured part of the body. The pneuma technikon within such talismans provides an ongoing direct healing effect upon the patient. Healing potions are typically comprised of herbs, stone/crystals, and pneuma technikon specific to the working. Similarly, washes, oils and incenses contain pneuma and materiae specific to the intended healing.

DIAGNOSIS

Discussion of the nature of the ailment with the patient is the first step of diagnosis. Such discussion is used to help identify the body part or system that requires healing. Etheric Perception and Tactile Casting are then used to obtain a deeper understanding of the patient's ailment at the etheric level. During

Etheric Perception the centers of Mind, Emotion and Power allow the healer to perceive the patient's etheric body in a visual, emotive and energetic capacity. Streams of energy are then extended into the patient from the etheric centers in the palms of the hands and fingertips. This extended energy is used to scan the body of the patient to perceive malign energy, damaged body parts, energy blockages or energy deficiencies. The extended energy streams from the hands provide a direct, tactile perception of the patient's body. Simultaneous use of these two techniques provides the healer with a comprehensive perception of the patient's body.

EXTRACTION OF HARMFUL ENERGY

Energies possessing destructive or malignant properties can damage the etheric aspect of the human body. Such harmful energies are often associated with disease. Malign energies may enter the body if an individual's natural protective energy is weakened. Harmful energy may also be self generated by an individual's own destructive thoughts and emotions. Additionally, damaged or diseased body parts may produce malign energy. In all such cases, removal of the harmful energy may greatly improve recovery.

ETHERIC REGENERATION

Affecting the etheric aspect of a body part in turn affects the material aspect of that body part through the action of Etheric Convergence. Advanced Energy Casting techniques are used by the magus to regenerate or improve the etheric aspect of organs, systems, and body parts. When the etheric aspect of an injured or diseased part of the body is improved through etheric healing, the material aspect will follow suit.

ADDITION OF HEALING ENERGY

Energies that are harmonious in nature have the ability to heal. Such energies build up, nurture, and fortify the etheric body. Healing energies are generated by the magus or gathered from external sources. These energies are then skillfully directed into the body of the patient. Healing energy is applied to a specific body part, or circulated through the entire body.

ENERGY CIRCULATION

In healthy individuals, energy flows freely through the body's energy channels. Blockages in this energy flow can cause deficiencies and stagnation resulting in disease. The magus uses Energy Casting techniques to remove blockages and guide energy throughout the body. The energy is circulated through the etheric centers and directed to specific body systems. Energy circulation may be combined with other practices or used as a standalone healing technique. As a standalone, it is particularly useful in treating poor circulation, energy blockages or energy stagnation. Energy Circulation combined with Energy Cultivation is also used as preventive medicine to maintain health.

REMOTE HEALING

Remote healing is used for situations in which physical proximity to the patient is not possible. This practice makes use of Spirit Projection to transport the etheric body of the magus to the location of the patient. Once at the remote location, the magus is able to treat the patient as if physically present.

SAFETY ISSUES

With practice of the healing arts comes the responsibility to do no harm. In order to safely work on patients, mastery of Etheric Perception and Energy Casting is necessary. Additionally, extreme care must be taken to avoid causing harm to the patient. Excessive use of force can damage the etheric body of the patient. The etheric body is delicate. Experienced healers achieve a deep understanding of the patient's body through Etheric Perception. This enables the healer to assess the right amount and type of energy an injured organ or area may need. Too much will damage a body part, too little will not yield benefit. During extraction, the magus must take care to remove only harmful energy. Very subtle energetic differences may exist between harmful energy and vital energy. Vital energies must be left intact. Care should also be taken when circulating energy. Circulation must be done at the correct stage in the healing, after the harmful energies have been removed. Circulating prior to this stage can infect additional body systems with malign energy. The skilled healer will perceive and assess energy flow in the patient and circulate accordingly.

The act of etheric healing presents a variety of hazards for the healer. Special care should be taken to ensure safety, including proper handling of malign energy, using energy from external sources and maintaining healthy energy stores. By necessity, the healer is frequently in contact with malign energy. The experienced magus will fortify the etheric form to prevent absorption of this harmful energy. Once extraction is complete, banishing is essential. Banishing removes any trace of harmful energy that may have penetrated the etheric form. It also removes any residual energy clinging to the outer layers of the form. The act of healing can deplete the energy reserves of the healer. Rather than tapping into stores of internal energy, external sources should be accessed whenever possible. External energy sources are typically accessed during the Preliminary Techniques, but may be accessed in between healing techniques if necessary. The healing energies used for the patient may also be used to replenish the reserves of the healer. Additionally, the healer should not undertake a working when ill or in a low energetic state.

The healing techniques presented are modular and may be used alone or combined as needed. If used in succession, the steps of the Preliminary Techniques and Closing Techniques are repetitive. These steps need only be completed once. When using these healing techniques in succession, perform the Preliminary Techniques at the beginning of the working and the closing techniques at the end of the working. It is important to banish the self of all malign energies during the closing techniques.

TECHNIQUE Healing – Extraction of Harmful Energy

	PROCEDURES	ANNOTATION
1	**Preliminary Techniques** Perform the Artes Praeviae.	*When performing the Artes Praeviae, generate thoughts and emotions of healing and compassion.*
2	**Fortify the Etheric Form** Use the mind and breath to direct energy into the hands. Use the breath to condense this energy into the outer layers of the etheric form of the hands and arms.	*The etheric form of the hands and arms is fortified to shield the etheric body from malign energies present in the patient.*

Sigil of Healing

3	**Perceive** Use Etheric Perception to perceive the etheric aspect of the patient's body.	*Use the Etheric Perception attained during the Preliminary Techniques to perceive the patient's etheric body and the energies present during the working. Etheric Perception allows direct perception of the patient at the etheric level and awareness of the energetic and emotive tone of energies present within the patient.*
4	**Extend Energy into the Patient** Hold the hands over the injured or diseased area of the patient's body. Use the mind and breath to emit streams of energy from the etheric centers in the palms of the hands and fingertips. Extend this energy into the body of the patient.	*The extended energy streams from the hands provide a direct, tactile perception of the patient's body. Simultaneous use of Etheric Perception and these extended streams provides the healer with an ongoing, comprehensive perception of the patient's body.* *Physical contact with the patient is often beneficial.* *Etheric Reading may be used to gauge the patient's comfort level with this contact.*

| 5 | **Scan for Malign Energies** Use the energy extended from the hands to scan for malign energies in the body of the patient. | *It is important that the healer feel the difference between malign and vital energies. Malign energies feel intrinsically dissonant, destructive, "hot", or harmful. When encountered, such energies may elicit an instinctive feeling of revulsion, pain, or disgust. Such malign energies may also be perceived as "out of place" within the etheric body of the patient. Malign energies may be encountered within the layers of the etheric form or embedded deeper within the core of the etheric body. Such energies can at times be strongly attached to the patient and be difficult to remove. These malign energies may also easily become attached to the healer, as such, careful banishing is required after each healing.*

Vital energies may be encountered at any point in the working. These are the core energies that sustain the etheric body. They flow strongest through the body's major etheric channels and centers but are present to some degree throughout the body. The definitive quality of vital energies is their harmonious resonance with the etheric body of the patient. These energies must be left intact. |
| 6 | **Extract** Once the malign energy is located, use energy extended from the hands to collect the malign energy and pull it from the body. | |

7	**Dispose of Malign Energy** Push this malign energy from your hands deep into the Earth.	*Use the mind and breath to dispose of the malign energy. Upon inhale direct energy into the hands. Upon exhale strongly project the malign energy deep into the Earth.*
8	Repeat this process until all harmful energy has been extracted.	*The extraction process cannot be rushed. It may take some time to remove all of the malign energy. It is important to scan surrounding areas, as the harmful energy can take refuge in adjacent areas of the patient's body.*
9	**Closing Techniques** Perform the Artes Concludendi.	*Thorough banishing is essential to the health of the healer.*

TECHNIQUE Healing – Etheric Regeneration

	PROCEDURES	*ANNOTATION*
1	**Preliminary Techniques** Perform the Artes Praeviae.	*When performing the Artes Praeviae, strongly envision the diseased or injured body part becoming healed. This focus may be enhanced by silently or verbally intoning a simple chant that reflects the healing. An example would be "your arm shall heal". Emotions generated are those of compassion, and benevolence.*
2	**Perceive** Use Etheric Perception to perceive the etheric aspect of the diseased or injured body part or system.	*Use the Etheric Perception attained during the Preliminary Techniques to perceive the patient's etheric body and the energies present during the working. Etheric Perception allows direct perception of the patient at the etheric level and awareness of the energetic and emotive tone of energies present within the patient.*

3	**Extend Energy into the Patient** Hold the hands over the diseased or injured area of the patient's body. Use the mind and breath to emit streams of energy from the etheric centers in the palms of the hands and fingertips. Extend this energy into the body of the patient.	*The extended energy streams from the hands provide a direct, tactile perception of the patient's body. Simultaneous use of Etheric Perception and these extended streams provides the healer with an ongoing, comprehensive perception of the patient's body.*
4	**Regenerate the Body Part or System** Use the extended streams to repair damage to the etheric aspect of the body part or system.	*At the etheric level, things may be easily reshaped by force of mind and energy. The extended energy streams function as the etheric appendages of the healer and may be used to reshape the etheric aspect of the diseased or injured body part or system into a healthy state, free of disease or injury.*
5	**Fortify the Diseased or Injured Area** Become aware of the pneuma generated during the Preliminary Techniques. Use the mind and breath to gently project this energy into the diseased or injured area.	*Project this energy from the etheric centers in the palms of the hands and fingertips.* *Fortifying the diseased or injured area with the pneuma generated during the Preliminary Techniques speeds the healing process. Adding additional energy to the etheric aspect also intensifies the effect of etheric convergence upon the material aspect.*

6	**Circulate Energy through the Regenerated Body Part or System (Optional)** Use the extended streams from the hands to gently draw the patient's internal energy through the energy channels and etheric centers. (See the modular practice of Healing – Energy Circulation for further detail.)	*If performing Etheric Regeneration within the linear series of healing practices, omit this step. If using this technique as a standalone practice, include this step.*
7	Move this energy through the regenerated area, reinforcing its connection to the entire etheric body.	
8	**Closing Techniques** Perform the Artes Concludendi.	*Thorough banishing is essential to the health of the healer.*

TECHNIQUE Healing – Addition of Healing Energy

	PROCEDURES	ANNOTATION
1	**Preliminary Techniques** Perform the Artes Praeviae.	*When performing the Artes Praeviae, strongly envision the patient becoming healed. This focus may be enhanced by silently or verbally intoning a simple chant that reflects the healing. An example would be "your arm shall heal" or "you will be healed of this infection". Emotions generated are those of compassion and benevolence. Such focus during the Preliminary techniques generates pneuma technikon specifically crafted to heal the malady of the patient.*

2	**Direct Healing Energy into the Patient** Use the mind and breath to gently project healing pneuma into the patient. Project this energy from the etheric centers in the palms of the hands and fingertips.	*Become aware of the powerful healing energy generated during the Preliminary Techniques. This pneuma may be emitted as currents of energy, or radiant emanations. Gently introduce the energy into the body of the patient. This pneuma technikon is an extension of the self. When projecting the energy, envision this life force actively healing the patient.*
3	This healing pneuma may be circulated through the patient's entire body to treat generalized maladies such as infections. It may also be condensed directly into the injured or diseased area.	*When circulating healing energy throughout the body, gently introduce energy into the Center of Power, then guide this energy through the patient's etheric channels and centers. Healing pneuma may be guided through the patient by extending streams of energy from the etheric centers in the fingertips and palms.* *When saturating a specific area with healing pneuma, gently project pneuma from the etheric centers in the palms. Use the mind and breath to circulate and condense energy into the body part or system.*
4	**Closing Techniques** Perform the Artes Concludendi.	*Thorough banishing is essential to the health of the healer.*

TECHNIQUE Healing – Energy Circulation

	PROCEDURES	ANNOTATION
1	**Preliminary Techniques** Perform the Artes Praeviae.	*When performing the Artes Praeviae, generate thoughts and emotions of healing and compassion.*

2	**Perceive** Use Etheric Perception to perceive the etheric aspect of the patient's body.	*Use the Etheric Perception attained during the Preliminary Techniques to perceive the patient's etheric body and the energies present during the working. Etheric Perception allows direct perception of the patient at the etheric level and awareness of the energetic and emotive tone of energies present within the patient.*
3	**Extend Energy into the Patient** Hold the hands over the patient's Center of Power (located just below the navel). Use the mind and breath to emit streams of energy from the etheric centers in the palms of the hands and fingertips. Extend this energy into the body of the patient.	*The extended energy streams from the hands provide a direct, tactile perception of the patient's body. Simultaneous use of Etheric Perception and these extended streams provides the healer with an ongoing, comprehensive perception of the patient's body.*
4	**Circulate Energy** Beginning at the Center of Power, use the extended streams to gently draw the patient's internal energy through the major etheric channels and centers. Move energy up the dorsal/spinal channel and down the ventral channel. Extend circulation through the body to move healing energy through the major channels in the arms and legs, the minor etheric channels, and the internal organs.	*Alternatively, any number of esoteric systems may be studied and implemented for the purpose of circulation. In lieu of an orthodox system, energy may also be circulated through the body in whichever manner feels intuitive and natural.*

5	**Perceive Blockage** As you pull the energy along this path feel for any energy blockages that may present.	*When a blockage is present, the flow of energy will slow, causing the energy to back-up and pool.*
6	**Remove Blockage** If a blockage is present, circulate energy at the blockage site until the obstruction dissipates.	*Move energy at this site in a circular motion to gradually disperse the blockage.*
7	**Continue Circulation** Continue circulating energy through the patient's etheric channels and centers.	*Continue circulating energy through the body of the patient, removing blockages as they are encountered, allowing the energy to flow freely.*
8	**Return energy to the Center of Power** Guide energy back to the patient's Center of Power. Use the mind and breath to circulate and condense energy into the center of power.	
9	**Closing Techniques** Perform the Artes Concludendi.	*Thorough banishing is essential to the health of the healer.*

MAGICKAL INFLUENCE
Auctoritas Magica

The technique of magickal influence allows the magus to powerfully influence the mind, emotions, and energy of another being. The magus first opens the etheric centers of Mind, Emotion and Power. Doing so facilitates perception of the subject's cognitive, emotive, and energetic states. The magus then powerfully projects thoughts, emotions, and energies from these centers into the subject's corresponding etheric centers. The greater the power and focus of the magus, the greater the influence upon the subject. Influence is achieved when the thoughts and emotions of the subject are supplanted by those of the magus. This influence is maintained by continually perceiving the subject's cognitive, emotive, and energetic states while using the projected thoughts, emotions, and energies to guide the subject. In extending consciousness, emotion and energy into the subject, the magus may powerfully guide the subject's flow of consciousness. This is accomplished by banishing the subject's thoughts and emotions that are antithetic to the desired behavior, while bringing desired thoughts and emotions into the forefront of consciousness. This technique is typically used to influence others during face-to-face, verbal interactions. It may also be used to influence others in one's general proximity without verbal interaction. Mastery of this technique is achieved when the magus appears to carry on a normal conversation with the subject while exerting powerful influence. This technique offers temporary influence, not total control over the subject. The level of influence gained is dependent upon the subject's openness, susceptibility, and resistance. This influence is typically experienced at a semiconscious level. The practice of Magickal Influence raises many ethical concerns. The magus must apply wisdom to the use of this technique.

Symbol Formula for Magickal Influence

TECHNIQUE Magickal Influence

	PROCEDURES	ANNOTATION
1	**Etheric Perception** Use the technique of Etheric Perception to become aware of the subject's cognitive, emotive, and energetic states.	*Center and banish, sequentially awaken and expand the centers of Power, Emotion and Mind. Enter Stillness and shift consciousness to the etheric aspect of existence.*

2	**Project Thoughts and Emotions Into the Subject** Strongly project your thoughts, emotions, and energies into the etheric centers of the subject.	*Thoughts, emotions, and energies may be emitted as radiant emanations, currents, or streams of energy. Cognitive pneuma is directed from your Center of Mind to that of the subject. Emotive pneuma is directed from your Center of Emotions to that of the subject, similarly raw pneuma is directed from your Center of Power to that of the subject.*
3	**Saturate the Subject** Continue to generate powerful thoughts and emotions to influence the subject. Intensely focus these cognitive and emotive energies upon the subject's center of Mind and Emotion.	*Pour your thoughts and emotions into the subject. This powerful flow of thoughts and emotions supplants the subject's with those generated by the magus.*
4	**Guide the Subject** Use the projected thoughts, emotions, and energies to guide those of the subject. Energy may be extended from the Center of Power to establish direct tactile influence of the subject's core energies and actions.	*Use the opened etheric centers to perceive the cognitive, emotive, and energetic states of the subject. Use your own projected consciousness, emotions, and energies to guide the subject's mind, emotions, and actions. This is accomplished by banishing the subject's thoughts and emotions that are antithetic to the desired behavior, while bringing desired thoughts and emotions into the forefront of consciousness.*
5	**Disengage from the Subject** Cease the generation and projection of influencing thoughts, emotions, and energies.	

6	Center and Return to Normal Consciousness	As the centers contract, shift the awareness back to material reality. Set the awareness within the etheric centers and become acutely aware of the moment at hand.
	Become aware of the internal energy raised to awaken the etheric centers. Use the mind and breath to draw this energy down the body from the Centers of Mind and Emotion, collecting it in the Center of Power. As the energy leaves these centers, contract them sequentially. Upon the inhale, gather and circulate energy within the center. Upon the exhale, contract the center as energy is drawn down the ventral channel. As the energy reaches the Center of Power, contract the center to its normal size and cultivate internal energy for future use.	

BLESSING
Benedictio

Blessing is the practice of magically attracting beneficial phenomena to a person or place. This is accomplished by use of Expansive Union. The magus becomes one with the selected region, then draws beneficent energies and phenomena toward the subject. Typically blessings are bestowed to attract prosperity or induce general happiness and well-being.

TECHNIQUE Blessing via Expansive Union

	PROCEDURES	ANNOTATION
1	**Preliminary Techniques** Perform the Artes Praeviae.	*During the Preliminary Techniques, intensely focus upon the desired beneficent effect on the subject. Hold this focus throughout the working.*

2	**Expansive Union** Use the technique of Expansive Union to expand into a state of union with the region surrounding the subject.	*Expansion into a local region, such as a city, is typically sufficient for most workings. The talented magus may however expand further to effect change on a global scale.*
3	**Draw Beneficial Phenomena** Use the technique of Expansive Union to draw beneficial phenomena towards the subject.	*Become aware of beneficent phenomena surrounding the subject. This typically includes beneficent energy currents, harmonious individuals, and the fortuitous flow of events. Use the expanded mind and energies to draw these phenomena towards the subject. Blessing may also entail shifting these phenomena into configurations that bring good fortune to the subject.*
4	**Return Etheric Body to a Normal State** Contract the etheric body back into the material body.	
5	**Closing Techniques** Perform the Artes Concludendi.	

LOVE MAGICK
Magia Amatoria

In the classical sense, love magick typically refers to charms and enchantments designed to force the love or sexual compliance of an unwilling subject. This type of application brings up obvious ethical concerns. Using magick to force romantic compliance is not only unethical, but ultimately leads to resentment and hatred. In the context of Vercanus, love magick refers to altering the self and resonating with compatible lovers. Magickal disciplines are used to transform the self into one whom is attractive to the desired lover. These disciplines allow the magus to add desired traits to the self, while removing unwanted traits. Additionally, the techniques of Expansive Union and Etheric Communication are used to attract potential lovers who are in resonance with the magus. Expansion Union is used to shift complex interactions on a large scale and draw potential lovers. Etheric Communication is used to attract potential partners via communication through the Universal Etheric Field at close proximity during daily interactions. The following techniques may be used alone or in any combination, it is however recommended that they be used together in the order given.

TECHNIQUE Recasting of the Self to Attract a Lover

	PROCEDURES	ANNOTATION
1	**Identify Desired Lover's Traits** Meditate upon the type of lover whom you wish to attract.	*Envision the primary traits that this individual would possess.*
2	**Identify Self Transformation Required** Meditate upon the type of person that you would have to become to attract this ideal lover.	*Become aware of aspects of yourself that would have to be added, altered, or enhanced.*
3	**Etheric Perception** Use Etheric Perception to perceive your etheric body.	*Center and banish, sequentially awaken and expand the centers of Power, Emotion and Mind. Enter Stillness and shift consciousness to the etheric aspect of existence. Focus inward to perceive the etheric aspect of self.*
4	**Identify Unwanted Aspects of the Self** Become fully aware of unwanted traits, emotions, and behaviors within yourself. From the clarity of Stillness, selectively allow unwanted aspects of the self to reemerge. Acknowledge the reason they exist and experience them completely.	*Typical traits include anger, fear, jealousy, hate, grief, attachment, anxiety, and insecurity.*

Simple Sigil to Transform the Self and Attract Love

5	**Locate the Unwanted Trait Within the Body** Identify where these unwanted traits are located within the body.	*Psychological and emotional traits are often perceived to reside in specific parts of the body or in specific etheric centers. For example, grief is often in the chest or Center of Emotion, fear is often in the stomach or Center of Power, and pathological thoughts are often in the head or Center of Mind. These traits may however be found anywhere in the body.*

| 6 | **Banish Unwanted Aspects of the Self**
Become aware of the internal energy raised to awaken the etheric centers. Remaining in a state of Stillness, use the mind and breath to draw this energy from the Center of Mind down the ventral channel back to the Center of Power. Beginning at the Center of Power, use the mind, breath, and energy to remove unwanted thoughts, emotions, and energies from the body. Upon inhale, circulate energy within this center. Upon exhale, radiate energy out from the center. Use this energy to push unwanted elements out of the center and away from the body. Raise internal energy from the Center of Power up the dorsal channel and repeat this process of purification for each etheric center and/or each area of the body where unwanted traits reside. Once all unwanted traits have been banished, move energy from the Center of Mind down the ventral channel back to the Center of Power. Circulate purified undifferentiated internal energy up the dorsal channel and down the ventral channel for one to two rounds, returning it to the Center of Power. | *Use the mind and breath to draw internal energy up the dorsal channel into each etheric center. Upon the inhale, circulate energy within the center. Upon exhale, radiate energy out from the center. Use this energy to push unwanted elements out of and away from the body. Perform this process of purification upon any etheric center or area of the body where unwanted traits reside. Multiple traits may be sequentially banished in a single session, or a single trait may be banished in a single session.* |

7	**Energy Summoning** Use the mind and breath to circulate and intensify the powerful energy stored within the Center of Power.	
8	Move this powerful internal energy through the body's etheric channels and out through one or more etheric center.	
9	Use the mind and breath to powerfully project streams of energy into an external energy source.	
10	Retract this extended energy back in through the etheric centers, bringing with it a current of energy from the external source. Use the mind and breath to draw this energy into the body.	
11	**Circulation** Circulate the external energy through the body's energy channels and etheric centers. Move energy up the dorsal/spinal channel and down the ventral channel. With each circulation draw additional external energy into the body.	

12	**Generate Pneuma Associated with the Desired Traits** Powerfully generate the thoughts and emotions associated with the desired trait. Feel these powerful energies merge with the circulating raw energy to produce potent pneuma technikon.	*Typical traits include confidence, strength, courage, compassion, love, passion, and peace. Each trait is associated with a particular type of cognitive or emotive pneuma.* *Invocation of deity energy or that of a power animal may be used in lieu of generation. In this case the magus would invoke deities or power animals that possess the desired traits and attributes.*
13	**Set Traits into Body** Use the mind and breath to condense and concentrate this circulating pneuma technikon into its proper place within the body. Continue to generate thoughts and emotions, as these energies are set into place.	*It may be beneficial to replace removed traits with their energetic opposites. For example, the magus may remove anger from the Center of Emotion in the chest and replace it with love. This has a balancing, therapeutic effect.* *Multiple desired traits may be sequentially added in a single session, or a single desired trait may be added in a single session*
14	**Closing Techniques** Perform the Artes Concludendi. The closing step of Banishing is typically omitted. Leave all desired traits present within the body.	
15	Repeat this process until each undesirable trait has been removed and each desirable characteristic has been added.	*This process may take time to complete. Typically, transformation of the self requires multiple sessions carried out over weeks or months.*

TECHNIQUE Attracting a Lover via Expansive Union

	PROCEDURES	*ANNOTATION*
1	**Preliminary Techniques** Perform the Artes Praeviae.	*When performing the Artes Praeviae, generate thoughts and emotions of love and passion.*
2	**Expansion and Union** Use the technique of Expansive Union to become one with your larger surroundings.	*Expand the etheric body into union with the region to be affected. Typically this would be one's city, state, or general geographic region. The magus may however, choose to attract lovers on a global scale.*
3	**Become Aware of Potential Lovers** Feel the presence of individuals with whom you are in resonance.	*Perceive the thoughts, emotions and energy of people possessing the traits that you desire in a partner.*
4	**Draw Potential Partners** Use the mind and energy to draw these potential partners to you.	*Become aware of the surrounding potential lovers within the larger region. Use the mind and energy to shift circumstances to draw these individuals into your life. Gently pull their minds and emotions toward yours.*
5	**Return Etheric Body to a Normal State** Contract the etheric body back into the material body.	
6	**Closing Techniques** Perform the Artes Concludendi.	

TECHNIQUE Etheric Communication to Attract a Lover

	PROCEDURES	ANNOTATION
1	**Generate Thoughts and Emotions** Generate thoughts, feelings and emotions of passion, romance and desire.	*Conjure your deepest romantic and erotic desires. Become inflamed with these thoughts and feelings; a passionate reflection of your newly created self.*
2	**Radiate Thoughts and Emotions** Use the technique of Etheric Communication to strongly project these thoughts and emotions outward through the Universal Etheric Field.	*Radially project your passion and desire out into your surroundings.*
3	**Listen for Resonance** Cease the generation of thought and emotion. Listen for a mental and emotive response to your desire.	*Those in resonance with your desire will respond to you even if only at a semiconscious level. This response is typically perceived as a visceral feeling of being drawn to an individual. It may also be experienced as a feeling of the awareness being pulled towards an individual.*
4	**Communicate** When an individual with whom you are in resonance is encountered, strongly direct a message to that person.	*Typical messages would include "see me", "come to me", "I want you", or "we are the same".*
5	Continue Etheric Communication to draw the potential lover to you.	*Communicate your passion to the potential lover, this is a sensual experience. For more intimate communication, streams of energy may be extended from the centers of Mind, Emotion, and Power into the corresponding centers of the subject.*

6	Center and Return to Normal Consciousness	As the centers contract, shift the awareness back to material reality.
	Become aware of the internal energy raised to awaken the etheric centers. Use the mind and breath to draw this energy down the body from the Centers of Mind and Emotion, collecting it in the Center of Power. As the energy leaves these centers, contract them sequentially. Upon the inhale, gather and circulate energy within the center. Upon the exhale, contract the center as energy is drawn down the ventral channel. As the energy reaches the Center of Power, contract the center to its normal size and cultivate internal energy for future use.	Set the awareness within the etheric centers and become acutely aware of the moment at hand.

SEX MAGICK
Magia Sexualis

Sex is a powerful augmentation to magickal techniques and practices. The sex act alters consciousness and generates large amounts of energy. Sex is a familiar and accessible way to generate the large amount of raw energy needed to power magickal acts. Focus upon the magickal goal during sex generates both cognitive and emotive pneuma. Through the sex act, these three energies are circulated through both partners creating potent pneuma. Energy is doubled when both partners direct their efforts towards a common goal. The explosive nature of orgasm lends itself to the release and deployment of pneuma. Energy Casting techniques are used to direct this explosive pneuma to a large region or a nearby talisman.

TECHNIQUE Sex Magick to Saturate a Talisman or Sigil

	PROCEDURES	ANNOTATION
1	**Centering** Gather and focus the cognitive, emotive, and energetic awareness into the centers of Mind, Emotion, and Power.	*Each partner should center individually.*
2	**Banishing** Banish unwanted thoughts, energies and emotions.	*Each partner should banish individually.*
3	**Protective Barrier** Expand a sphere of protective energy to encompass the entire magickal space.	*It is only necessary for one partner to create a barrier.*
4	**Begin Sex** Initiate the sex act.	*The talisman or sigil should be in close physical proximity to the partners.*
5	**Circulate Energy with Partner** Become aware of the Center of Power and the energy stored therein. Use the mind and breath to circulate and intensify the energy stored within this center. Move energy from the Center of power down to the Sex Center.	
6	Use the mind and breath to emit energy from the Sex Center into your partner. Draw your partner's energy back into your body along with your partner's breath.	*The etheric center located at the genitals is used to powerfully project and receive energy. In drawing your partner's energy in with your breath, a circuit of moving energy is formed.*

7	Circulate this energy through your partner's body and back through your own body.	*Allow this pneuma to flow naturally through the energy channels and centers of the body.* *During sex, energy may be exchanged between partners in any manner that feels intuitive. The power of sex magick is not affected by sexual preference.*
8	**Generate Cognitive and Emotive Pneuma.** Focus upon the magickal goal while maintaining circulation with your partner.	*Become immersed in the focus upon the magickal goal to generate potent cognitive and emotive pneuma.*
9	Circulate cognitive, emotive, and raw sexual pneuma until both partners are inflamed with potent pneuma technikon.	
10	**Saturate Talisman** At the moment of orgasm, each partner strongly projects pneuma into the talisman or sigil.	*Pneuma may be emitted from any desired etheric center. Commonly used centers include those within the palms of the hands and fingertips, the Sex Center, and major etheric centers. Project the energy in a way that feels powerful without interrupting the natural flow of sex.*

11	**Banishing** Beginning at the Center of Power, use the mind, breath, and energy to remove unwanted thoughts, emotions, and energies from the body. Upon inhale, circulate energy within this center. Upon exhale, radiate energy out from the center. Use this energy to push unwanted elements out of and away from the body. Raise internal energy from the Center of Power up the dorsal channel and repeat this process of purification for all of the etheric centers. Once all centers have been purified, move energy from the Center of Mind down the ventral channel back to the Center of Power. Circulate purified undifferentiated internal energy up the dorsal channel and down the ventral channel for one to two rounds, returning it to the Center of Power.	*Use the mind and breath to draw internal energy up the dorsal channel into each etheric center. Upon the inhale, circulate energy within the center. Upon exhale, radiate energy out from the center. Use this energy to push unwanted elements out of and away from the body.*

TECHNIQUE Sex Magick to Saturate a Large Area

	PROCEDURES	ANNOTATION
1	**Centering** Gather and focus the cognitive, emotive, and energetic awareness into the centers of Mind, Emotion, and Power.	*Each partner should center individually.*
2	**Banishing** Banish unwanted thoughts, energies and emotions.	*Each partner should banish individually.*
3	**Protective Barrier** Expand a sphere of protective energy to encompass the entire magickal space.	*It is only necessary for one partner to create a barrier.*
4	**Begin Sex** Initiate the sex act.	
5	**Circulate Energy with Partner** Become aware of the Center of Power and the energy stored therein. Use the mind and breath to circulate and intensify the energy stored within this center. Move energy from the Center of power down to the Sex Center.	
6	Use the mind and breath to emit energy from the Sex Center into your partner. Draw your partner's energy back into your body along with your partner's breath.	*The etheric center located at the genitals is used to powerfully project and receive energy. In drawing your partners energy in with your breath, a circuit of moving energy is formed.*

7	Circulate this energy through your partner's body and back through your own body.	*Allow this pneuma to flow naturally through the energy channels and centers of the body.* *During sex, energy may be exchanged between partners in any manner that feels intuitive. The power of sex magick is not affected by sexual preference.*
8	**Generate Cognitive and Emotive Pneuma** Focus upon the magickal goal while maintaining circulation with your partner.	*Become immersed in the focus upon the magickal goal to generate potent cognitive and emotive pneuma.*
9	Circulate cognitive, emotive, and raw sexual pneuma until both partners are inflamed with potent pneuma technikon.	
10	**Saturate the Area** At the moment of orgasm, each partner explosively expands pneuma from the Sex Center.	*Allow the force of orgasm to expand a radial pulse of pneuma technikon outward from the Sex Center to encompass the entire area of enchantment. The area may include immediate surroundings or an entire geographic region.*

| 11 | **Banishing**
Beginning at the Center of Power, use the mind, breath, and energy to remove unwanted thoughts, emotions, and energies from the body. Upon inhale, circulate energy within this center. Upon exhale, radiate energy out from the center. Use this energy to push unwanted elements out of and away from the body. Raise internal energy from the Center of Power up the dorsal channel and repeat this process of purification for all of the etheric centers. Once all centers have been purified, move energy from the Center of Mind down the ventral channel back to the Center of Power. Circulate purified undifferentiated internal energy up the dorsal channel and down the ventral channel for one to two rounds, returning it to the Center of Power. | *Use the mind and breath to draw internal energy up the dorsal channel into each etheric center. Upon the inhale, circulate energy within the center. Upon exhale, radiate energy out from the center. Use this energy to push unwanted elements out of and away from the body.* |

CURSING
Maledictio

Typically cursing involves harming another being via magickal means. It may also entail harming an entire group or region. The topic of cursing brings up serious ethical concerns. In most cases, curses are used for revenge, punishment, or selfish gain. Such actions typically lead to suffering, isolation, and self degradation. For these reasons, the cursing arts are not included in this work. The arts of magickal self defense offer an ethical solution to dealing with adversity.

DEFENSIVE MAGICK
Magia Defensiva

Defensive or protection magick is used to prevent harm from being done to the self or others. Various potential threats exist. Magickal attack from another magus, although rare, may present a valid concern. More common are attacks from non-magickal individuals intending physical, mental or emotional harm. Attacks from hostile etheric entities also present a very real threat. Whatever the source of the threat, personal safety and well-being may be maintained via mastery of the defensive arts.

Magickal self defense begins with the ability to perceive surrounding dangers. In becoming aware of potential threats, the magus takes appropriate action to avoid being harmed. Expanded Perception and Etheric Perception are used to ascertain if a suspected threat indeed exists, and if so, to analyze the threat. Defensive techniques are then used to address the identified threat.

TECHNIQUE Etheric Perception of Immediate Surroundings to Perceive Potential Threats

	PROCEDURES	ANNOTATION
1	**Scan the Area** Use Etheric Perception to observe your immediate surroundings at the etheric level. Center and banish, sequentially awaken and expand the centers of Power, Emotion and Mind. Enter Stillness and shift consciousness to the etheric aspect of existence.	*Scan your immediate surroundings for malign phenomena.*

2	**Observe and Analyze Malign Phenomena** If a malign phenomenon is perceived, use Etheric Perception to analyze the phenomenon.	*Typical sources of harm include harmful energy currents, negative etheric traces, malign power spots, hostile entities and malign pneuma from an enchantment, individual or object. Analyze the energetic tone, conscious objective, and behavior of these phenomena to determine the appropriate defensive response.*
3	**Center and Return to Normal Consciousness** Become aware of the internal energy raised to awaken the etheric centers. Use the mind and breath to draw this energy down the body from the Centers of Mind and Emotion, collecting it in the Center of Power. As the energy leaves these centers, contract them sequentially. Upon the inhale, gather and circulate energy within the center. Upon the exhale, contract the center as energy is drawn down the ventral channel. As the energy reaches the Center of Power, contract the center to its normal size and cultivate internal energy for future use.	*As the centers contract, shift the awareness back to material reality. Set the awareness within the etheric centers and become acutely aware of the moment at hand.*
4	**Proceed to Defensive Technique if Needed** If malign phenomena were detected, proceed to the defensive technique that best addresses the nature of the threat.	

TECHNIQUE Etheric Perception of the Self to Perceive Potential Threats

	PROCEDURES	ANNOTATION
1	**Scan the Body for Malign Phenomena** Use Etheric Perception to observe your etheric body. Center and banish, sequentially awaken and expand the centers of Power, Emotion and Mind. Enter Stillness and shift consciousness to the etheric aspect of existence. Focus inward to perceive the etheric aspect of self.	*Close the eyes. Focus the awareness approximately six inches above the head. Scan for harmful energies or entities. Use the palms of the hands to assist in this perception. Slowly move this focus down the entire body. Pay special attention to the centers of Mind, Emotion and Power.*

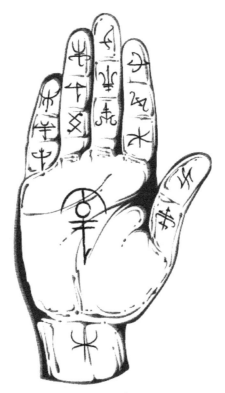

Talismanic Hand

2	**Observe and Analyze Malign Phenomena** If a malign phenomenon is perceived, use Etheric Perception to analyze the phenomenon.	*Typical sources of harm include harmful energies from naturally occurring sources, malign pneuma from an enchantment and harmful entities. The presence of powerful pneuma exhibiting unusually potent cognitive and emotive tone may indicate a curse. Pneuma from a curse may be perceived as intrinsically harmful, repulsive, destructive, or malevolent energy. Such energy generated via magick may be further identified by its semi-sentient and reactive behavior. Direct perception of this malign pneuma allows the magus to "read" the intent of the curse. This is accomplished through observation of the behavior of the pneuma and perception of its conscious objective and emotive tone. This perception may be experienced as a sudden flash of insight, disjointed images, powerful emotions, or a fully immersive visionary experience.*
		Identify any entities that may have attached to the etheric body. Harmful entities may be observed draining energy or parasitizing the etheric body.

3	Center and Return to Normal Consciousness Become aware of the internal energy raised to awaken the etheric centers. Use the mind and breath to draw this energy down the body from the Centers of Mind and Emotion, collecting it in the Center of Power. As the energy leaves these centers, contract them sequentially. Upon the inhale, gather and circulate energy within the center. Upon the exhale, contract the center as energy is drawn down the ventral channel. As the energy reaches the Center of Power, contract the center to its normal size and cultivate internal energy for future use.	*As the centers contract, shift the awareness back to material reality. Set the awareness within the etheric centers and become acutely aware of the moment at hand.*
4	Proceed to Defensive Technique if Needed If malign energies or parasitic entities are detected, proceed to the technique of Full Banishing.	*When banishing is complete, use divination to determine the source of the malign phenomenon. If necessary proceed to the defensive techniques to prevent further harm.*

TECHNIQUE
Divination via Expanded Perception to Perceive Potential Threats

	PROCEDURES	ANNOTATION
1	Perceive Use the technique of Expanded Perception to perceive the interconnectivity of all things through the Universal Etheric Field.	*Shift the awareness to perceive reality on a large scale.*

2	**Perceive Potential Threats** Perceive potentially harmful phenomena in your expanded surroundings.	*Become aware of the inertial flow of events and phenomena that surround you. Identify phenomena that could potentially harm you. Potentially harmful phenomena include malign energy currents, etheric shifts caused by curses, the inertial flow of potentially harmful events, and the harmful intentions of others.*
3	**Comprehend Interaction** Comprehend the way in which these phenomena may cause harm.	*Observe the way in which these phenomena are harming you or may potentially do you harm.*
4	**Center and Return to Normal Consciousness** Become aware of the internal energy raised to awaken the etheric centers. Use the mind and breath to draw this energy down the body from the Centers of Mind and Emotion, collecting it in the Center of Power. As the energy leaves these centers, contract them sequentially. Upon the inhale, gather and circulate energy within the center. Upon the exhale, contract the center as energy is drawn down the ventral channel. As the energy reaches the Center of Power, contract the center to its normal size and cultivate internal energy for future use.	*As the centers contract, shift the awareness back to material reality. Set the awareness within the etheric centers and become acutely aware of the moment at hand.*

5	**Proceed to Defensive Techniques if Needed** If malign phenomena are detected, proceed to the defensive technique that best addresses the nature of the threat.	

Sigil of Protection

TECHNIQUE Divination of the Future to Perceive Potential Threats

	PROCEDURES	*ANNOTATION*
1	**Expanded Perception** Use the technique of Expanded Perception to perceive the larger environment that surrounds you. Become aware of phenomena that interact with and directly affect you. Expanded Perception may be used to perceive both local and distance phenomena.	*Feel and perceive the flow of events that surround you.*
2	**Project Awareness Forward in Time** Project the awareness forward in time.	*Project the awareness forward in the time stream along with the flow of events that surround you.*

3	**Identify Potential Future Dangers**	*Become immersed in the inertial flow of events as they interact and move forward in time. Perceive potential futures as they take shape.*

Identify Potential Future Dangers

Perceive the energy currents, emanations, and waves of force sent forward in the time stream by your actions in the present. Become aware of the movement, interaction, and configuration of these emanations as they move forward in time. Use this perception to comprehend the future outcome of circumstances and events that surround and affect you in the present. Perception of this future may be experienced as a sudden flash of insight, disjointed images, premonitory intuition, powerful emotions, or a fully immersive visionary experience. The future is in a constant state of flux due to action and change in the present. Visions of the future fade and change as events in the present shift course. The visions perceived reflect the outcome of the current flow of events.

Become immersed in the inertial flow of events as they interact and move forward in time. Perceive potential futures as they take shape.

Divination of future danger may include visions of tragic potential futures that are currently being shaped in the present, perception of malign energy currents shifting towards you, or an overwhelming sensation that something bad is about to happen.

4	**Center and Return to Normal Consciousness** Become aware of the internal energy raised to awaken the etheric centers. Use the mind and breath to draw this energy down the body from the Centers of Mind and Emotion, collecting it in the Center of Power. As the energy leaves these centers, contract them sequentially. Upon the inhale, gather and circulate energy within the center. Upon the exhale, contract the center as energy is drawn down the ventral channel. As the energy reaches the Center of Power, contract the center to its normal size and cultivate internal energy for future use.	*As the centers contract, shift the awareness back to material reality. Set the awareness within the etheric centers and become acutely aware of the moment at hand.*
5	**Proceed to Defensive Techniques if Needed** If potential future dangers are perceived, proceed to the defensive technique that best addresses the nature of the threat.	*If possible, isolate the specific threat and take every action necessary to prevent that potential future from coming to pass. If the specific threat cannot be clearly perceived, generalized defensive and protective magicks should be implemented, such as Deflection of Harmful Phenomena via Expansive Union, Shielding, or the creation of a protective talisman.*

SHIELDING

Preventing harmful energies from entering the body is fundamental to magickal defense. Additionally, the magus must keep hostile entities at bay. This is primarily accomplished by constructing magickal shields and fortifying the etheric form. Magickal shields are spheres of energy that surround an individual or area. Created from pneuma technikon, shields are more than passive barriers. They may act to defend the magus by extending streams of energy, exerting waves of force, and emitting radiant emanations. A shield is an extension of the self, a barrier of living energy. This unique composition renders the sphere semi-permeable in nature. The magus may selectively allow benign energies and entities to pass through the barrier while maintaining defense against hostile phenomena. The strength of the shield is dependent upon the power of the magus who created it. The next line of defense is the etheric form. The etheric form is an energy field of varying densities that encompasses the etheric body. The innermost layers typically conform to the shape of the material body, while outer layers tend to be elliptical in shape. The etheric form provides natural defense against intruding energies. Energy may be condensed into the innermost layers of the form to strengthen this natural defense. Powerful shields and a well fortified etheric form render the magus impervious to most magickal attacks and harmful etheric phenomena.

TECHNIQUE Defense – Shielding the Self

	PROCEDURES	ANNOTATION
1	**Preliminary Techniques** Perform the technique of Artes Praeviae, omitting the step of forming a protective barrier (step 5).	*When performing the Artes Praeviae the magus generates thoughts and emotions that are defensive and martial in nature.* *Step 5 of the Artes Praeviae is omitted due to the fact that a powerful barrier will be created at the end of this technique.*
2	Performing the last step in the Preliminary Techniques, continue to draw in external energy while generating cognitive and emotive pneuma. Circulate these energies until the body is filled to the point of overflowing with potent pneuma technikon.	

3	**Concentrate Pneuma into the Center of Power** Use the mind and breath to concentrate this circulating pneuma into the Center of Power.	*As the energy is concentrated into the Center of Power, feel the energy circulate and intensify.*
4	Continue to concentrate pneuma into this center until it is inflamed with power.	
5	**Expand Shield** Use the mind and breath to expand a powerful sphere of this pneuma out from the Center of Power to just beyond the outermost layers of the etheric form. These layers typically extend just beyond the fingertips of the outstretched arms.	*Take a single deep breath. Upon inhale, feel the pneuma concentrated in the Center of Power become powerful to the point of growing beyond containment. Upon exhale expand a powerful sphere of pneuma slightly beyond the outer etheric form. Feel this sphere merge with the outermost layers of the etheric form to create a barrier of living energy around the body.*
6	**Fortify Shield** Fortify the shield by extending streams of energy from the etheric centers in the palms of the hands and fingertips into the sphere. Use these extended streams as a conduit to send energy into the shield.	*Continually radiate pneuma through these extended streams and into the sphere. This increases the strength and power of the shield. This fortification may be enhanced by envisioning the formation of protective symbols on the surface of the sphere. Words of power and chant may also be used to enhance fortification of the shield.*
7	**Disconnect from the Sphere** Retract these extended streams when the sphere is sufficiently fortified.	

8	**Re-absorb the Shield (Optional)** The shield may be re-absorbed into the Center of Power if no longer needed.	*The magus may leave the shield intact to act as a permanent, protective barrier around the self. If the shield is no longer needed it may be reabsorbed.*
9	**Closing Techniques** Perform the Artes Concludendi.	*Closing Techniques*

TECHNIQUE Defense – Impromptu Shielding the Self

	PROCEDURES	*ANNOTATION*
1	**Energy Summoning** Become aware of the Center of Power and the energy stored therein. Use the mind and breath to circulate and intensify the energy stored within this center.	*Upon inhale, feel energy circulate within this center. Upon exhale, feel the energy intensify.*
2	**Expand Shield** Use the mind and breath to expand a powerful sphere of this pneuma out from the Center of Power to just beyond the outermost layers of the etheric form. These layers typically extend just beyond the fingertips of the outstretched arms.	*Take a single deep breath. Upon inhale, feel the pneuma concentrated in the Center of Power become powerful to the point of growing beyond containment. Upon exhale expand a powerful sphere of pneuma slightly beyond the outer etheric form. Feel this sphere merge with the outermost layers of the etheric form to create a barrier of living energy around the body.*

3	**Fortify Shield (Optional)** If necessary, the shield may be fortified by extending streams of energy from the etheric centers in the palms of the hands and fingertips into the sphere. Use these extended streams as a conduit to send energy into the shield. Fortifying an impromptu shield is typically only necessary if the magus is under attack or exposed to particularly harmful emanations.	*Continually radiate pneuma through these extended streams and into the sphere. This increases the strength and power of the shield.* *Words of power and chant may be used to enhance fortification of the shield.*
4	**Disconnect from the Sphere (Optional)** Retract these extended streams when the sphere is sufficiently fortified.	
5	**Re-absorb the Shield** When the threat has passed, use the mind and breath to re-absorb the shield into the Center of Power.	

TECHNIQUE Defense – Shielding an Individual

	PROCEDURES	*ANNOTATION*
1	**Preliminary Techniques** Perform the technique of Artes Praeviae, omitting the step of forming a protective barrier (step 5).	*When performing the Artes Praeviae the magus generates thoughts and emotions that are defensive and martial in nature.* *Step 5 of the Artes Praeviae is omitted due to the fact that a powerful barrier will be created at the end of this technique.*

2	Performing the last step in the Preliminary Techniques, continue to draw in external energy while generating cognitive and emotive pneuma. Circulate these energies until the body is filled to the point of overflowing with potent pneuma technikon.	
3	**Direct Energy to the Palms** Use mind and breath to direct this energy to the palms of the hands.	
4	**Create a Sphere of Pneuma** Use mind and breath to create a sphere of pneuma between the palms.	*Start with the palms facing each other, slightly apart. Upon inhale, feel energy circulate through the body. Upon exhale, move this energy through the hands to expand a sphere of energy between the palms. Expand the sphere upon each successive exhale. Move the hands with the sphere as it expands.*
5	**Expand Shield to Encompass the Subject** Standing in front of the subject, continue to expand the sphere just beyond the outermost layers of the subject's etheric form.	*As the sphere expands, turn the palms slightly outward. Expand the sphere to completely contain the subject within the protective shield. Merge the sphere with the outermost layers of the etheric form.*
6	**Fortify Shield** Fortify the shield by moving energy through the hands and into the sphere.	*Continually radiate pneuma from the etheric centers in the palms directly into the sphere to increase the strength and power of the shield. This fortification may be enhanced by envisioning the formation of protective symbols on the surface of the sphere. Words of power and chant may also be used to enhance fortification of the shield.*

7	**Disconnect from the Shield** Move the hands away from the sphere when it has been sufficiently fortified.	
8	The magus may leave the shield intact to act as a permanent protective barrier around the individual. If the shield is no longer needed it may be reabsorbed into the Center of Power via the hands.	*This defensive sphere will continue to actively protect the individual by exerting waves of force, extending streams of energy, and emitting radiant emanations. Additionally the shield will provide a powerful barrier against malign energies and entities.*
9	**Closing Techniques** Perform the Artes Concludendi.	*Closing Techniques*

TECHNIQUE Defense – Shielding a Location

	PROCEDURES	*ANNOTATION*
1	**Preliminary Techniques** Perform the technique of Artes Praeviae, omitting the step of forming a protective barrier (step 5).	*When performing the Artes Praeviae the magus generates thoughts and emotions that are defensive and martial in nature.* *Step 5 of the Artes Praeviae is omitted due to the fact that a powerful barrier will be created at the end of this technique.*
2	Performing the last step in the Preliminary Techniques, continue to draw in external energy while generating cognitive and emotive pneuma. Circulate these energies until the body is filled to the point of overflowing with potent pneuma technikon.	

3	**Concentrate Pneuma into the Center of Power** Use the mind and breath to concentrate this circulating pneuma into the Center of Power.	*As the energy is concentrated into the Center of Power, feel the energy circulate and intensify.*
4	Continue to concentrate pneuma into this center until it is inflamed with power.	
5	**Expand Shield** Use the mind and breath to expand a powerful sphere of this pneuma out from the Center of Power to encompass the entire area of protection.	*Take a single deep breath. Upon inhale, feel the pneuma concentrated in the Center of Power become powerful to the point of growing beyond containment. Upon exhale expand a powerful sphere of pneuma to encompass the area of protection.* *Typically, the area of protection would be the size of a home, building or sacred space. The talented magus may also create a shield large enough to protect a neighborhood, city, or nation.*
6	**Fortify Shield** Fortify the shield by extending streams of energy from the etheric centers in the palms of the hands and fingertips into the sphere. Use these extended streams as a conduit to send energy into the shield.	*Continually radiate pneuma through these extended streams and into the sphere. This increases the strength and power of the shield. This fortification may be enhanced by envisioning the formation of protective symbols on the surface of the sphere. Words of power and chant may also be used to enhance fortification of the shield.*
7	**Disconnect from the Sphere** Retract these streams when the sphere is sufficiently fortified.	

| 8 | The shield may be left permanently in place to protect a specific location. | *This defensive sphere will continue to actively protect the space by exerting waves of force, extending streams of energy, and emitting radiant emanations. This shield of pneuma technikon is an extension of the self, a barrier of living energy. This unique composition renders the sphere semi-permeable in nature. The magus may selectively allow energies and entities to pass through the barrier while maintaining defense against hostile phenomena.* |
| 9 | **Closing Techniques** Perform the Artes Concludendi. | |

TECHNIQUE Defense - Fortifying the Etheric Form

	PROCEDURES	ANNOTATION
1	**Preliminary Techniques** Perform the Artes Praeviae.	*When performing the Artes Praeviae, generate thoughts and emotions of strength and power.*
2	Performing the last step in the Preliminary Techniques, continue to draw in external energy while generating cognitive and emotive pneuma. Circulate these energies until the body is filled to the point of overflowing with potent pneuma technikon.	

3	**Concentrate and Condense Energy into the Etheric Form** Use the mind and breath to concentrate and condense energy into the innermost layers of the etheric form. Upon inhale draw energy in from the external power source and circulate it through the body. Upon exhale concentrate and condense pneuma into the etheric form. This is repeated until the form has become densely fortified with pneuma technikon.	*The innermost layers of the etheric form typically conform to the shape of the material body. These inner layers typically extend up to several inches from the body.*
4	**Perform Regularly** Repeat often to maintain the fortitude of the etheric form.	*Fortification of the etheric form is not typically used to counter a direct attack. It is used to maintain the body's natural defenses against malign energy. Performing this technique on a monthly basis is typically sufficient to maintain a fortified etheric form.*
5	**Closing Techniques** Perform the Artes Concludendi.	

DEFLECTION

Harmful energies and phenomena may be deflected away from the magus prior to causing harm. Energy Casting techniques are used to deflect malign energy and phenomena at close range. The interaction of daily living brings the magus into frequent contact with both harmful and benign energies. Many individuals inadvertently project harmful thoughts, emotion, and energies. Etheric beings, hostile magi, and even certain locations or objects are capable of emitting malign energies. As such, it is a good practice to continually deflect malign energies while drawing in beneficent energies. Harmful energies and phenomena may also be deflected on a large scale via the technique of Expansive Union.

TECHNIQUE Deflection of Harmful Phenomena via Tactile Casting

	PROCEDURES	ANNOTATION
1	**Energy Summoning** Become aware of the Center of Power and the energy stored therein. Use the mind and breath to circulate and intensify the energy stored within this center.	
2	As energy radiates from the awakened center, circulate it through the body's energy channels.	
3	**Emit Pneuma** Powerfully emit pneuma from the selected etheric centers.	*Pneuma is typically emitted from the etheric centers in the palms of the hands and fingertips. It may also be emitted from any of the major etheric centers.* *This pneuma is typically emitted as powerful waves of force or currents of energy.*
4	**Deflect Harmful Phenomena** Use this energy to forcibly push harmful energies and phenomena safely away from yourself.	*This technique should be performed immediately upon sensing the presence of harmful phenomena.*

TECHNIQUE Deflection of Harmful Phenomena via Expansive Union

	PROCEDURES	ANNOTATION
1	**Preliminary Techniques** Perform the Artes Praeviae.	*When performing the Artes Praeviae, generate thoughts and emotions that are defensive and martial in nature.*

2	**Expansive Union** Use the technique of Expansive Union to expand into union with existence on a large scale.	*Expansion into a local region, such as a city, is typically sufficient for most workings. However, the experienced magus may expand further to deflect harm on a global scale.*
3	**Become Aware of Harmful Phenomena** Become aware of phenomena that are currently harming you or may potentially cause you harm.	*Become aware of the inertial flow of events and phenomena that surround you. Identify phenomena that are currently causing you harm or may harm you in the future. Common harmful phenomena include malign energy currents, etheric shifts caused by curses, the inertial flow of potentially harmful events, and the harmful intentions of others.*
4	**Deflect Harmful Phenomena** Use the mind and energy to move harmful phenomena away from you.	*Having become one with reality on a large scale, use the mind and energy to shift phenomena within your extended surroundings. This typically entails deflecting harmful phenomena away from yourself or another subject. Defense may also entail shifting these phenomena into configurations that prevent harm from occurring.*
5	**Return to Normal Consciousness** Contract the etheric body back into the material body.	
6	**Closing Techniques** Perform the Artes Concludendi.	

BANISHING

While shields and a fortified form provide a great deal of protection, they do not render the magus invincible. An energetic exchange occurs when interacting with surroundings and other beings. During such interactions, defensive shields may be opened to some degree. Even the best defenses don't guarantee total protection from unwanted phenomena. For this reason, routine banishing is necessary. Such banishing removes unwanted enchantments, energies and etheric phenomena that may penetrate the defenses of the magus. The technique below is an extension of the Banishing provided in the Artes Praeviae. It may be used for both routine banishing and in the event of exposure to malign energies or entities.

TECHNIQUE Full Banishing

	PROCEDURES	ANNOTATION
1	**Extend Energy from the Hands** Use the mind and breath to extend streams of energy from the etheric centers in the palms of the hands and the fingertips.	
2	**Collect Malign Phenomena** Starting several inches above the head slowly move the hands down the length of the body. As the hands move, extend these streams of energy into the body to collect all harmful energies, emotions, thoughts, and entities. Draw these malign elements down the body.	*Harmful energies feel intrinsically malign and detrimental to the body.* *Special attention should be given to the etheric centers of Mind, Emotion, and Power and the major etheric channels.* *If a parasitic entity is present it may be carefully removed using the energy extended from the fingertips. Once the entity is removed, use the technique Banishing a Hostile Spirit to dispatch the entity.*
3	**Project Malign Elements into the Earth** When the arms are fully extended at each downward sweep, use the mind and breath to project the malign elements deep into the Earth.	*When the arms become fully extended, energy may be further extended from the hands to cleanse the legs and feet. Each arm may be cleansed separately.*

4	**Repeat** Repeat this process until all malign elements have been removed. This may require several sweeps of the body.	*It is important to sweep the entire body, as malign elements may take refuge in various areas.*

Symbol for Bind

BINDING

Binding entails the use of magick to dissuade an individual from causing harm. This technique offers lasting influence, not total control over the subject. This influence is typically experienced at a semiconscious level. Binding is accomplished by thoroughly saturating the subject's etheric centers with pneuma. The pneuma technikon used is specifically crafted to prevent the subject from enacting a particular harmful behavior. This pneuma typically consists of commanding thoughts and emotions such as "you will not harm (name)" or "you will treat (name) well". The conscious, emotive, and energetic tone of the pneuma exerts a lasting effect upon the subject's behavior. Once saturated with this pneuma, the subject is overwhelmed with feelings of compassion, remorse, or fear at the thought of doing harm to the intended victim. This dissuades the attacker from taking hostile action against the intended victim. This technique requires the generation of large amounts of pneuma technikon and an extended period of time to complete. It therefore may be impractical to perform while in close physical proximity to the subject. As such, this technique makes use of Spirit Projection to enact the binding. This facilitates the production of large amounts of pneuma technikon and ample time to perform the working. The greater the amount of pneuma technikon present, the greater the effect upon the subject. Like any form of offensive magick, binding brings up serious ethical concerns and should only be used when all other options have been exhausted.

TECHNIQUE Binding

	PROCEDURES	*ANNOTATION*
1	**Preliminary Techniques** Perform the Artes Praeviae.	*When generating pneuma, intensely focus upon commanding thoughts and emotions to prevent the subject from enacting the specific unwanted behavior. Strongly envision the subject complying with the desired change.*
2	Performing the last step in the Preliminary Techniques, continue to draw in external energy while generating cognitive and emotive pneuma. Circulate these energies until the body is filled to the point of overflowing with potent pneuma technikon.	
3	**Spirit Projection** Use the technique of Spirit Projection to travel to the subject.	
4	**Bind the Subject** Upon arrival at the subject's location, focus upon on the pneuma created during the Preliminary Techniques. Feel this potent energy as it flows through the etheric body.	
5	Use the technique of Primary Energy Casting to project this pneuma into the subject's centers of Mind, Emotion, and Power.	*Passionately pour the entirety of your binding command and all of its associated thoughts, emotions, and energies into the subject's etheric centers. This energy is typically emitted from the etheric centers in the palms or the Center of Mind.*
6	Thoroughly saturate the subject's etheric centers with pneuma.	*Continue to pour pneuma into the subject's centers until they are completely saturated.*

7	**Guide the Subject** Use the projected thoughts, emotions, and energies to realign the consciousness of the subject into accordance with the desired behavior.	*Use the opened etheric centers to perceive the cognitive, emotive, and energetic states of the subject. Use your own projected consciousness, emotions, and energies to shift those of the subject into accordance with the desired behavior. This is accomplished by banishing the subject's thoughts and emotions that are antithetic to the desired behavior, while bringing desired thoughts and emotions into the forefront of consciousness.*
8	**Disengage from the Subject** Cease the generation and projection of influencing thoughts, emotions, and energies.	
9	**Return to the Material Body** Travel back to the material body.	*Slowly re-integrate the etheric body with the material body.*
10	**Closing Techniques** Perform the Artes Concludendi.	

ENLISTING THE AID OF SPIRITS

The magus may enlist the aid of spirits to defend against curses and magickal attacks. Spirits are valuable in that they are autonomous beings that may work tirelessly to defend the magus. In a defensive capacity, spirits may be assigned the task of continually deflecting magickal attacks. Spirits typically deflect malign energy by emitting waves of force, currents, or streams of energy. Complex spirits may make use of a variety of magickal techniques to defend the magus. Such defensive spirits may be tasked to protect a specific location or individual. In an offensive capacity, spirits may be sent to an attacker to prevent further hostilities. In such instances, the spirit continually works to counter and block any attempt to harm the magus. The single minded nature of simple spirits and cultivated spirits makes them particularly well suited to defensive magick.

Guardian spirits and spirit allies of any nature may also be called upon. Full instructions for interacting with spirits may be found in the Interacting With Etheric Entities section of this chapter.

BANISHING A HOSTILE SPIRIT

Magickal shields are quite effective in keeping hostile entities at bay. However, it is sometimes necessary to take a more offensive approach. Banishing a hostile or malign spirit involves permanently driving it away from a specific location. This is accomplished by forcibly bombarding the spirit with energy. This explosive flood of martial pneuma disrupts the spirit's energy. Etheric entities are unable to withstand sustained bombardment without incurring damage to and dissipation of their etheric body. As such, the spirit is driven from the area. As the spirit retreats, Etheric Communication may be used to deliver a warning not to return. Entities banished in such a fashion rarely return to the region from which they were banished due to the continued threat of dissipation and the strong aversion to the negative experience of having been bombarded with destructive pneuma.

TECHNIQUE Banishing a Hostile Spirit

	PROCEDURES	ANNOTATION
1	**Preliminary Techniques** Perform the Artes Praeviae.	*When performing the Artes Praeviae, generate thoughts and emotions that are martial in nature.*
2	Performing the last step in the Preliminary Techniques, continue to draw in external energy while generating cognitive and emotive pneuma. Circulate these energies until the body is filled to the point of overflowing with potent pneuma technikon.	
3	**Perceive the Spirit** Use Etheric Perception to become aware of the spirit.	*The receptive state of Etheric Perception was initiated during the Preliminary Techniques. Attune the centers of mind, emotion and power to directly perceive the spirit.*

4	**Banish the Spirit** Use the technique of Primary Energy Casting to bombard the spirit with martial pneuma.	*Upon inhale feel the body become inflamed with martial pneuma. Upon exhale emit an explosive flood of this energy from the etheric centers in the palms of the hands and fingertips. This pneuma is typically emitted as waves of force or currents of energy.*
5	Continue to bombard the spirit with energy, driving it far from your local environment.	*Typically, spirits retreat quickly when under such bombardment.*
6	**Cease Bombardment** Discontinue bombardment of the spirit once it has been driven far from your local environment.	*Prolonged bombardment is not recommended as it could ultimately damage or dissipate the spirit's etheric body.*
7	**Etheric Communication (Optional)** As the spirit flees, Etheric Communication may be used to deliver a warning not to return.	*The continued threat of dissipation and the strong aversion to the negative experience of having been bombarded with destructive pneuma typically prevents entities from returning to the location.*
8	**Closing Techniques** Perform the Artes Concludendi.	

TECHNIQUE Banishing a Hostile Spirit via Impromptu Casting

	PROCEDURES	*ANNOTATION*
1	**Perceive the Spirit** Use Etheric Perception to become aware of the spirit.	*Center and banish, sequentially awaken and expand the centers of Power, Emotion and Mind. Enter Stillness and shift consciousness to the etheric aspect of existence.*

2	**Impromptu Casting** Use the technique of Impromptu Casting to become inflamed with martial pneuma.	*Become aware of the internal energy raised to awaken the etheric centers. Use the mind and breath to draw this energy from the Center of Mind down the ventral channel back to the Center of Power.*
3	Intensely generate thoughts and emotions of a defensive martial nature. Become aware of the Center of Power and the energy stored therein. Use the mind and breath to circulate and intensify the energy stored within this center. Briefly circulate this energy through the body's energy channels.	
4	**Banish the Spirit** Use the technique of Impromptu Casting to bombard the spirit with this pneuma.	*Upon inhale feel the body become inflamed with martial pneuma. Upon exhale emit an explosive flood of this energy from the etheric centers in the palms of the hands and fingertips. This pneuma is typically emitted as waves of force or currents of energy.*
5	Continue to bombard the spirit with energy, driving it far away from your local environment.	*Typically, spirits retreat quickly when under such bombardment.*
6	**Cease Bombardment** Discontinue bombardment of the spirit once it has been driven far from your local environment.	*Prolonged bombardment is not recommended as it could ultimately damage or dissipate the spirit's etheric body.*
7	**Etheric Communication (Optional)** As the spirit flees, Etheric Communication may be used to deliver a warning not to return.	*The continued threat of dissipation and the strong aversion to the negative experience of having been bombarded with destructive pneuma typically prevents entities from returning to the location.*

| 8 | **Banishing (Optional)** Beginning at the Center of Power, use the mind, breath, and energy to remove unwanted thoughts, emotions, and energies from the body. Upon inhale, circulate energy within this center. Upon exhale, radiate energy out from the center. Use this energy to push unwanted elements out of and away from the body. Raise internal energy from the Center of Power up the dorsal channel and repeat this process of purification for all of the etheric centers. Once all centers have been purified, move energy from the Center of Mind down the ventral channel back to the Center of Power. Circulate purified undifferentiated internal energy up the dorsal channel and down the ventral channel for one to two rounds, returning it to the Center of Power. | *Use the mind and breath to draw internal energy up the dorsal channel into each etheric center. Upon the inhale, circulate energy within the center. Upon exhale, radiate energy out from the center. Use this energy to push unwanted elements out of and away from the body.* |

DEFENSIVE TALISMANS AND AMULETS

Talismans and amulets may be created and saturated with pneuma technikon to powerfully deflect harm. Full instructions for the creation of talismans and amulets may be found in the Working with Magickal Substances section of this chapter.

COUNTERING CURSES AND MAGICKAL ATTACKS

Actual curses and magickal attacks are relatively rare, but not unheard of. Living an honorable life, keeping good company, and practicing basic defensive magick will in most cases deter magickal attack. Nevertheless, the ability to identify and remove a curse or defend against a magickal attack is a traditional and valuable component of magickal training. The presence of a curse may be ascertained via Etheric Perception and Expanded Perception. When determining the presence of a curse it is important to remain objective. Etheric Perception is used to scan the etheric body and general surroundings for malign pneuma from an enchantment. Surroundings should also be scanned for the presence of hostile spirits. Expanded Perception is used to identify the presence of malign etheric shifts or harmful energy currents surrounding the magus.

If the magus determines that a curse has been cast, immediate defensive action should be taken. Shielding techniques provide defense against further attacks. Banishing is used to thoroughly remove all traces of malign pneuma from the body and the immediate surroundings. The technique of Expansive Union may be used to counter malign etheric shifts or harmful phenomena on a large scale. Hostile spirits may be banished. If performed correctly, these countermeasures will neutralize the curse. Curses are typically crimes of passion and rarely repeated on a regular basis. If, however, it is determined that a continuing threat exists and the person or entity responsible for the curse is positively identified, offensive measures may be considered. Binding may be used to prevent the attacker from doing further harm. The magus may also task a spirit with blocking the attacker from taking further action.

A direct magickal attack in close proximity may be countered by the immediate use of shielding and deflection techniques. Shielding is first employed to block hostile energies and phenomena. When properly performed, shielding techniques protect the magus from harm. Energy Casting is then used to deflect the attack. When countering attacks at close range the deflecting energy is typically emitted as powerful waves of force or currents of energy. This energy is may be emitted from the etheric centers in the palms of the hands and fingertips. It may also be emitted from any of the major etheric centers. Deflecting energies are projected directly towards the attacker. Such deflection typically renders the attack ineffective.

Options When Encountering Malign Energies or Objects

Object Containing Malign Pneuma from an Enchantment or a Harmful Etheric Trace

Option 1 – Safely Leave: Immediately leave the proximity of the object. Then perform Full Banishing to remove any residual energies from your body.

Option 2 - Destroy: Use a utensil or tool to place the object in a container to avoid coming into physical contact. Then burn or bury the object. Lastly, perform Full Banishing to remove any residual energies from your body.

Option 3 – Recover Object: Banish the object using the Banish Specific Objects technique delineated in the Closing Techniques in chapter two. Then perform Full Banishing to remove any residual energies from your body.

Area Containing Malign Pneuma from an Enchantment or Etheric Trace

Option 1 – Safely Leave: Immediately leave the area. Then perform Full Banishing to remove any residual energies from your body.

Option 2 – Safely Remain: If leaving immediately is not an option, create a defensive shield around the self. Once you have left the area, perform Full Banishing to remove any residual energies from your body.

Option 3 - Banish: Use the Banish Immediate Surroundings technique delineated in the Closing Techniques in chapter two. Then perform Full Banishing to remove any residual energies from your body.

Malign Energy Current

Option 1 – Safely Leave: Immediately leave the area. Then perform Full Banishing to remove any residual energies from your body.

Option 2 – Redirect Current: If relocation is not possible, use the defensive technique of Deflection of Harmful Phenomena via Expansive Union to shift the current away from the location. Perform Full Banishing to remove any residual energies from your body.

Malign Power Spot

Option 1 – Safely Leave: Immediately leave the area. Then perform Full Banishing to remove any residual energies from your body.
Option 2 – Redirect Energy: If relocation is not possible, use the defensive technique of Deflection of Harmful Phenomena via Expansive Union to redirect the upwelling of power to discharge at another location. Perform Full Banishing to remove any residual energies from your body.

Malign Entity

Option 1 – Safely Leave: Immediately leave the area.
Option 2 – Banish Spirit: Use the defensive technique of Banishing a Hostile Spirit.

Unintended Harmful Emanations from an Individual

Option 1 – Safely Leave: Immediately leave the area. Then perform Full Banishing to remove any residual energies from your body.
Option 2 – Shield and Remain: If leaving immediately is not an option, create a defensive shield around the self. Once you have left the area, perform Full Banishing to remove any residual energies from your body.
Option 3 – Calm Individual: Use the technique of Magickal Influence to affect the mental and emotional states of the subject. This act is beneficial for both the subject and individuals in the immediate surroundings. Then perform Full Banishing to remove any residual energies from your body.

DREAM MAGICK
Magia Somniorum

Sleep induces profoundly altered states of consciousness collectively known as dreaming. During ordinary states of consciousness the etheric centers are narrowly focused upon material reality. During sleep the centers expand, shifting consciousness away from material reality and towards etheric reality. This shift in consciousness and complete dissociation from the material self naturally induces Spirit Projection and Expanded Perception.

The Spirit Projection and Expanded Perception induced during sleep are initiated from an unconscious state. As such the spirit may randomly project through the Universal Etheric Field to various material and etheric environments. Likewise, the expanded perception is opened to a flood of uncontrolled information. As the spirit projects, the dreamer may become immersed in traces of the past, visions of the future, or emanations of consciousness within the Universal Etheric Field. This open, semiconscious state may also evoke thoughts and imagery from deep within the dreamer's own psyche. The cognitive pneuma produced by the dreamer's internal thoughts may directly shape and become manifest in the surrounding ambient pneuma of the Universal Etheric Field. During the disembodied dream state these externalized manifestations are tangibly and directly experienced. As such the dream experience consists of subjective, internal etheric projections manifested within the ambient pneuma, objective, external etheric phenomena, and emanations of collective consciousness. The art of lucid dreaming lies in gaining control of the awareness and controlling the dream experience. This entails distinguishing internally projected phenomena from external phenomena, and maintaining focus and volition. Spirit Projection, Focused Awareness and Energy Casting are used to control the dream state and maintain lucidity. Once this control is gained, the magus may explore the dream state with intention. Such exploration may include travel to etheric or material environments, interaction with other dreamers, etheric entities or even spirits of the departed. Dream magick is also conducive to the practice of divination. Divination while dreaming typically manifests as visions of the future, or past. It may also entail the remote viewing of distant locations or events. Advanced dream magick may include directly affecting reality at the etheric level during dream projections.

Magickal techniques are used before and during sleep to gain control of the dream experience. Preliminary Techniques used just prior to sleep transition the consciousness into the dream state while maintaining focus upon the magickal goal. The technique of Banishing is used to clear unwanted thoughts and emotions that would otherwise occlude the dream experience. The etheric centers are expanded to shift consciousness towards the etheric aspect of reality. Stillness is used to enter a deep meditative state free of thought. The technique of Focused Awareness is then used to concentrate upon the intent of the dream on entering sleep. This establishes the single minded awareness that allows the dreamer to recall the magickal goal while in the dream state. This focused state also allows the dreamer to realize that one is dreaming and thus achieve lucidity. When actively dreaming, the technique of Spirit Projection is used to willfully move through the dreamscape. The magus uses the etheric body, energy casting techniques, and the intensely focused consciousness to directly shape and affect phenomena encountered within the dream environment.

Symbol for Dream

When dreaming, the magus perceives via etheric means. Such perception is subjective, as etheric reality is directly perceived and interpreted by the mind. Dreams intensify this subjectivity as they are entered from an unconscious state. Perception of the dreamscape is shaped by the internal symbolism of the dreamer. Therefore dream settings, characters and events may appear strange or completely unrelated to the task at hand, yet symbolically reflect phenomena relevant to the magickal goal. Similarly, divinatory visions experienced while dreaming may be highly symbolic, yet reflect meaningful information. It is important to recognize the meaning behind such symbolic imagery and experiences. Acquiring a deep understanding of one's internal symbolism facilitates this process.

TECHNIQUE Dream Magick

	PROCEDURES	ANNOTATION
1	**Preliminary Techniques** Perform the Artes Praeviae.	*Banish to clear unwanted thoughts and emotions, shift consciousness towards the etheric aspect of reality, and enter Stillness to induce a deep meditative state free of thought.* *The thoughts and emotions generated are in accordance with the goal of the working.*
2	Feel your internal energy (previously summoned during the Preliminary Techniques) surging through and strengthening your etheric body. Gather this energy to the Center of Power.	
3	**Become Aware of the Etheric Body** The receptive state of Etheric Perception was initiated during the Preliminary Techniques. Use the heightened state of Etheric Perception to feel your etheric body within your material body.	
4	**Sleep** Enter the sleep state while maintaining focus upon the magickal goal.	

Symbol for Project

5	**Control the Dream State** Use the techniques of Energy Casting and Spirit Projection to control the dream state.	*The focus resulting from the Preliminary Techniques will naturally shape the dream in accordance with the magickal goal. The dream state is further controlled via use of Energy Casting to affect etheric phenomena and Spirit projection to travel. Through energy casting, phenomena encountered may be affected by emitting streams of energy or waves of force from the etheric body. Spirit Projection allows the magus to move through the dreamscape with intent, as opposed to being randomly pulled through various dream scenes. Controlling the flow of the dream is essential to achieving the magickal goal.*

6	**Perform the Magickal Goal** Perceive or alter dream phenomena in accordance with the magickal goal.	*Use the techniques of Energy Casting and Spirit Projection to actively engage dream phenomena. Magickally altering such phenomena profoundly affects both the etheric and material aspects of reality. It is by affecting these phenomena that the magickal goal is realized. Common goals include Etheric Perception, Divination, Remote Viewing, Etheric Communication, Etheric Exploration, and direct enchantment.* *It is important to remember that dream phenomena tend to be subjective and symbolic in nature. As such, phenomena experienced in the dream state may initially seem irrelevant to the magickal goal. Upon deeper examination, such phenomena often prove to be symbolic reflections of elements relevant to the magickal goal.*
7	**Recall the Dream** Upon awakening recall every detail of the dream.	
8	**Closing Techniques** Perform the Artes Concludendi.	

WORKING WITH MAGICKAL SUBSTANCES
Opus Materiae Magicae

Certain material substances contain unique types of pneuma that exert specific effects upon reality at the etheric level. Magickal substances typically consist of plant, mineral, or animal material. Etheric Perception is used to identify magickal substances and determine the properties of the pneuma contained therein. Substances possessing properties beneficial to the magickal goal are carefully selected. Energy Casting techniques are then used to saturate these substances with pneuma technikon specific to the magickal goal. This greatly increases the potency of the substance by blending its natural energy with that of the pneuma technikon. Magickal substances affect reality through the basic etheric mechanisms of radiant emanations, resonance / dissonance, saturation, and the behaviors of pneuma technikon. Magickal substances may also be used to store, transport, and deliver magickal energies. Throughout the centuries, volumes describing the properties of various magickal substances have been compiled. These compendiums may further assist the magus in identifying, selecting, and formulating materiae magicae.

Materiae magicae may be fashioned into a variety of forms per the intended goal of the working. Oils, powders, incense, candles, potions, washes, talismans and amulets are the forms most commonly used. A materia magica may be used alone or combined into a formula. In each case, the materia magica used is saturated with pneuma technikon.

OILS

Magickal oils typically consist of essential oils and magickal plants infused in a carrier oil. This oil is then saturated with pneuma technikon. These oils are used to transfer pneuma to objects or people with which they come into contact. When worn by the magus, oils can alter consciousness or magickally affect the self. Additionally, oils may be heated to disperse pneuma technikon into the surrounding air.

POWDERS

Powders of the art are typically composed of ground magickal plants with the occasional addition of mineral or animal components. They are often infused with essential oils to increase potency. These powders are then saturated with pneuma technikon. Such powders may be poured on the ground to form a magickal circle, sprinkled to alter the etheric nature of an area, or blown from the palm of the hand to deliver pneuma to a subject.

INCENSE

Magickal incense typically consists of aromatic herbs, woods, and resins. This blend is then saturated with pneuma technikon. When burned, these substances release their magickal energies, altering the immediate surroundings by infusing the air with pneuma. Incense may also be used as an offertory to spirits and deities.

CANDLES

Magickal candles typically consist of wax blended with magickal plants and essential oils. These candles are saturated with pneuma technikon. Burning such candles produces magickal flame which radiates etheric emanations merged with candle light. If the candle contains essential oils, their properties are diffused into the surrounding air. Candles may be colored or left uncolored in their natural state. The use of color is based upon the internal symbolism of the magus.

POTIONS

The term potion refers to a magickal drink. Potions are consumed to alter or transform the drinker. These elixirs may confer health, courage, meditative states, happiness, success, etc. Such drinks are typically created by saturating traditional herbal remedies and formulas with pneuma technikon. Most herbs used in traditional medicinal and culinary teas possess magickal properties. The pneuma added to the potion works synergistically with the natural properties of the herbs. Potions typically consist of herbs and stones infused in water and alcohol.

WASHES

Washes typically consist of herbs and essential oils infused in water and alcohol. Pneuma technikon is then added to this aqueous concoction. The wash is splashed or rubbed upon the body to transport the properties of the wash to the user.

TALISMANS AND AMULETS

Talismans or amulets are material objects that have been saturated with pneuma technikon. The etheric emanations from such talismans exert a powerful effect upon surrounding beings and phenomena. Via action of resonance / dissonance, phenomena of similar energetic tone to the talisman will be drawn and opposing phenomena repelled. Through this action, the talisman is surrounded by entities and energies conducive to the magickal goal. Additionally, such pneuma may directly shape and alter reality at the etheric level, producing a profound effect upon surrounding beings and phenomena. These objects are typically made from gem stones, crystals, wood, roots, metal or clay. They are often fashioned into jewelry or statuettes. Talismans may even take the form of a magickal symbol written on a piece of paper. Typically these charms are small enough to be carried or worn on the person.

TECHNIQUE Perceiving the Etheric Properties of Material Substances

	PROCEDURES	*ANNOTATION*
1	**Perceive the Substance** Use Etheric Perception to perceive all aspects of the substance. Center and banish, sequentially awaken and expand the centers of Power, Emotion and Mind. Enter Stillness and shift consciousness to the etheric aspect of existence. Focus inward to perceive the etheric aspect of self.	*This is typically accomplished by holding or touching the substance. This allows the magus to use the etheric centers in the hands to directly perceive the etheric properties of the substance. Become completely immersed in the perception of the substance. Allow its smell, appearance and tactile qualities to flood the senses. Perceive the material and etheric aspects of the substance together as one.*
2	**Analyze Properties** Use the state of Etheric Perception to analyze the etheric properties of the substance.	*Observe the nature of the pneuma contained within the substance. Dynamic, radiant energy may indicate a substance suited towards more aggressive or active magicks such as protection or defense. Harmonious tranquil energy may indicate a substance suited towards more beneficent magicks such as healing or love. Destructive, malign energy may indicate a harmful substance.* *Become aware of the way that the substance makes you feel. This is ultimately the best indication of its magickal use.*

| 3 | **Center and Return to Normal Consciousness** Become aware of the internal energy raised to awaken the etheric centers. Use the mind and breath to draw this energy down the body from the Centers of Mind and Emotion, collecting it in the Center of Power. As the energy leaves these centers, contract them sequentially. Upon the inhale, gather and circulate energy within the center. Upon the exhale, contract the center as energy is drawn down the ventral channel. As the energy reaches the Center of Power, contract the center to its normal size and cultivate internal energy for future use. | *As the centers contract, shift the awareness back to material reality. Set the awareness within the etheric centers and become acutely aware of the moment at hand.* |

TECHNIQUE Creation of a Magickal Oil

	PROCEDURES	*ANNOTATION*
1	**Select Container** Select the container to be used for the magickal oil.	*Magickal oils are not intended for internal use.* *Typically this is a glass bottle one to four inches in height. The bottle should include a tight fitting cork, stopper, or lid.*
2	**Select Plant and/or Mineral Materiae** Select a blend of plants and/or minerals possessing properties beneficial to the magickal goal.	*Formulating this blend is a true art. The magus selects substances that are in resonance with the magickal goal and complementary to each other.*

3	**Add the Materiae** Place the selected plant and/or mineral material into the bottle.	*Do not completely fill the bottle with these substances. Magickal plants and minerals are quite potent, typically only a small amount is used. Powdered plant and mineral material should be avoided as these will create an oil with a muddy texture. Cut leaf, root, and resin pieces should be used.*
4	**Add the Carrier Oil** Fill the container with a carrier oil until it is approximately two thirds full.	*A carrier oil is a natural plant based oil that is used as the basis of the magickal oil. Traditional carrier oils include olive oil, sweet almond oil, and sesame oil.*
5	**Add the Essential Oils** Add a blend of essential oils as needed to strongly scent the oil.	*Essential oils are the distilled essence of magickal plants. These oils are remarkably potent, containing the concentrated pneuma of the plant. The magus selects a blend of essential oils that are in resonance with the magickal goal and complementary to each other.*
6	**Fill the Container** Add carrier oil as needed to fill the remainder of the container.	
7	**Preliminary Techniques** Perform the Artes Praeviae.	*When performing the Artes Praeviae, generate thoughts and emotions in accordance with the intended use of the oil.*
8	Performing the last step in the Preliminary Techniques, continue to draw in external energy while generating cognitive and emotive pneuma. Circulate these energies until the body is filled to the point of overflowing with potent pneuma technikon.	

9	**Saturate the Oil with Pneuma** Use the technique of Primary Energy Casting to saturate the oil with this pneuma.	*Hold the bottle with both hands. Use the mind and breath to emit pneuma from the palms and fingertips into the oil. Concentrate and condense this pneuma into the oil. Continue to pour your thoughts, emotions, and energies into the oil until it is completely saturated.* *This pneuma technikon is an extension of the self. When saturating the oil envision this life force powerfully affecting reality in accordance with the goal of the working.*
10	**Closing Techniques** Perform the Artes Concludendi.	*During the closing techniques banish only yourself, do not banish the oil.*

TECHNIQUE Creation of a Magickal Powder

	PROCEDURES	*ANNOTATION*
1	**Select the Plant and/ or Mineral Materiae** Select a blend of plants and/or minerals possessing properties beneficial to the magickal goal.	*Magickal powders are not intended for internal use.* *Formulating this blend is a true art. The magus selects substances that are in resonance with the magickal goal and complementary to each other.*
2	**Pulverize the Materiae** Place the selected plant and/or mineral material into a mortar and pestle. Grind the materiae into a coarse powder.	*If the material is too difficult to grind by hand, an electric grinder may be used. Some herbs may also be purchased pre-powdered for convenience.*

3	**Select Essential Oils** Select a blend of oils with properties beneficial to the magickal goal.	*Essential oils are the distilled essence of magickal plants. These oils are remarkably potent, containing the concentrated pneuma of the plant. The magus selects a blend of essential oils that are in resonance with the magickal goal and complementary to each other.*
4	**Add the Essential Oils** Add a blend of essential oils to the powdered materiae. Mix the powder.	*Use only enough oil to strongly scent the powder, using too much will render the powder soggy. Too little oil produces a weak powder of poor consistency. Thoroughly blend the oil and powder mixture until a consistent texture is achieved.*
5	**Place Powder into Container** Typically this is a glass bottle two to five inches in height. The bottle should include a tight fitting cork, stopper, or lid.	
6	**Preliminary Techniques** Perform the Artes Praeviae.	*When performing the Artes Praeviae, generate thoughts and emotions in accordance with the intended use of the powder.*
7	Performing the last step in the Preliminary Techniques, continue to draw in external energy while generating cognitive and emotive pneuma. Circulate these energies until the body is filled to the point of overflowing with potent pneuma technikon.	

8	**Saturate the Powder with Pneuma** Use the technique of Primary Energy Casting to saturate the powder with this pneuma.	*Hold the bottle with both hands. Use the mind and breath to emit pneuma from the palms and fingertips into the powder. Concentrate and condense this pneuma into the powder. Continue to pour your thoughts, emotions, and energies into the powder until it is completely saturated. This pneuma technikon is an extension of the self. When saturating the powder envision this life force powerfully affecting reality in accordance with the goal of the working.*
9	**Closing Techniques** Perform the Artes Concludendi.	*During the closing techniques banish only yourself, do not banish the powder.*

TECHNIQUE Creation of a Magickal Incense

	PROCEDURES	*ANNOTATION*
1	**Select Plant Materiae** Select a blend of herbs, barks, and resins possessing properties beneficial to the magickal goal.	*Formulating this blend is a true art. The magus selects substances that are in resonance with the magickal goal and complementary to each other.*
2	**Pulverize the Plant Materiae** Place the selected plant material into a mortar and pestle. Grind the materiae into a coarse powder.	*If the material is too difficult to grind by hand, an electric grinder may be used. Herbs may also be purchased pre-powdered for convenience.*

3	**Select Essential Oils (Optional)** Select a blend of oils with properties beneficial to the magickal goal.	*The addition of essential oils is optional.* *Essential oils are the distilled essence of magickal plants. These oils are remarkably potent, containing the concentrated pneuma of the plant. The magus selects a blend of essential oils that are in resonance with the magickal goal and complementary to each other.*
4	**Add the Essential Oils (Optional)** Add a blend of essential oils to the powdered materiae. Mix the powder.	*Use only enough oil to strongly scent the incense, using too much will render the incense soggy.*
5	**Place Incense into Container** Typically this is a glass bottle two to five inches in height. The bottle should include a tight fitting cork, stopper, or lid.	
6	**Preliminary Techniques** Perform the Artes Praeviae.	*When performing the Artes Praeviae, generate thoughts and emotions in accordance with the intended use of the incense.*
7	Performing the last step in the Preliminary Techniques, continue to draw in external energy while generating cognitive and emotive pneuma. Circulate these energies until the body is filled to the point of overflowing with potent pneuma technikon.	

8	**Saturate the Incense with Pneuma** Use the technique of Primary Energy Casting to saturate the incense with this pneuma.	*Hold the bottle with both hands. Use the mind and breath to emit pneuma from the palms and fingertips into the incense. Concentrate and condense this pneuma into the incense. Continue to pour your thoughts, emotions, and energies into the incense until it is completely saturated. This pneuma technikon is an extension of the self. When saturating the incense envision this life force powerfully affecting reality in accordance with the goal of the working.*
9	**Burning the Incense** This type of loose incense is burnt upon lit charcoals.	*Specially formed charcoal discs for incense may be purchased at occult supply shops. This charcoal is lit then placed in an incense burner filled with sand. When working indoors, only use charcoal specifically made for use with incense.*
10	**Closing Techniques** Perform the Artes Concludendi.	*During the closing techniques banish only yourself, do not banish the incense.*

TECHNIQUE Creation of a Magickal Candle – Method 1

	PROCEDURES	*ANNOTATION*
1	**Obtain Candle Making Supplies** You will need wax, candle molds, wicks, coloring, a pouring pot, and a pot to boil water.	*When using these supplies, follow all usage and safety instructions included with the products.*
2	**Select Plant and/or Mineral Materiae** Select a blend of plants and/or minerals possessing properties beneficial to the magickal goal.	*Formulating this blend is a true art. The magus selects substances that are in resonance with the magickal goal and complementary to each other.*

3	**Blend the Materiae** Thoroughly mix a small amount of the selected materiae. Do not use finely powdered materiae as this may clog the wick and interfere with the burning process. Whole leaf, root, and resin pieces should be used.	
4	**Prepare the candle Mold** Prepare the mold and wick per instructions included with the products.	
5	**Melt the Wax** Place the wax inside the pouring pot. Place the pouring pot into the boiling pot. Add an inch or two of water to the boiling pot. Simmer until the wax melts.	*Be mindful of all safety precautions, wax is highly flammable.*
6	**Add Color** Add candle coloring to the melted wax. Follow usage instructions included with the product.	*Select a color that is appropriate to the intended use of the magickal candle. Candles may be colored or left uncolored in their natural state. The use of color is based upon the internal symbolism of the magus.*
7	**Add the Plant and/ or Mineral Materiae** Turn off heating source. Place the selected plant and/or mineral material into the melted wax. Use only a small amount.	
8	**Add the Essential Oils** Add a blend of essential oils to the melted wax. Use only enough oil to strongly scent the wax. Typically the candle consists of eight to ten percent essential oil.	*Essential oils are the distilled essence of magickal plants. These oils are remarkably potent, containing the concentrated pneuma of the plant. The magus selects a blend of essential oils that are in resonance with the magickal goal and complementary to each other.*

9	**Pour the Wax into the Mold** Be mindful of all safety precautions. Follow usage instructions included with the products.	
10	**Remove Candle from Mold** Allow the candle to cool completely before removing from mold. This may take several hours. Follow usage instructions included with the mold.	
11	**Apply Symbols (Optional)** Paint or carve a symbol or group of symbols onto the candle. Symbols may be used to amplify the power of the candle.	*When painting a candle use only melted candle coloring, do not use paint. This is accomplished by melting pure candle coloring wax at a low temperature in a double boiler. The melted coloring wax may then be quickly applied to the candle using a paintbrush.* *A set of symbols customized for magickal use is presented in this chapter.*
12	**Preliminary Techniques** Perform the Artes Praeviae.	*When performing the Artes Praeviae, generate thoughts and emotions in accordance with the intended use of the candle.*
13	Performing the last step in the Preliminary Techniques, continue to draw in external energy while generating cognitive and emotive pneuma. Circulate these energies until the body is filled to the point of overflowing with potent pneuma technikon.	

14	**Saturate the Candle with Pneuma** Use the technique of Primary Energy Casting to saturate the candle with this pneuma.	*Hold the candle with both hands. Use the mind and breath to emit pneuma from the palms and fingertips into the candle. Concentrate and condense this pneuma into the candle. Continue to pour your thoughts, emotions, and energies into the candle until it is completely saturated. This pneuma technikon is an extension of the self. When saturating the candle envision this life force powerfully affecting reality in accordance with the goal of the working.*
15	**Closing Techniques** Perform the Artes Concludendi.	*During the closing techniques banish only yourself, do not banish the candle.*

TECHNIQUE Creation of a Magickal Candle – Method 2

	PROCEDURES	*ANNOTATION*
1	**Select Candle** Obtain a quality candle.	*Select a color that is appropriate to the intended use of the magickal candle. The candle selected may be colored or uncolored in its natural state. The use of color is based upon the internal symbolism of the magus. Unscented candles are preferable.*
2	**Apply Symbols (Optional)** Paint or carve a symbol or group of symbols onto the candle. Symbols may be used to amplify the power of the candle.	*When painting a candle use only melted candle coloring, do not use paint. This is accomplished by melting pure candle coloring wax at a low temperature in a double boiler. The melted coloring wax may then be quickly applied to the candle using a paintbrush.* *A set of symbols customized for magickal use is presented in this chapter.*

3	**Select Plant and/or Mineral Materiae** Select a blend of plants and/or minerals possessing properties beneficial to the magickal goal.	*Formulating this blend is a true art. The magus selects substances that are in resonance with the magickal goal and complementary to each other.*
4	**Grind Materiae** Place a small amount of the selected materiae into a mortar and pestle. Grind the materiae into a coarse powder.	*If the material is too difficult to grind by hand, an electric grinder may be used. Herbs may also be purchased pre-powdered for convenience.* *Do not use finely powdered material as this may clog the wick and interfere with the burning process.*
5	**Blend Essential Oils** In a small shallow dish, blend essential oils. Select a blend of oils with properties beneficial to the magickal goal.	*Essential oils are the distilled essence of magickal plants. These oils are remarkably potent, containing the concentrated pneuma of the plant.*
6	**Mix Oil and Plant Materiae** Add a small amount of the powdered plant materiae to the dish of essential oils. Use a finger to thoroughly mix the plants and oils.	
7	**Anoint the Candle** Use the hands to rub a thin layer of the oil and plant mixture upon the candle.	*This infuses the candle wax with the energy of the essential oils and plant materiae.*
8	**Preliminary Techniques** Perform the Artes Praeviae.	*When performing the Artes Praeviae, generate thoughts and emotions in accordance with the intended use of the candle.*

9	Performing the last step in the Preliminary Techniques, continue to draw in external energy while generating cognitive and emotive pneuma. Circulate these energies until the body is filled to the point of overflowing with potent pneuma technikon.	
10	**Saturate the Candle with Pneuma** Use the technique of Primary Energy Casting to saturate the candle with this pneuma.	*Hold the candle with both hands. Use the mind and breath to emit pneuma from the palms and fingertips into the candle. Concentrate and condense this pneuma into the candle. Continue to pour your thoughts, emotions, and energies into the candle until it is completely saturated. This pneuma technikon is an extension of the self. When saturating the candle envision this life force powerfully affecting reality in accordance with the goal of the working.*
11	**Closing Techniques** Perform the Artes Concludendi.	*During the closing techniques banish only yourself, do not banish the candle.*

Sigil of Fertility

199

Symbol for Enchantment

TECHNIQUE Creation of a Magickal Potion

	PROCEDURES	*ANNOTATION*
1	**Select the Plant Materiae** Select a blend of herbs and/ or stones that are in resonance with the magickal goal and complementary to each other.	*It is important to use only herbs that are safe for human consumption. This is accomplished by choosing herbs that are used in traditional culinary or medicinal teas. Most herbs use in these traditional blends possess magickal properties. It is also important to use only stones or crystals that are nontoxic as infusions made from some stones may contain harmful substances.*
2	**Simmer Herbs** Simmer the herbs for fifteen to twenty minutes in purified or spring water to produce a strong tea.	
3	**Filter the Herbs** Use a strainer to filter the herbs out of the tea.	
4	**Reduce the Tea** Return the tea to the pot. Gently simmer the tea until it has reduced in volume by two thirds. Allow the tea to fully cool.	*Slowly reduce the tea to produce a concentrated herbal decoction.*

5	**Place Alcohol into the Potion Container** Add quality eighty proof vodka to the potion container. Add enough vodka to fill exactly seventy percent of the container. Typically this is a glass bottle one to four inches in height. The bottle should include a tight fitting cork, stopper, or lid.	*It is important to use only eighty proof vodka in a seventy percent ratio of vodka to tea. Lower alcohol content will fail to preserve the potion.*
6	**Add Herbal Decoction to Container** Fill the remaining thirty percent of the container with the concentrated herbal decoction. Tightly cap the container. Shake the container to thoroughly mix the vodka with the herbal decoction.	
7	**Add Stone/Crystal (Optional)** Add one or more stone/crystal that is in resonance with the working at hand.	
8	**Preliminary Techniques** Perform the Artes Praeviae.	*When performing the Artes Praeviae, generate thoughts and emotions in accordance with the intended use of the potion.*

Symbol for Pneuma

9	Performing the last step in the Preliminary Techniques, continue to draw in external energy while generating cognitive and emotive pneuma. Circulate these energies until the body is filled to the point of overflowing with potent pneuma technikon.	
10	**Saturate the Potion with Pneuma** Use the technique of Primary Energy Casting to saturate the potion with this pneuma.	*Hold the bottle with both hands. Use the mind and breath to emit pneuma from the palms and fingertips into the potion. Concentrate and condense this pneuma into the potion. Continue to pour your thoughts, emotions, and energies into the potion until it is completely saturated. This pneuma technikon is an extension of the self. When saturating the potion envision this life force powerfully affecting reality in accordance with the goal of the working.*
11	**Closing Techniques** Perform the Artes Concludendi.	*During the closing techniques banish only yourself, do not banish the potion.*

| 12 | **Reconstitute the Potion** The elixir produced in the above steps is a very concentrated magickal potion. Small amounts of this concentrate are used to produce a magickal drink.

Fill a tea cup with boiling water. Shake the potion before each use. Add two tablespoons of potion to the water, and stir. If a stone was used, ensure the stone remains in the bottle. Let the reconstituted potion stand for five minutes before drinking. Two tablespoons of the concentrate may also be added to a glass of wine or beer to create a magickal draught. | *Typically the concentrate is added to hot water, this reconstitutes the potion and removes the alcohol. This concentrate may however, be added to any type of drink.* |

TECHNIQUE Creation of a Magickal Wash

	PROCEDURES	ANNOTATION
1	**Select the Plant Materiae** Select a blend of herbs and essential oils that are complementary to the magickal goal.	*Magickal washes are intended for external use only.*
2	**Simmer Herbs** Simmer the herbs for fifteen to twenty minutes in purified or spring water to produce a strong tea.	
3	**Filter the Herbs** Use a strainer to filter the herbs out of the tea.	

4	**Reduce the Tea** Return the tea to the pot. Gently summer the tea until it has reduced in volume by two thirds. Allow the tea to fully cool.	*Slowly reduce the tea to produce a concentrated herbal decoction.*
5	**Add the Essential Oils** Add a blend of essential oils to the tea. Use only enough oil to strongly scent the wash.	*Essential oils are the distilled essence of magickal plants. These oils are remarkably potent, containing the concentrated pneuma of the plant. The magus selects a blend of essential oils that are in resonance with the magickal goal and complementary to each other.* *When creating a wash, use only pure essential oils. Using essential oils mixed with a carrier oil will produce an unpleasant, greasy wash.*
6	**Place Alcohol into the Wash Container** Add quality eighty proof vodka to the potion container. Add enough vodka to fill exactly seventy percent of the container. Typically this is a glass bottle one to four inches in height. The bottle should include a tight fitting cork, stopper, or lid.	*It is important to use only eighty proof vodka in a seventy percent ratio of vodka to tea. Lower alcohol content will fail to preserve the wash.*
7	**Add Herbal Decoction to Container** Fill the remaining thirty percent of the container with the concentrated herbal and oil decoction. Tightly cap the container. Shake the container to thoroughly mix the vodka with the herbal decoction.	

8	**Preliminary Techniques** Perform the Artes Praeviae.	*When performing the Artes Praeviae, generate thoughts and emotions in accordance with the intended use of the wash.*
9	Performing the last step in the Preliminary Techniques, continue to draw in external energy while generating cognitive and emotive pneuma. Circulate these energies until the body is filled to the point of overflowing with potent pneuma technikon.	
10	**Saturate the Wash with Pneuma** Use the technique of Primary Energy Casting to saturate the wash with this pneuma.	*Hold the bottle with both hands. Use the mind and breath to emit pneuma from the palms and fingertips into the wash. Concentrate and condense this pneuma into the wash. Continue to pour your thoughts, emotions, and energies into the wash until it is completely saturated. This pneuma technikon is an extension of the self. When saturating the wash envision this life force powerfully affecting reality in accordance with the goal of the working.*
11	**Closing Techniques** Perform the Artes Concludendi.	*During the closing techniques banish only yourself, do not banish the wash.*

| 12 | **Reconstitute the Wash** The wash produced in the above steps is a very concentrated magickal tincture. Small amounts of this concentrate are used to produce a magickal wash. Shake well, add roughly three tablespoons of concentrated wash to one cup of pure clean water. | *This wash may be splashed or rubbed upon the face, head, neck, chest, or body as needed.* |

Symbol for Saturate

TECHNIQUE Creation of a Talisman or Amulet

	PROCEDURES	*ANNOTATION*
	Stage One of the Working, Find and Prepare the Material Basis	
1	**Select or Create the Material Basis for the Talisman** Procure or create a small object that is suitable for use as a talisman.	*The object selected should reflect the intended function of the talisman or be composed of a substance that possesses properties beneficial to the intended use. These objects are typically made from gem stones, crystals, wood, roots, metal or clay. They are often fashioned into jewelry or statuettes.*

2	**Banish the Talisman (Optional)** Jewelry, statuettes, and material objects that have been purchased or the history of which is unknown may contain energies antithetic to the intended use of the talisman. Banishing may be used to cleanse the material basis of any unwanted energies. Crystals should be carefully banished before use. When banishing a crystal it is important to remove only the unwanted energies perceived within the stone, all native energies must be left intact. Delicate materiae magicae such as roots should not be banished as this would diminish the etheric properties innate to such substances.	*Etheric Perception is used to determine if the material basis contains unwanted energies.*
3	Use the mind and breath to emit streams of energy from the etheric centers in the palms of the hands and fingertips. Extend this energy into the Talisman.	
4	Use this energy to scan for unwanted energies within the Talisman.	
5	If unwanted energy is detected, use the energy extended from the hands to collect and pull it from the Talisman.	
6	Push this energy from your hands deep into the Earth.	

7	Repeat until all of the unwanted energy has been extracted.	
8	**Apply Symbols (Optional)** Paint, carve, or etch a symbol or group of symbols onto the talisman.	*A set of symbols customized for magickal use is presented in this chapter. Symbols may be used to amplify the power of the talisman.*

Stage Two, Saturate the Talisman

1	**Preliminary Techniques** Perform the Artes Praeviae.	*When performing the Artes Praeviae, generate thoughts and emotions in accordance with the intended use of the talisman.*
2	Performing the last step in the Preliminary Techniques, continue to draw in external energy while generating cognitive and emotive pneuma. Circulate these energies until the body is filled to the point of overflowing with potent pneuma technikon.	
3	**Saturate the Talisman with Pneuma** Use the technique of Primary Energy Casting to saturate the talisman with this pneuma.	*Hold the talisman with both hands. Use the mind and breath to emit pneuma from the palms and fingertips into the talisman. Concentrate and condense this pneuma into the talisman. Continue to pour your thoughts, emotions, and energies into the talisman until it is completely saturated. This pneuma technikon is an extension of the self. When saturating the talisman envision this life force powerfully affecting reality in accordance with the goal of the working.*

	Saturate the Talisman with Pneuma *(Continued)*	*The talisman may be anointed with magickal oils and infused with magickal incense to increase its potency.*
4	**Closing Techniques** Perform the Artes Concludendi.	*During the closing techniques banish only yourself, not the talisman.*

WORKING WITH SYMBOLS
Magia Symbolica

Within the context of magick, symbols may be used as gateways to pools of energy and consciousness within the Universal Etheric Field, meditative focal points, or receptacles for pneuma technikon. Certain symbols possess innate power. These symbols of power are typically ancient glyphs used repeatedly by magi over time to produce specific magickal effects. Pentagrams, runes, yantras, and deity images are examples of ancient symbols of power. Throughout the ages, magi have focused upon such symbols of power while performing acts of magick or invoking etheric entities. Over time this leaves a powerful etheric trace within the Universal Etheric Field. This trace eventually becomes a potent reservoir of pneuma technikon. The symbol of power acts as a conduit to the larger reservoir of power with which it is associated. In focusing upon the symbol, the magus may tap directly into this store of power via action of cognitive and emotive resonance through the Universal Etheric Field. This resonance is experienced by the onlooker as fascination. The sympathetic emanations produced by such resonance draw power through the symbol toward the onlooker and into the surroundings. Symbols of power may also be intentionally created by focusing upon a symbol while generating pneuma specific to its intended use. This pneuma is then radiated out into the Universal Etheric Field. In focusing the awareness upon a symbol the magus may also saturate the symbol with pneuma technikon specific to the magickal goal. Symbols saturated in this way act as powerful talismans. As meditative focal points, symbols may be used during the Focused Awareness stage of the preliminary techniques or as a powerful augmentation to enhance the focus of any practice.

TECHNIQUE Saturating a Symbol with Pneuma

	PROCEDURES	ANNOTATION
1	**Preliminary Techniques** Perform the Artes Praeviae.	*When performing the Artes Praeviae, generate thoughts and emotions in accordance with the intended use of the symbol.*
2	Performing the last step in the Preliminary Techniques, continue to draw in external energy while generating cognitive and emotive pneuma.	*Circulate these energies until the body is filled to the point of overflowing with potent pneuma technikon.*
3	**Saturate the Symbol with Pneuma** Use the technique of Primary Energy Casting to saturate the symbol with this pneuma.	*Pneuma may be emitted from any desired etheric center. Commonly used centers include those within the palms of the hands and fingertips, and the major etheric centers. Concentrate and condense this pneuma into the symbol. Continue to pour your thoughts, emotions, and energies into the symbol until it is completely saturated. This pneuma technikon is an extension of the self. When saturating the symbol envision this life force powerfully affecting reality in accordance with the goal of the working.*
4	**Closing Techniques** Perform the Artes Concludendi.	*During the closing techniques banish only yourself, do not banish the symbol.*

TECHNIQUE Creating a Symbol of Power

	PROCEDURES	ANNOTATION
1	**Preliminary Techniques** Perform the Artes Praeviae.	*When performing the Artes Praeviae, generate thoughts and emotions in accordance with the intended use of the symbol.*

2	Performing the last step in the Preliminary Techniques, continue to draw in external energy while generating cognitive and emotive pneuma. Circulate these energies until the body is filled to the point of overflowing with potent pneuma technikon.	*Focus upon the image of the symbol while generating and circulating this pneuma.*
3	**Concentrate Pneuma into the Center of Power** Use the mind and breath to concentrate this circulating pneuma into the Center of Power.	*As the energy is concentrated into the Center of Power, feel the energy circulate and intensify.*
4	**Radiate Pneuma** Use the technique of Radiant Casting to expand pneuma into the Universal Etheric Field. In a single, explosive release, radiate the pneuma concentrated in the Center of Power outward into the Universal Etheric Field.	*Take a single deep breath. Upon inhale, feel the pneuma concentrated in the Center of Power become powerful to the point of growing beyond containment. Upon exhale expand a radial pulse of pneuma outward into the Universal Etheric Field.*
5	**Closing Techniques** Perform the Artes Concludendi.	*During the closing techniques banish only yourself, do not banish the symbol.*

TECHNIQUE Awaken a Symbol of Power

1	PROCEDURES	*ANNOTATION*
2	**Become Aware of the Symbol** Focus the awareness upon the local copy of the symbol	

3	**Become Aware of Power Associated with the Symbol** Use Expanded Perception to become aware of the larger pool of energy and consciousness associated with the symbol of power.	*Shift awareness into the Universal Etheric Field to perceive the power of the symbol.*
4	**Focus Upon the Symbol of Power** Focus upon the symbol to the exclusion of all other things. Allow yourself to become immersed in the perception of the symbol, and the larger pool of consciousness and power associated with it.	
5	**Resonate with the Symbol** Merge into a state of resonance with the power of the symbol.	*Become completely immersed in the consciousness and power associated with the symbol.*
6	**Draw Power through the Symbol** Feel the symbol's power flow through the symbol into you and the surrounding area.	*In resonating with the symbol, the magus opens an energetic gateway. This gateway moves the power of the symbol into the self and the surrounding area.*
7	**Use the Power of the Symbol as Needed** The awakened symbol of power may be used as an augmentation to a magickal working, as a talisman, or left in place to alter the energetic nature of the surroundings.	

| 8 | **Center and Return to Normal Consciousness** Become aware of the internal energy raised to awaken the etheric centers. Use the mind and breath to draw this energy down the body from the Centers of Mind and Emotion, collecting it in the Center of Power. As the energy leaves these centers, contract them sequentially. Upon the inhale, gather and circulate energy within the center. Upon the exhale, contract the center as energy is drawn down the ventral channel. As the energy reaches the Center of Power, contract the center to its normal size and cultivate internal energy for future use. | *As the centers contract, shift the awareness back to material reality. Set the awareness within the etheric centers and become acutely aware of the moment at hand.* |
| 9 | **Banishing (Optional)** If desired, a banishing may be performed to remove any unwanted energies from the self. | |

The following pages contain a selection of custom symbols derived from ancient Greek magickal kharakteres (characters). Such symbols are ubiquitous within the corpus of Western occult practices. Examples of kharakteres may be found within the Greco-Egyptian magickal papyri, astrological symbolism, alchemical symbolism, and throughout the various grimoires. Each symbol below embodies a specific conceptual building block pertinent to magickal use. These symbols encompass core concepts and actions used within the art of magick. The magus may endeavor to create an original symbol system or expand upon these existing symbols as needed.

SYMBOLS OF THE ART

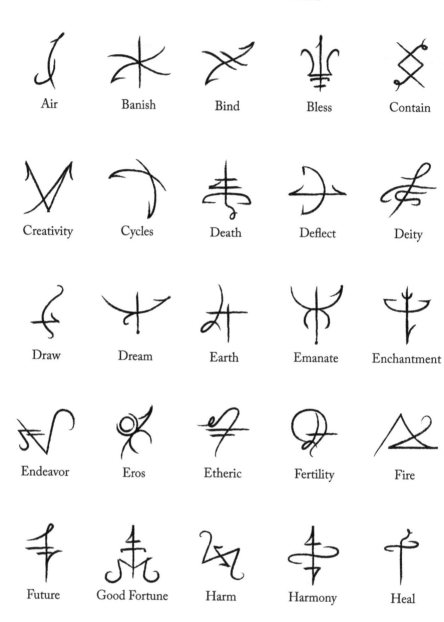

Air	Banish	Bind	Bless	Contain
Creativity	Cycles	Death	Deflect	Deity
Draw	Dream	Earth	Emanate	Enchantment
Endeavor	Eros	Etheric	Fertility	Fire
Future	Good Fortune	Harm	Harmony	Heal

Symbols of the Art

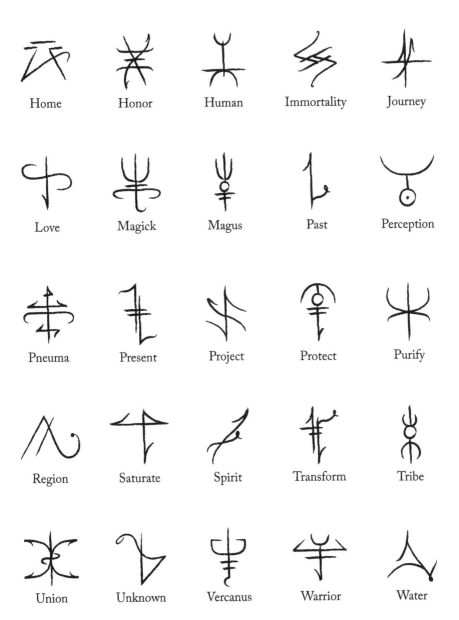

Home

Honor

Human

Immortality

Journey

Love

Magick

Magus

Past

Perception

Pneuma

Present

Project

Protect

Purify

Region

Saturate

Spirit

Transform

Tribe

Union

Unknown

Vercanus

Warrior

Water

CHANTS AND WORDS OF POWER
Carmina et Verba Potentia

The spoken word possesses great symbolic and emotive power. Words inspire specific thoughts and emotions. When combined with the rhythmic, mind altering qualities of chant, words become a powerful tool for the generation and transmission of potent pneuma technikon. Additionally, the rhythmic quality of chant serves to focus the awareness upon the magickal goal. Similar to symbols of power, words of power are links to large reservoirs of pneuma possessing a specific energetic tone. These words are made more powerful over time through repeated magickal use. Examples of words of power include god names, spoken runes, mantras, and the Ephesia Grammata. Examples of chant include mantras, sacred hymn, and the aforementioned words of power arranged into rhythmic succession.

Certain words possess intrinsic power. Similar to symbols of power, these words of power are links to large reservoirs of pneuma possessing a specific energetic tone. Such words are made more powerful over time through repeated magickal use. The addition of words of power to chants, recited spells, and spoken magickal formulae greatly increases potency. Such words may be used alone or arranged into rhythmic succession to produce a chant, spell, incantation, or hymn.

TECHNIQUE Using Chant to Generate and Project Pneuma

	PROCEDURES	ANNOTATION
1	**Preliminary Techniques** Perform the Artes Praeviae.	*When performing the Artes Praeviae, generate thoughts and emotions in accordance with the magickal goal.*

2	Performing the last step in the Preliminary Techniques, continue to draw in external energy while generating cognitive and emotive pneuma. Circulate these energies until the body is filled to the point of overflowing with potent pneuma technikon.	*Feel the words of the chant resonate and become one with this pneuma.* *If words of power are being used, use the Etheric Perception attained during the Preliminary Techniques to become immersed in the power connected to the words. Feel the pneuma of the chant resonate with the larger energy reservoir linked to the words of power. Draw this flood of energy into the chant.*
3	**Project Pneuma** Use the power of the chant and the technique of Energy Casting to project this pneuma from the body.	*Feel the chant well up from deep within the self. Allow the chant to become one with the breath and energy. Use the mind and breath to project the pneuma of the chant through the voice and out of the body. This pneuma may also be projected from etheric centers such as the palms of the hands, fingertips, and major etheric centers.*
4	**Closing Techniques** Perform the Artes Concludendi.	

Working With Magickal Tools
Instrumenta Magica

Magickal tools are an integral part of ritual. Each tool serves a specific purpose. Projecting tools such as the dagger, rod, sword, and staff serve to amplify and project the magickal energies of the magus. Receptive tools such as the chalice, censer and cauldron serve to transform, consecrate, or increase the power of the substance which they contain.

TECHNIQUE Creation of a Projecting Tool

	PROCEDURES	ANNOTATION
1	**Select the Tool** Select an item that is stylistically and pragmatically suited to the use of the tool.	*Common projecting tools include the dagger, rod, sword, and staff.*
2	**Apply Symbols (Optional)** Paint, carve, or etch a symbol or group of symbols onto the tool. Symbols may be used to amplify the power of the tool.	*A set of symbols customized for magickal use is presented in this chapter.*
3	**Banish the Tool** Cleanse the tool of any unwanted energies.	
4	Use the mind and breath to emit streams of energy from the etheric centers in the palms of the hands and fingertips. Extend this energy into the tool.	
5	Use this energy to scan for unwanted energies within the tool.	
6	If unwanted energy is detected, use the energy extended from the hands to collect and pull it from the tool.	
7	Push this energy from your hands deep into the Earth.	
8	Repeat this process until all of the unwanted energy has been extracted.	

9	**Preliminary Techniques** Perform the Artes Praeviae.	*When performing the Artes Praeviae envision the tool powerfully amplifying and projecting magickal energies.* *The creation of this tool may not require emotive pneuma. In this instance, the step of emotive generation may be omitted during the Preliminary Techniques.*
10	Performing the last step in the Preliminary Techniques, continue to draw in external energy while generating cognitive and emotive pneuma. Circulate these energies until the body is filled to the point of overflowing with potent pneuma technikon.	
11	**Saturate the Tool with Pneuma** Use the technique of Primary Energy Casting to saturate the tool with this pneuma.	*Hold the tool with both hands. Use the mind and breath to emit pneuma from the palms and fingertips into the talisman. Concentrate and condense this pneuma into the tool. Continue to pour your thoughts, emotions, and energies into the tool until it is completely saturated. This pneuma technikon is an extension of the self. When saturating the tool, envision this life force powerfully amplifying and projecting energies through the tool.*
12	**Project Pneuma from the Tool** Direct pneuma through the tool and out of its projecting end.	*This establishes the proper flow of energy through the tool. With regular use the tool will accrue energy and acquire the ability to powerfully project energies.*
13	**Closing Techniques** Perform the Artes Concludendi.	*During the closing techniques banish only yourself, do not banish the tool.*

TECHNIQUE Creation of a Receptive Tool

	PROCEDURES	ANNOTATION
1	**Select the Tool** Select an item that is stylistically and pragmatically suited to the use of the tool.	*Common receptive tools include the chalice, censer, and cauldron.*
2	**Apply Symbols (Optional)** Paint, carve, or etch a symbol or group of symbols onto the tool. Symbols may be used to amplify the power of the tool.	*A set of symbols customized for magickal use is presented in this chapter.*
3	**Banish the Tool** Cleanse the tool of any unwanted energies.	
4	Use the mind and breath to emit streams of energy from the etheric centers in the palms of the hands and fingertips. Extend this energy into the tool.	
5	Use this energy to scan for unwanted energies within the tool.	
6	If unwanted energy is detected, use the energy extended from the hands to collect and pull it from the tool.	
7	Push this energy from your hands deep into the Earth.	
8	Repeat this process until all of the unwanted energy has been extracted.	
9	**Preliminary Techniques** Perform the Artes Praeviae.	*When performing the Artes Praeviae envision the tool powerfully transforming substances placed into it. The nature of the transformation is specific to the intended use of the tool.*

10	Performing the last step in the Preliminary Techniques, continue to draw in external energy while generating cognitive and emotive pneuma. Circulate these energies until the body is filled to the point of overflowing with potent pneuma technikon.	
11	**Saturate the Tool with Pneuma** Use the technique of Primary Energy Casting to saturate the tool with this pneuma.	*Hold the tool with both hands. Use the mind and breath to emit pneuma from the palms and fingertips into the talisman. Concentrate and condense this pneuma into the tool. Continue to pour your thoughts, emotions, and energies into the tool until it is completely saturated. This pneuma technikon is an extension of the self. When saturating the tool envision this life force powerfully transforming substances placed into the tool.*
12	**Closing Techniques** Perform the Artes Concludendi.	*During the closing techniques banish only yourself, do not banish the tool.*

GROUP MAGICK
Magia Complurium

Group magick is used to focus the power of many magi upon a single magickal goal. Group work forges bonds, builds fellowship, and produces powerful magick. Group workings typically make use of the techniques of Radiant Casting and Distance Casting. When using these techniques the group forms a circle around a main operator. The main operator guides the working and directs group energies towards the magickal goal.

TECHNIQUE Group Magick – Radiant Casting

	PROCEDURES	*ANNOTATION*
1	**Form a Circle** The group stands in a circle facing the main operator who stands in the center.	*During this working members in circle generate a large amount of energy which is directed into the main operator. This energy is absorbed and concentrated by the main operator then redirected towards the magickal goal. The main operator is also responsible for guiding the group through the each step of the working. This is typically choreographed via the use of gesture, chant, or recitation.*
2	**Preliminary Techniques** The entire group performs the Artes Praeviae in unison.	*The main operator guides the group through the various stages of the Preliminary Techniques.* *When performing the Artes Praeviae the magus generates thoughts and emotions in accordance with the goal of the magickal working.* *During the Preliminary Techniques a powerful protective barrier is formed. It is only necessary for the main operator to create a barrier. The barrier should be large enough to encompass the entire group.*
3	Performing the last step in the Preliminary Techniques, continue to draw in external energy while generating cognitive and emotive pneuma. Circulate these energies until the body is filled to the point of overflowing with potent pneuma technikon.	

4	**Project Pneuma to the Main Operator** Members in the circle use the technique of Primary Energy Casting to project this pneuma into the main operator.	*When the moment is right, the main operator gives a cue to the group to project pneuma. The members in the circle use the mind and breath to project this energy into the main operator. It is typically emitted from the etheric centers in the palms and fingertips. Pneuma may also be emitted from the Center of Power.*
5	**Concentrate Pneuma into the Center of Power** The main operator uses the mind and breath to concentrate this pneuma into the Center of Power.	*Feel this flood of energy pour into and circulate through the body. As the energy is concentrated into the Center of Power, feel the energy circulate and intensify.*
6	Continue to concentrate pneuma into this center until it is inflamed with power.	
7	**Saturate the Area** The main operator uses the mind and breath to powerfully emit a radial pulse of this pneuma outward from the Center of Power.	*Take a single deep breath. Upon inhale, feel the pneuma concentrated in the Center of Power become powerful to the point of growing beyond containment. Upon exhale expand a radial pulse of this pneuma to encompass the entire area of enchantment. This area may encompass immediate surroundings or a large geographic region. As this pneuma technikon saturates the region, envision this life force powerfully affecting reality in accordance with the goal of the working.*
8	As the main operator radiates pneuma, the members of the circle assist its expansion.	*As the pneuma radiates the members of the circle turn away from the main operator. Facing outward, they use the mind, breath, and gesture to assist in the expansion of pneuma.*

| 9 | **Closing Techniques**
The main operator guides the group though performing the Artes Concludendi. | *Do not banish energies that you wish to remain present.* |

TECHNIQUE Group Magick – Distance Casting

	PROCEDURES	*ANNOTATION*
1	**Form a Circle** The group stands in a circle facing the main operator who stands in the center.	*During this working members in the circle generate a large amount of energy which is directed into the main operator. This energy is absorbed and concentrated by the main operator then redirected towards the magickal goal. The main operator is also responsible for guiding the group through the each step of the working. This is typically choreographed via the use of gesture, chant, or recitation.*
2	**Preliminary Techniques** The entire group performs the Artes Praeviae in unison.	*The main operator guides the group through the various stages of the Artes Praeviae.* *When performing the Artes Praeviae the magus generates thoughts and emotions in accordance with the goal of the magickal working.* *During the Preliminary Techniques a powerful protective barrier is formed. It is only necessary for the main operator to create a barrier. The barrier should be large enough to encompass the entire group.*

3	Performing the last step in the Preliminary Techniques, continue to draw in external energy while generating cognitive and emotive pneuma. Circulate these energies until the body is filled to the point of overflowing with potent pneuma technikon.	
4	**Project Pneuma to the Main Operator** Members in the circle use the technique of Primary Energy Casting to project this pneuma into the main operator.	*When the moment is right, the main operator gives a cue to the group to project pneuma. The members in the circle use the mind and breath to project this energy into the main operator. It is typically emitted from the etheric centers in the palms and fingertips. Pneuma may also be emitted from the Center of Power.*
5	**Concentrate Pneuma** The main operator uses the mind and breath to concentrate this pneuma into the body.	*Feel this flood of energy pour into the body. Employ the inhalation and exhalation of the breath to circulate and intensify this energy within the body.*
6	Become inflamed with this potent pneuma.	
7	**Expanded Perception** Use the technique of Expanded Perception to locate and perceive the distant subject.	*Omit the first and last steps of Expanded Perception. These steps are redundant with the Preliminary and Closing Techniques used within this practice.*
8	**Emit Pneuma From the Body** Select an etheric center or centers from which to project pneuma.	*Commonly used centers include those within the palms of the hands and fingertips, and the major etheric centers.*

9	Use the mind, breath and gestures to project pneuma through the Universal Etheric Field and into the subject.	*The sensation of projecting energy across the Universal Etheric Field is unique due to the spatial ambiguity of etheric reality. The distant subject is typically perceived to be in proximity to the magus. There is however, a distinct sensation of distance as energies are projected across the Universal Etheric Field and into the subject.* *Pneuma may be emitted as currents of energy, or radiant emanations.*
10	**Saturate the Subject** Saturate the subject of the working with pneuma.	*Use the mind and breath to concentrate and condense pneuma into the subject of the working. Continue to pour your thoughts, emotions, and energies into the subject until it is completely saturated. As this pneuma technikon saturates the subject, envision this life force powerfully affecting reality in accordance with the goal of the working.*
11	As the main operator saturates the subject with pneuma, the members of the circle assist in directing pneuma to the subject.	*Circle members use the mind, breath, and gesture to move pneuma through the main operator and into the distant subject.*
12	**Closing Techniques** The main operator guides the group through performing the Artes Concludendi.	*Do not banish energies that you wish to remain present.*

TRAINING
Disciplina

Training induces a profound transformation in the magus while producing the magickal requisites of power, perception, and control. In the context of Vercanus Magick, training consists of a Core Training Technique, an Energy Casting technique, and the regular training of a wide variety of magickal practices. The Core Training Technique, Principalis Disciplina, incorporates steps from the Preliminary and Closing Techniques with special emphasis on Energy Summoning and Cultivation. Regular practice of this core technique facilitates mastery of the Preliminary Techniques, which are the cornerstone of magickal practice. Proficiency in the generation and projection of pneuma is also essential to the magickal arts. The Energy Casting technique is used to repeatedly bombard an inanimate target with various types of pneuma for the purpose of training. A schedule is given to train multiple practices on a regular basis. Such training confers mastery of the magickal practices.

When performing the Core Training Technique, the magus makes use of enhanced perception to perceive the self within a vast etheric ecology of energy and consciousness. This perception is used to tap into powerful external energy sources and increase internal power. A clear and unwavering state of mind is maintained throughout training as internal and external energies are accessed, intensified and cultivated. The thoughts and emotions generated are those of power and strength, as the sole focus is that of increasing internal energies.

Benefits of Regular Training

STEP	BENEFIT CONFERRED BY REGULAR USE
Centering	Through the practice of Centering, awareness is aligned within the self and rooted in the moment at hand. This facilitates the transition into the altered states of consciousness required to perform magick. Regular practice confers the ability to be present in the moment and align the awareness within the self even in the face of adversity and distraction.
Banishing	Removes unwanted thoughts, energies and emotions that have built up within one's consciousness and etheric body over the course of daily life.

Etheric Perception	Produces the Magickal Requisite of Perception.
Stillness	Produces the Magickal Requisites of Perception and Control and facilitates a clear state of mind that is free of internal distraction.
Energy Summoning	Produces the Magickal Requisite of Power, increases the amount of energy flowing within the body, and facilitates control of internal and external energies.
Circulation	Intensifies internal energies, strengthens the energy channels, and facilitates the free flow of internal energies without blockages or stagnation. Regular practice facilitates the ability to channel an ever increasing amount of power from external sources.
Focused Awareness	Produces the Magickal Requisite of Control and facilitates a disciplined mind.
Emotive Generation	Facilitates the ability to harness the power of emotion for magickal use.
Culmination	Upon reaching the stage of Culmination, the magus has cleared and focused the mind, enhanced the perception, and become inflamed with powerful energies. In maintaining this focused, powerful, heightened state, the magus produces the three Magickal Requisites of Power, Perception, and Control.
Banishing (Optional)	The closing step of banishing is typically not performed during training due to the fact that specific thoughts, emotions or energies are not generated. Banishing may, however, be used if the tone or potency of energies accessed or called upon are deemed to be disruptive or too powerful for normal states of being.
Circulation	Balances and normalizes the flow of internal energies.
Centering	Returns the magus to normal states of consciousness after performing magical acts. Regular practice confers the ability to transition smoothly to and from altered states of consciousness.
Cultivation	Produces the Magickal Requisite of Power and increases the amount of stored energy within the body.

TECHNIQUE Core Training Technique – *Principalis Disciplina*

	PROCEDURES	*ANNOTATION*
1	**Centering** Gather and focus the cognitive, emotive, and energetic awareness into the centers of Mind, Emotion, and Power. Feel the awareness become centered within these axial, etheric nexuses. Become acutely aware of the moment at hand perceived via these etheric centers.	*Beginning at the Center of Power and moving up to the center of Mind, gather and focus the awareness within the etheric centers.*
2	**Banishing** Use the mind and breath to extend streams of energy from the etheric centers in the palms of the hands and the fingertips.	
3	Starting just above the head slowly move the hands down the length of the body. As the hands move, extend these streams of energy into the body to collect all unwanted thoughts, energies and emotions. Draw these unwanted elements down the body.	
4	When the arms are fully extended downward, turn palms to face the ground. Use the mind and breath to project the unwanted elements deep into the Earth.	*The alternate Banishing technique, free of gestures, may be used if discretion is preferred.*

5	**Protective Barrier** Become aware of the Center of Power and the energy stored therein. Use the mind and breath to circulate and intensify the energy stored within this center.	*Use the inhalation and exhalation of the breath to circulate and intensify the energy within this center.*
6	Take a single deep breath. Upon exhale expand a sphere of protective energy outward from this center to include the entire magickal space. As the sphere expands, envision the area being cleared of unwanted energies while retaining any desired energies that may be present. If the operation requires that you be physically mobile, a smaller barrier may be extended just beyond the material body. In this case, the barrier merges with the outer layers of the body's etheric form. Through this merging, the barrier is attached to the body of the magus and moves with it.	*The barrier is an extension of the self, a sphere of pneuma technikon directly controlled by the magus. This renders the barrier semi-permeable in nature. The magus may selectively allow energies and entities to pass through the barrier while maintaining defense against hostile phenomena.* *If desired for the purpose of training, the barrier may be strengthened by fortifying the sphere with additional energy. This is accomplished by extending streams of energy from the etheric centers in the palms of the hands and fingertips into the sphere. Use these extended streams as a conduit to send energy into the shield. Fortifying of the magickal barrier is typically only necessary if the magus is under attack or exposed to particularly harmful emanations.*
7	**Etheric Perception** Use the mind and breath to awaken and expand the Center of Power. Employ the inhalation and exhalation of the breath to circulate and intensify energy within this center. Upon the exhale gradually expand the center to a size of seven to ten inches in diameter.	*Awakening and expanding the centers may be performed using several breaths or a single deep inhalation and exhalation.* *As this center expands it becomes receptive to the energetic intensity of surrounding phenomena.*

8	Use the mind and breath to move the energy awakened at the Center of Power upward along the dorsal channel to awaken the Center of Emotion. Use the inhalation and exhalation of the breath to circulate and intensify energy within this center. Upon the exhale gradually expand the center to a size of seven to ten inches in diameter.	*As this center expands it becomes receptive to the emotive tone of surrounding phenomena.*
9	Use the mind and breath to move energy awakened at the Center of Emotion upward along the dorsal channel to awaken the Center of Mind. Use the inhalation and exhalation of the breath to circulate and intensify energy within this center. Upon the exhale gradually expand the center to a size of seven to ten inches in diameter.	*As the center of Mind expands allow your awareness to shift from the tight, hard focus upon material reality to a softer, expanded focus upon the etheric aspect of reality. Allow the expanded Center of Mind to induce a receptive, light trance.* *Upon expanding, the Center of Mind becomes receptive to surrounding emanations of consciousness and induces clairvoyance.*
10	**Stillness** Become aware of the breath. Upon inhale, feel the mind become still.	
11	Upon exhale, use the energy within the Center of Mind to radially push emerging thoughts out of and away from the body.	*Push the thoughts away from the body until completely dissipated.*
12	Continue this process to hold the mind in a still state free of all thought.	
13	Immerse the mind in this state of Stillness.	

14	Use Etheric Perception to perceive the vast ecology of energy and consciousness that surrounds you and to become aware of external energy sources.	
15	**Energy Summoning** Remaining in a state of Stillness, move energy from the Center of Mind down the ventral channel back to the Center of Power.	
16	Use the mind and breath to circulate and intensify the powerful energy stored within this center.	*Use the inhalation and exhalation of the breath to circulate and inflame the energy within this center.*
17	Move this powerful flow of internal core energy through the body's etheric channels and out through one or more etheric center.	*Centers commonly used to project energy from and draw energy into the body include:* *The palms of the hands* *Soles of the feet* *The Center of Mind at the brow* *Crown Center at the top of the head* *Commonly used paths to project internal energy from the body include:* *Up the dorsal channel, then through the arms and out through the etheric centers in the palms.* *Down the legs and out through the etheric centers in the soles of the feet.* *Up the dorsal channel, and out through the etheric center in the crown.*

18	Use the mind and breath to powerfully project streams of this energy into an external energy source.	*Use the altered states of Etheric Perception and Stillness to directly perceive external energy sources.* *External energy sources may include power from within the earth, celestial energies such as those from the moon, sun, and skies, energies drawn from the elements of nature, and those from naturally occurring energy currents and power spots.*
19	Retract this extended energy back in through the etheric centers, bringing with it a current of energy from the external source. Use the mind and breath to draw this energy into the body.	*As the extended energy is retracted, feel the external energy flow into the body. This energy may be absorbed through any of the etheric centers. It may also be drawn into the body with the breath. This powerful current of energy may be maintained throughout the working or allowed to subside at will.*
20	**Circulation** Circulate the external energy through the body's energy channels and etheric centers. Move energy up the dorsal/spinal channel and down the ventral channel. With each circulation draw additional external energy into the body. Maintain circulation as you move through the remaining steps of the Preliminary Techniques.	*Alternatively, any number of esoteric systems may be studied and implemented for the purpose of circulation. The arts of Chi Gong, Tibetan Tummo, Yogic Pranayama, and Kundalini Yoga provide excellent examples for energy circulation. In lieu of an orthodox system, energy may also be circulated through the body in whichever manner feels intuitive and natural.*

21	**Focused Awareness** Moving from the clarity previously attained through Stillness, focus solely upon increasing internal power as external energies are drawn into the body and intensified.	*When using the Preliminary Techniques to perform acts of magick the focus is solely upon the goal of the magickal working. When training, the sole focus is upon increasing internal power.*
22	Maintain focus upon drawing in, circulating, and intensifying energies to the exclusion of all else.	
23	**Emotive Generation** When training Emotive Generation, generate feelings of strength and power.	*When using the Preliminary Techniques to perform acts of magick the emotion generated pertains to the goal of the specific working. For training purposes, the emotions generated are feelings of strength and power. These feelings amplify and increase the potency of energies generated and stored during this training.*
24	Use the mind and breath to become inflamed with these emotions.	

25	**Culmination** Continue to draw in external energy and circulate it throughout the body. The clear, unwavering focus is directed upon gathering and circulating energies. The enhanced perception facilitates an awareness of the self within a vast etheric ecology, drawing upon powerful external forces. The emotions generated are those of strength and power. Maintain this circulation, focus, and clarity as you become inflamed with potent pneuma.	*Feel and perceive your connection to the vast network of energy and consciousness that surrounds you. Draw these powerful external energies into your body and circulate them through your etheric channels.*
26	Hold this inflamed, focused state as long as desired to gather power and maintain enhanced states of focus and perception.	*The stage of Culmination is typically held from fifteen minutes to one hour.*
27	**Banishing (Optional)** Typically, the closing step of banishing is not performed during training. If required, banish yourself of any remaining unwanted thoughts, energies, and emotions. (See banishing under Preliminary Techniques chapter two.)	*The closing step of banishing is typically not performed during training due to the fact that undesired thoughts, emotions or energies are not generated. Banishing may, however, be used if the tone or potency of energies accessed or called upon are deemed to be disruptive or too powerful for normal states of being.* *Do not banish any energies that you wish to retain.*

28	**Circulation** Cease drawing in energy from the external power source. Allow the internal energy circulation to become more relaxed as you begin to normalize the flow of energy within the body. Feel the powerful energies gathered and generated via this training flow freely through the body's etheric channels and centers. Continue to circulate these powerful internal energies until the flow of energy feels balanced, unblocked, and free of buildups. Feel the power gathered and generated during this training become integrated into your etheric body.	*The step of Circulation typically entails briefly moving energy through the body to establish a natural, balanced flow of energy throughout the body. Circulate energy up the dorsal channel and down the ventral channel. Alternately, any traditional paths of energy circulation may be used or energy may be circulated through the body in a manner that feels intuitive.*
29	**Centering** Use the mind and breath to draw these powerful circulating energies down the body from the Centers of Mind and Emotion, collecting them in the Center of Power. As the energy leaves these centers, contract them sequentially. Upon the inhale, gather and circulate energy within the center. Upon the exhale, contract the center as energy is drawn down the ventral channel. As these energies reach the Center of Power, contract the center to its normal size.	*As the centers contract, shift the awareness back to material reality. Set the consciousness within the etheric centers and become aware of the moment at hand.*

30	**Cultivation** Upon contracting the center of Power, cultivate internal energies within this center for future use. Feel the abundance of power gathered and generated during this practice become rooted within the Center of Power.	*Use the mind and breath to condense internal energies into the Center of Power. Feel this energy intensify as it is concentrated into the center.*
31	Use the mind and breath to reabsorb the protective barrier generated during the Preliminary Techniques back into the Center of Power.	*Upon inhale draw the sphere into the Center of Power. Upon exhale condense the sphere into the Center of Power.*

The following training makes use of Energy Casting techniques to perfect the generation and projection of pneuma.

TECHNIQUE Energy Casting Training - *Virium Emissio Disciplina*

	PROCEDURES	ANNOTATION
1	**Select Suitable Target** Select a target that may safely be bombarded by a variety of etheric energies.	*Typical targets include good sized stones or pieces of wood. The target may also be a symbol inscribed upon paper or cloth.*
2	**Preliminary Techniques** Perform the Artes Praeviae.	*It is recommended that various types of pneuma be produced in the course of training. With each new training session, produce a specific type of pneuma by generating the appropriate thoughts, emotions, and energies. Only a single type of pneuma should be generated in any given session. Typical categories include healing energies, defensive energies, beneficent energies, erotic energies, and specific enchantments.*

3	Performing the last step in the Preliminary Techniques, continue to draw in external energy while generating cognitive and emotive pneuma. Circulate these energies until the body is filled to the point of overflowing with potent pneuma technikon.	
4	**Emit Pneuma** Select an etheric center from which to emit this pneuma.	*Commonly used centers include those within the palms of the hands and fingertips, and the major etheric centers.*
5	Use the mind, breath and gestures to project pneuma into the target.	*Pneuma may be emitted as currents of energy, waves of force, or radiant emanations.*
6	**Saturate the Target** Saturate the target with pneuma.	*Use the mind and breath to concentrate and condense pneuma into the target. Continue to pour your thoughts, emotions, and energies into the target until it is completely saturated.*
7	**Closing Techniques** Perform the Artes Concludendi.	
8	**Banish the Target** Use the mind and breath to emit streams of energy from the etheric centers in the palms of the hands and fingertips. Extend this energy into the target.	*If the target is not regularly banished, it could become an unstable talisman or cultivated spirit due to the various and conflicting types of pneuma with which it has been saturated. Without proper banishing such a target may become harmful to those in close proximity.*
9	Use this energy to feel the pneuma within the target.	

10	Use the energy extended from the hands to collect and pull the pneuma from the target.	
11	Push this energy from your hands deep into the Earth.	
12	Repeat this process until all of the unwanted energy has been extracted.	

Mastery of the magickal arts is gained through regular training. Below is a suggested training schedule for the core magickal techniques and practices. Training the techniques of Spirit Projection, Expansive Union and Etheric Perception simply entails using the techniques. Spirit Projection is trained by regularly leaving the body to explore etheric realms. Expansive Union is trained through frequent use of the technique to alter reality on a large scale in accordance with desired goals. Etheric Perception is trained by using the technique to explore etheric surroundings.

Training Schedule

TECHNIQUE	TRAINING
Core Training	Once per week.
Etheric Perception	Daily, through perception of, and interaction with etheric surroundings.
Energy Casting	Three times per month.
Spirit Projection	Three times per month.
Expansive Union	Three times per month.
Arts of Perception	One or more of the Arts of Perception should be trained at least once per month.
Magickal Practices	One or more of the Magickal Practices should be trained at least once per month.
Transformation	Ongoing, as needed to transform the self.

TRANSFORMATION
Transformatio

Transformation is the highest goal of magick. The arts of transformation entail altering the self via magickal means. Through transformation the magus may become more than human. In altering the self, the magus pushes the limits of human potential and fundamentally redefines the boundaries of existence. The following practices present multiple paths to transformation. The magus may master all of these practices, or focus solely upon one.

EXPANDED AWARENESS
Sensus Expansus

The technique of Sensus Expansus allows the magus to expand awareness on a continual basis. Unlike the technique of Expanded Perception which is used to temporarily shift awareness, this transformation is used to continually hold the expanded state. This is accomplished by slightly expanding the etheric centers and shifting awareness into the Universal Etheric Field. This technique induces a mildly altered state of consciousness allowing the magus to continually perceive reality on a larger scale. It facilitates awareness of surrounding events and phenomena, both in close proximity and at a distance. The technique also facilitates a continual awareness of the interconnectivity of all things. Additionally, this expanded state induces generalized prescience as it expands awareness forward into the Time Stream. Phenomena perceived via this technique are not typically in the forefront of consciousness, but rather at a semiconscious level. This expanded state is powerful, yet light enough to permit the magus to carry out the activities of daily life. The practice may be initiated in the morning or called upon as needed throughout the day.

TECHNIQUE Expanded Awareness

	PROCEDURES	ANNOTATION
1	**Center and Banish** Per instructions in the technique for Expanded Perception in chapter two.	

2	**Etheric Perception** Use the mind and breath to awaken and expand the Center of Power. Employ the inhalation and exhalation of the breath to circulate and intensify energy within this center. Upon the exhale slightly expand the center to a size of four to six inches in diameter.	*Awakening and expanding the centers may be performed using several breaths or a single deep inhalation and exhalation.* *As this center expands it becomes receptive to the energetic intensity of surrounding phenomena.*
3	Use the mind and breath to move the energy awakened at the Center of Power upward along the dorsal channel to awaken the Center of Emotion. Use the inhalation and exhalation of the breath to circulate and intensify energy within this center. Upon the exhale slightly expand the center to a size of four to six inches in diameter.	*As this center expands it becomes receptive to the emotive tone of surrounding phenomena.*
4	Use the mind and breath to move energy awakened at the Center of Emotion upward along the dorsal channel to awaken the Center of Mind. Use the inhalation and exhalation of the breath to circulate and intensify energy within this center. Upon the exhale slightly expand the center to a size of four to six inches.	*As the center of Mind expands allow your awareness to shift from the tight, hard focus upon material reality to a softer, expanded focus upon the etheric aspect of reality. Upon expanding, the Center of Mind becomes receptive to surrounding emanations of consciousness and induces clairvoyance.*

5	**Shift the Awareness into the Universal Etheric Field** Attune the awareness to the Universal Etheric Field and the interconnectedness of all things. Shift the outermost edges of awareness into perception of existence on a large scale.	*This mildly altered state of consciousness allows the magus to perceive the flow of events and interaction of phenomena on a large scale. Things perceived at this level are not typically in the forefront of consciousness, but rather at a semiconscious level.*
6	**Maintain this Expanded State** This state may be continually maintained. In doing so the magus expands the awareness at a fundamental level. Alternately, the centers may be contracted and returned to a normal state as desired. This is accomplished by returning the raised energy to the Center of Power and contracting each center sequentially beginning at the Center of Mind.	

Union
Communio

In attaining states of union the magus expands the self to experience existence beyond that of an individuated being. Through such union the magus becomes one with a larger ecology of life, energy and consciousness. The practice of union may be used to induce states of bliss, expand consciousness, and experience altered states of being. Boundless Union and Regional Union make use of Expansive Union to induce a deep, immersive experience. This entails expanding the entirety of the etheric self into union with existence at large. Union via Sacred Sex makes use of internal alchemy and enhanced perception to attain states of nondual bliss and union. These profoundly meditative experiences vary in scope from union with existence in its entirety or union with a local region.

Boundless Union
Communio Infinita

Through the technique of Boundless Union the magus may transcend duality and unify with existence at large. This is accomplished by expanding the entirety of the etheric self into union with all things at the etheric level. This expansion reunites the individuated consciousness/energy with the universal consciousness/ energy that permeates, surrounds and extends beyond all things. Terms such as Nirvana, Moksha, and Nirvikalpa Samadhi are used within Eastern Mysticism to describe similar sates of union. Such union confers liberation from the illusion of separation, freedom from individuated existence, and a direct experience of the essential unity of all things. Upon returning to a state of individuated existence, the magus retains the perception of the fundamental unity of all things. With repeated practice of this technique, the consciousness is profoundly expanded as the illusory division between the individuated self and the greater reality is diminished. The etheric centers may be left slightly expanded to maintain this enhanced perception continually. Within Hindu mysticism, those who attain similar states of continual union are described as Jivanmukta.

The technique of Boundless Union entails using core energies to awaken and expand the etheric centers and merge internal energies with powerful external energies to induce a profound nondual state of bliss in which the magus is con- nected to a larger ecology of energy and consciousness. This altered state and intensified energy is then used to powerfully expand the entirety of the spirit body beyond the individuated self and into union with the totality of existence. Several energy based meditations such as Kundalini Yoga, Chi Gong, and Tummo, make use of similar techniques to attain nondual states of being and union beyond the individuated self. During the preliminary phase of this technique, internal energy is used to awaken and expand the etheric centers. The technique of Boundless Union entails the awakening of an additional etheric center located at the top of the head. This Crown Center is the etheric body's connection point linking the individuated consciousness to the larger collective consciousness. It is at this interface that internal consciousness/energy is tangibly connected to the ocean of consciousness/energy that surrounds us. Raising internal energies to and awakening this center, powerfully shifts the awareness into nondual states of consciousness. This shift of awareness facilitates a profound expansion of the self into union with existence at large.

The technique presented below includes the individual steps of the Preliminary Techniques as they pertain to the use of Boundless Union.

TECHNIQUE Boundless Union

	PROCEDURES	ANNOTATION
	PRELIMINARY TECHNIQUES (Detailed Instruction)	
1	**Centering** Gather and focus the cognitive, emotive, and energetic awareness into the centers of Mind, Emotion, and Power.	
2	**Banishing** Banish unwanted thoughts, energies and emotions.	
3	**Protective Barrier** Expand a sphere of protective energy to encompass the entire magickal space.	
4	**Etheric Perception** Sequentially awaken and expand the centers of Power, Emotion, Mind, and Crown. Shift awareness to the etheric aspect of existence. When performing the step of Etheric Perception, continue to raise energy beyond the Center of Mind to awaken and expand the Crown Center at the top of the head.	*In moving energy to and awakening the Crown Center, perception is powerfully shifted away from individuated consciousness and towards nondual states of awareness.*

5	**Stillness** Use the mind and breath to dispel unwanted thoughts, becoming immersed in a state of Stillness.	
6	From this state of Stillness, use Etheric Perception to perceive the vast ecology of energy and consciousness that surrounds you and to become aware of external energy sources.	
7	**Energy Summoning** Remaining in a state of Stillness, move energy from the Crown Center down the ventral channel back to the Center of Power.	
8	Use the mind and breath to circulate and intensify the powerful energy stored within this center.	
9	Move this powerful internal energy up the dorsal channel, through the arms, and to the palms.	
10	Use the mind and breath to powerfully project streams of this energy through the etheric centers in the palms to connect to external energies deep within the earth.	*This step is typically performed in a standing position with the palms facing down.*
11	Retract this extended energy, bringing with it a current of energy from the earth. Use the mind and breath to draw this energy through the body.	

12	Draw the earth energy up the body. As the energy reaches the Crown Center, use the mind and breath to powerfully project streams of this energy upwards through the Crown Center and palms to connect with currents within the larger ecology of energy and consciousness that surrounds you.	*Connect to an energetic field, a pool of energy or one or more currents within the Universal Etheric Field.*
13	Retract this extended energy back in through the etheric centers of the hands and crown, bringing with it a current of energy from the surrounding cosmos. Use the mind and breath to draw this energy down through the body.	
14	**Circulation** As the universal energy is drawn down the ventral channel, reach down again and draw earth energy up the dorsal channel to meet universal energy. Draw down universal energy and continue this circulation.	
15	**Focused Awareness** The sole focus is upon the connection to the larger ecology of energy and consciousness as internal and external energies are circulated and merged into one.	
16	**Emotive Generation** Emotions generated are those of oneness, unity and bliss.	

17	**Culmination** Continue to draw in and circulate universal and earth energies through the body. The clear, unwavering focus is directed upon merging external and internal energies into one. The enhanced perception facilitates an awareness of the self within a vast etheric ecology, drawing upon and becoming one with powerful external forces. The feelings generated are those of oneness, unity and bliss. Maintain this circulation, focus, and clarity as internal and external energies merge and intensify to create powerful, nondual states of bliss.	*Chants or mantras may be used to facilitate this focus and emotive state.*
18	**Gather Energies to Center of Power** Draw the circulating energies down the ventral channel and into the Center of Power.	*Cease circulation and gather energies to the body's central nexus of power. Feel the earth and universal energies centered within the body's central core of power.*

| 19 | **Expansive Union** Use the mind, breath, and energy to expand the entirety of the etheric self into union with surrounding phenomena. Upon each inhale draw earth and universal energies into the core, feel these energies build and intensify within the body to create powerful, nondual states of bliss.

Upon each exhale use the intensified internal energy to expand the entirety of the etheric self through the Universal Etheric Field into ever widening union with surrounding phenomena. As the etheric self expands into union with existence at large, shift awareness beyond individuated consciousness into direct union with surrounding phenomena. Continue this expansion into the Universal Etheric Field, extending the awareness to the furthest reaches of the continuum of existence. | *This union may be experienced as expanding to great size, perception from a great height, or omnipresence. As the etheric body expands it becomes a protean field of living energy merging into the Universal Etheric Field, becoming one with the entirety of existence.* |

20	**Become Immersed in Union** Become immersed in this profound, nondual state of union. Perceive the entirety of existence within you and around you as an undivided part of yourself. Attune your spirit to the ebb and flow of consciousness and energy within existence at large as you breathe with the cosmos.	*Experience direct union with all things. Merge into one with universal consciousness.*
21	**Contract the Etheric Body** Use the mind and breath to contract the etheric self back into the material body. Upon each inhale, contract the etheric body back into the material body. Upon each exhale, further condense the expanded etheric body. As the etheric body contracts into the material body, shift consciousness away from the expanded unified state, and return to individuated awareness.	

| 22 | **Closing Techniques**
Perform the Artes Concludendi.

At the closing stage of Circulation, maintain awareness of the energies within the larger region that you accessed and merged with. At the stage of Cultivation, condense a portion of these energies into the Center of Power to retain a potent energetic link to the larger ecology of consciousness and energy.

When Centering, the etheric centers may be left slightly expanded to continually maintain the experience of union and perception of the interconnectedness of all things. | |

REGIONAL UNION
Communio Regionalis

Similar to Boundless Union, Regional Union allows one to transcend the individ-uated self to directly experience unity with a larger reality. Using the technique of Communio Regionalis, the Magus becomes one with the consciousness, energy and life present within a specific region. This is accomplished by expanding the entirety of the etheric self into union with a particular region. In becoming one with the region the magus experiences the phenomena and flow of energy within the region in a deep and profound way, a depth of experience greater than that provided by the perspective of an individuated being. This technique is typically used to become one with regions sacred in nature or possessing natural power including sacred sites, forests, deserts, mountains or seas. It may also be used to become one with the complex human landscape of a city, town, or group.

The technique presented below includes the individual steps of the Preliminary Techniques as they pertain to the use of Regional Union.

TECHNIQUE Regional Union

	PROCEDURES	ANNOTATION
	PRELIMINARY TECHNIQUES (Detailed Instruction)	
1	**Centering** Gather and focus the cognitive, emotive, and energetic awareness into the centers of Mind, Emotion, and Power.	
2	**Banishing** Banish unwanted thoughts, energies and emotions.	
3	**Protective Barrier** Expand a sphere of protective energy to encompass the entire magickal space.	
4	**Etheric Perception** Sequentially awaken and expand the centers of Power, Emotion, Mind, and Crown. Enter Stillness and shift consciousness to the etheric aspect of existence. When performing the step of Etheric Perception, continue to raise energy beyond the Center of Mind to awaken and expand the Crown Center at the top of the head.	*In moving energy to and awakening the Crown Center, perception is powerfully shifted away from individuated consciousness and towards nondual states of awareness.*

5	**Stillness** Use the mind and breath to dispel unwanted thoughts, becoming immersed in a state of Stillness.	
6	From this state of Stillness, use Etheric Perception to perceive the vast ecology of energy and consciousness that surrounds you and to become aware of external energy sources.	
7	**Energy Summoning** Remaining in a state of Stillness, move energy from the Crown Center down the ventral channel back to the Center of Power.	
8	Use the mind and breath to circulate and intensify the powerful energy stored within this center.	
9	Use the mind and breath to powerfully project a stream of this energy through etheric centers in the palms and soles of the feet to connect to external energies within the earth.	
10	Retract this extended energy back in through the etheric centers, bringing with it a current of energy from the earth. Use the mind and breath to draw this energy into the body.	

11	Draw the earth energy up the body. As the energy reaches the Crown Center, use the mind and breath to powerfully project streams of this energy upwards through the Crown Center and palms to connect with currents within the larger ecology of energy and consciousness that surrounds you.	*Connect to an energetic field, a pool of energy or one or more currents within the Universal Etheric Field.*
12	Retract this extended energy back in through the etheric centers, bringing with it a current of energy from the surrounding cosmos. Use the mind and breath to draw this energy down into the body.	
13	**Circulation** As the universal energy is drawn down the ventral channel, reach down again and draw earth energy up the dorsal channel to meet universal energy. Draw down universal energy and continue this circulation.	
14	**Focused Awareness** The sole focus is upon the connection to the larger ecology of energy and consciousness as internal and external energies are circulated and merged into one.	
15	**Emotive Generation** Emotions generated are those of oneness, unity and bliss.	

16	**Culmination** Continue to draw in and circulate universal and earth energies through the body. The clear, unwavering focus is directed upon merging external and internal energies into one. The enhanced perception facilitates an awareness of the self within the larger etheric ecology, drawing upon and becoming one with powerful external forces. The feelings generated are those of oneness, unity and bliss. Maintain this circulation, focus, and clarity as internal and external energies merge and intensify to create powerful, nondual states of bliss.	*Chants or mantras may be used to facilitate this focus and emotive state.*
17	**Gather Energies to Center of Power** Draw the circulating energies down the ventral channel and into the Center of Power.	*Cease circulation and gather energies to the body's central nexus of power. Feel the earth and universal energies centered within the body's central core of power.*

| 18 | **Expansive Union**
Use the mind, breath, and energy to expand the entirety of the etheric self into union with surrounding phenomena. Upon each inhale draw earth and universal energies into the core, feel these energies build and intensify within the body to create powerful, nondual states of bliss.

Upon each exhale use the intensified internal energy to expand the entirety of the etheric self through the Universal Etheric Field into ever widening union with surrounding phenomena. As the etheric self expands into union with existence at large, shift awareness beyond individuated consciousness into direct union with surrounding phenomena. Continue this expansion into the Universal Etheric Field, extending the awareness to encompass the entire region. | *This union may be experienced as expanding to great size, perception from a great height, or omnipresence throughout the region. As the etheric body expands it becomes a protean field of living energy merging into the Universal Etheric Field, becoming one with the entirety of existence.* |

19	**Become Immersed in Union** Become immersed in this profound, nondual state of union. Allow this expanded, unified state to dissolve the separation between yourself and surrounding phenomena within the larger region. Attune your spirit to the ebb and flow of consciousness and energy within the region as you breathe with the entirety of the region.	*Experience direct union with surrounding phenomena as you merge into the collective consciousness and energy of the region.*
20	**Contract the Etheric Body** Use the mind and breath to contract the etheric self back into the material body. Upon each inhale, contract the etheric body back into the material body. Upon each exhale, further condense the expanded etheric body. As the etheric body contracts into the material body, shift consciousness away from the expanded unified state, and return to individuated awareness.	

21	Closing Techniques	
	Perform the Artes Concludendi. At the closing stage of Circulation, maintain awareness of the energies within the larger region that you accessed and merged with. At the stage of Cultivation, condense a portion of these energies into the Center of Power to retain a potent energetic link to the larger ecology of consciousness and energy. When Centering, the etheric centers may be left slightly expanded to continually maintain the experience of union and perception of the interconnectedness of all things.	

UNION VIA SACRED SEX
Communio Sexualis Sacra

Through sacred sex, two partners merge together to experience existence beyond the individuated self. This practice entails exchanging male and female energies to create a powerful, nondual state of bliss. During this sacred sex each partner perceives the other as a localized manifestation of the divine universal male or female principal. As the female draws in male energy through her Sex Center and the male draws in energy through the female breath, a circuit of moving energy is formed. Alternately, any method of energy circulation that feels natural and intuitive may be used. Through continued energy exchange via sexual union the two partners become one. As the nondual state of bliss intensifies, the illusory division between the self, the partner and the larger ecology of consciousness and energy dissolves. As orgasm is reached, this profound transpersonal state of union is intensified and expanded, merging the lovers into one with each other and the greater collective of existence. The initial stages of this technique may be augmented with elements of ritual to bring the partners into a state of resonance. The efficacy of this technique is not affected by sexual preference. Depending upon the nature of each individual, same sex couples may embody the union of male/female universal energies or the union and intensification of same gender universal energies.

TECHNIQUE Union via Sacred Sex

	PROCEDURES	*ANNOTATION*
	PRELIMINARY TECHNIQUES (Detailed Instruction)	
1	**Centering** Gather and focus the cognitive, emotive, and energetic awareness into the centers of Mind, Emotion, and Power.	
2	**Banishing** Banish unwanted thoughts, energies and emotions.	
3	**Protective Barrier** Expand a sphere of protective energy to encompass the entire magickal space.	
4	**Etheric Perception** Sequentially awaken and expand the centers of Power, Emotion and Mind. Enter Stillness and shift consciousness to the etheric aspect of existence.	
5	**Stillness** Use the mind and breath to dispel unwanted thoughts, becoming immersed in a state of Stillness.	

6	From this state of Stillness use Etheric Perception to become aware of your partner's spirit and the connection that exists between the two of you. Perceive your partner as a localized manifestation of the divine universal male or female principle.	*Same sex couples may also embody the union of male/female universal energies or the union and intensification of same gender universal energies.*
7	**Energy Summoning** Remaining in a state of Stillness, move energy from the Center of Mind down the ventral channel back to the Center of Power.	
8	Use the mind and breath to circulate and intensify the powerful energy stored within this center.	
9	Move this intensified energy down from the Center of Power to the Sex Center.	*The etheric center located at the genitals is used to powerfully project and receive energy.*
10	Use the mind and breath to exchange energy with your partner via sexual union. The male partner projects a stream of energy from the Sex Center into his partner. The female partner draws this energy up through the entirety of her body and projects it into her partner via the breath. The male draws in this energy through the breath, moves it down the entirety of his body and projects it back into his partner via the Sex Center.	*Alternately, energy may be exchanged between partners in any manner that feels intuitive. The efficacy of this technique is not affected by sexual preference.*

11	**Circulation** Continue to exchange energy with your partner. Maintain circulation as you move through the remaining steps of this technique.	
12	**Focused Awareness** The sole focus is upon desire and admiration of your partner as a manifestation of the divine universal male or female principle as the exchanged energies are circulated and merged into one.	
13	**Emotive Generation** Emotions generated are those of passion, love, unity and bliss.	

Sigil of Union

14	**Culmination / Union** Continue to exchange energies with your partner. The clear, unwavering focus is directed upon merging male and female energies together. The enhanced perception facilitates an awareness of the partner as the divine universal male or female while the deep energetic connection binds the two together as one. The feelings generated are those of oneness, unity and bliss. Maintain this circulation, focus, and clarity as the nondual state of bliss intensifies, and dissolves the illusory division between the self, the partner and the larger ecology of consciousness and energy. Upon reaching orgasm, allow this profound transpersonal state of union to intensify and expand, merging the lovers into one with each other and the greater collective of existence.	

ETHERIC EXPLORATION
Exploratio Aetherica

Etheric Exploration is a particularly fascinating and liberating aspect of the occult arts. This practice entails using Spirit Projection, Dream Magick, and Etheric Perception to explore the etheric aspect of reality as well as distant material locations. We are surrounded by a boundless realm of etheric environments. These environments contain an intriguing array of etheric beings, phenomena, and form diverse in complexity. This rich aspect of reality goes unnoticed during ordinary states of consciousness. The art of magick allows the magus to transcend the borders of material reality and explore new worlds. The technique of Spirit Projection is used to journey to and interact with etheric environments. During such journeys the magus may interact with and explore these environments as if physically present. The skills gained via the Union practices may also be used to merge into one with any given aspect of the cosmos encountered during Etheric Exploration. Subjects of such exploration may include etheric environments, deity centered environments, vast etheric currents, energetic fields, and pools of consciousness within the multifaceted monad that is the cosmos. Spirit Projection may also be used to explore distant material locations. Similarly, the technique of Dream Magick may be used to explore etheric and material environments while sleeping. This allows the magus to lead a second life each night. The etheric aspect of existence may be directly explored via Etheric Perception. Such perception facilitates exploration of the immediate etheric surroundings without leaving the body. The transformational practice of Etheric Exploration liberates the magus from the confines of the material body and facilitates the experience of existence beyond the limitations of a physical being.

TECHNIQUE Etheric Exploration via Spirit Projection

	PROCEDURES	ANNOTATION
1	**Preliminary Techniques** Perform the Artes Praeviae.	*During the step of Focused Awareness, focus intensely upon the destination to be explored.*
2	**Project from the Body** Use the technique of Spirit Projection to leave the material body.	
3	**Project to the Destination** Using the technique of Spirit Projection, travel to the intended destination.	*This may be an etheric environment or a material location.* *Common destinations include the Upper-Worlds, Lower-Worlds, Heavens, Hells, abodes of the Gods, higher realms of existence, etc. described within the religion, mysticism, and mythology of various cultures.*

4	**Explore the Destination** The etheric body is now free to explore the destination from a first person perspective.	*Spirit Projection allows the magus to explore the location as if physically present.* *The skills gained via the Union practices may also be used to merge into one with any given aspect of the cosmos encountered during Etheric Exploration.*
5	**Return to the Material Body** Return to the material body and normal consciousness.	
6	**Closing Techniques** Perform the Artes Concludendi.	

TECHNIQUE Etheric Exploration via Dream Magick

	PROCEDURES	*ANNOTATION*
1	**Preliminary Techniques** Perform the Artes Praeviae.	*Banish to clear unwanted thoughts and emotions, shift consciousness towards the etheric aspect of reality, and enter Stillness to induce a deep meditative state free of thought.* *During the step of Focused Awareness, focus intensely upon the destination to be explored. Common destinations include the Upper-Worlds, Lower-Worlds, Heavens, Hells, abodes of the Gods, higher realms of existence, etc. described within the religion, mysticism, and mythology of various cultures.*

2	Feel your internal energy (previously summoned during the Preliminary Techniques) surging through and strengthening your etheric body. Gather this energy to the Center of Power.	
3	**Become Aware of the Etheric Body** The receptive state of Etheric Perception was initiated during the Preliminary Techniques. Use the heightened state of Etheric Perception to feel your etheric body within your material body.	
4	**Sleep** Enter the sleep state while maintaining focus upon the magickal goal.	
5	**Control the Dream State** Use the techniques of Energy Casting and Spirit Projection to control the dream state.	*The pneuma and focus resulting from the Preliminary Techniques will naturally shape the dream in accordance with the magickal goal. The dream state is further controlled by using Energy Casting to affect etheric phenomena and Spirit projection to travel. Through energy casting the very fabric of the dream may be reshaped by emitting streams of energy or waves of force from the etheric body. Spirit Projection allows the magus to move through the dreamscape with intent, as opposed to being randomly pulled through various dream scenes.*

6	**Explore** Interact with all phenomena encountered in the dream state.	*Willfully engage all beings and phenomena encountered in the dream. It is important to remember that dream phenomena tend to be subjective and symbolic in nature. As such, elements of the dream may manifest in unexpected yet entirely relevant forms.* *Hostile or malevolent entities may be dealt with via the techniques of Defensive Magick. Unpleasant dream states may be reshaped by Energy Casting or escaped from via Spirit Projection.*
7	**Recall the Dream** Upon awakening recall every detail of the dream.	
8	**Closing Techniques** Perform the Artes Concludendi.	

TECHNIQUE Etheric Exploration via Etheric Perception

	PROCEDURES	*ANNOTATION*
1	**Etheric Perception** Center and banish, sequentially awaken and expand the centers of Power, Emotion and Mind. Enter Stillness and shift consciousness to the etheric aspect of existence.	

2	**Explore Etheric Surroundings** Use the receptive, light trance state of Etheric Perception to directly perceive and interact with etheric phenomena in your immediate surroundings.	*The technique of Etheric Perception induces a receptive, visionary state. Use this light trance to become immersed in your etheric surroundings. Move the eyes into a soft focus. It may also be helpful to begin Etheric Perception with the eyes closed or half open. This limits perception of material reality, shifting perception to the Center of Mind. The eyes are then slowly opened, facilitating simultaneous perception of both etheric and material phenomena.* *Use your entire body to perceive surrounding phenomena. Smaller etheric centers throughout the body may be used to perceive etheric phenomena. The centers in the palms of the hands and fingertips are particularly useful.*

Symbol for Etheric

3	**Center and Return to Normal Consciousness** Become aware of the internal energy raised to awaken the etheric centers. Use the mind and breath to draw this energy down the body from the Centers of Mind and Emotion, collecting it in the Center of Power. As the energy leaves these centers, contract them sequentially. Upon the inhale, gather and circulate energy within the center. Upon the exhale, contract the center as energy is drawn down the ventral channel. As the energy reaches the Center of Power, contract the center to its normal size and cultivate internal energy for future use.	*As the centers contract, shift the awareness back to material reality. Set the awareness within the etheric centers and become acutely aware of the moment at hand.*

ENERGY CULTIVATION
Cultura Virium

Energy cultivation is the practice of drawing in, gathering, and storing etheric energy from a variety of powerful external sources. Through energy cultivation the magus becomes powerful. Possessing a large amount of energy allows the magus to exert a greater effect upon reality at the etheric level. As such, the magus may more effectively shape external phenomena and transform the self. Energy cultivation is also a key component of immortality practices (see Immortality). This practice entails tapping into a varied assortment of external power sources and performing protracted energy gathering sessions. Through accessing a variety of external power sources, the magus balances internal energies, and becomes connected to a wider ecology of energy. Typically accessed energy sources include power from within the earth, celestial energies such as those from the moon, sun, and skies, energies drawn from the elements, and those from naturally occurring energy currents and power spots. Energy may also be obtained from other humans via dual cultivation. Typically, dual cultivation is practiced in conjunction with sexual yoga or some form of sex magick. In such instances the two partners willingly exchange, increase, and balance each other's energy. The practice of Energy Cultivation makes use of the same techniques as the Core Training Technique. The fundamental difference is that in the case of Energy Cultivation, the magus seeks out a variety of power sources and spends a protracted amount of time connecting with and gathering energy from these sources.

TECHNIQUE Energy Cultivation

	PROCEDURES	ANNOTATION
1	**Centering** Gather and focus the cognitive, emotive, and energetic awareness into the centers of Mind, Emotion, and Power. Feel the awareness become centered within these axial, etheric nexuses. Become acutely aware of the moment at hand perceived via these etheric centers.	*Beginning at the Center of Power and moving up to the center of Mind, gather and focus the awareness within the etheric centers.*
2	**Banishing** Use the mind and breath to extend streams of energy from the etheric centers in the palms of the hands and the fingertips.	
3	Starting just above the head slowly move the hands down the length of the body. As the hands move, extend these streams of energy into the body to collect all unwanted thoughts, energies and emotions. Draw these unwanted elements down the body.	

4	When the arms are fully extended downward, turn palms to face the ground. Use the mind and breath to project the unwanted elements deep into the Earth.	*The alternate Banishing technique, free of gestures, may be used if discretion is preferred.*
5	**Protective Barrier** Become aware of the Center of Power and the energy stored therein. Use the mind and breath to circulate and intensify the energy stored within this center.	*Use the inhalation and exhalation of the breath to circulate and intensify the energy within this center.*
6	Take a single deep breath. Upon exhale expand a sphere of protective energy outward from this center to include the entire magickal space. As the sphere expands, envision the area being cleared of unwanted energies while retaining any desired energies that may be present. If the operation requires that you be physically mobile, a smaller barrier may be extended just beyond the material body. In this case, the barrier merges with the outer layers of the body's etheric form. Through this merging, the barrier is attached to the body of the magus and moves with it.	*The barrier is an extension of the self, a sphere of pneuma directly controlled by the magus. This renders the barrier semi-permeable in nature. The magus may selectively allow energies and entities to pass through the barrier while maintaining defense against hostile phenomena.*

7	**Etheric Perception** Use the mind and breath to awaken and expand the Center of Power. Employ the inhalation and exhalation of the breath to circulate and intensify energy within this center. Upon the exhale gradually expand the center to a size of seven to ten inches in diameter.	*Awakening and expanding the centers may be performed using several breaths or a single, deep inhalation and exhalation.* *As this center expands it becomes receptive to the energetic intensity of surrounding phenomena.*
8	Use the mind and breath to move the energy awakened at the Center of Power upward along the dorsal channel to awaken the Center of Emotion. Use the inhalation and exhalation of the breath to circulate and intensify energy within this center. Upon the exhale gradually expand the center to a size of seven to ten inches in diameter.	*As this center expands it becomes receptive to the emotive tone of surrounding phenomena.*
9	Use the mind and breath to move energy awakened at the Center of Emotion upward along the dorsal channel to awaken the Center of Mind. Use the inhalation and exhalation of the breath to circulate and intensify energy within this center. Upon the exhale gradually expand the center to a size of seven to ten inches in diameter.	*As the center of Mind expands allow your awareness to shift from the tight, hard focus upon material reality to a softer, expanded focus upon the etheric aspect of reality. Allow the expanded Center of Mind to induce a receptive, light trance.* *Upon expanding, the Center of Mind becomes receptive to surrounding emanations of consciousness and induces clairvoyance.*
10	**Stillness** Become aware of the breath. Upon inhale, feel the mind become still.	

11	Upon exhale, use the energy within the Center of Mind to radially push emerging thoughts out of and away from the body.	*Push the thoughts away from the body until completely dissipated.*
12	Continue this process to hold the mind in a still state free of all thought.	
13	Immerse the mind in this state of Stillness.	
14	Use Etheric Perception to perceive the vast ecology of energy and consciousness that surrounds you and to become aware of external energy sources.	
15	**Energy Summoning** Remaining in a state of Stillness, move energy from the Center of Mind down the ventral channel back to the Center of Power.	
16	Use the mind and breath to circulate and intensify the powerful energy stored within this center.	*Use the inhalation and exhalation of the breath to circulate and inflame the energy within this center.*
17	Move this powerful flow of internal core energy through the body's etheric channels and out through one or more etheric center.	*Centers commonly used to project energy from and draw energy into the body include:* ~ *The palms of the hands* ~ *Soles of the feet* ~ *The Center of Mind at the brow* ~ *Crown Center at the top of the head*

18	Use the mind and breath to powerfully project streams of this energy into an external energy source.	*External energy sources may include power from within the earth, celestial energies such as those from the moon, sun, and skies, energies drawn from the elements of nature, and those from naturally occurring energy currents and power spots.*
19	Retract this extended energy back in through the etheric centers, bringing with it a current of energy from the external source. Use the mind and breath to draw this energy into the body.	*As the extended energy is retracted, feel the external energy flow into the body. This energy may be absorbed through any of the etheric centers. It may also be drawn into the body with the breath. This powerful current of energy may be maintained throughout the working or allowed to subside at will.*
20	**Circulation** Circulate the external energy through the body's energy channels and etheric centers. Move energy up the dorsal/spinal channel and down the ventral channel. With each circulation draw additional external energy into the body. Maintain circulation as you move through the remaining steps of the Preliminary Techniques.	*Alternatively, any number of esoteric systems may be studied and implemented for the purpose of circulation. The arts of Chi Gong, Tibetan Tummo, Yogic Pranayama, and Kundalini Yoga provide excellent examples for energy circulation. In lieu of an orthodox system, energy may also be circulated through the body in whichever manner feels intuitive and natural.*
21	**Focused Awareness** Moving from the clarity previously attained through Stillness, focus solely upon increasing internal power as external energies are drawn into the body and intensified.	*When using the Preliminary Techniques to perform acts of magick the focus is solely upon the goal of the magickal working. When cultivating energy, the sole focus is upon increasing internal power.*

22	Maintain focus upon drawing in, circulating, and intensifying energies to the exclusion of all else.	
23	**Emotive Generation** When cultivating energy, generate feelings of strength and power.	*When using the Preliminary Techniques to perform acts of magick the emotion generated pertains to the specific magickal goal. When cultivating energy, the emotions generated are feelings of strength and power. These feelings serve to increase the power and potency of the energies generated and stored during this practice.*
24	Use the mind and breath to become inflamed with these emotions.	
25	**Culmination** Continue to draw in external energy and circulate it throughout the body. The clear, unwavering focus is directed upon gathering and circulating energies. The enhanced perception facilitates an awareness of the self within a vast etheric ecology, drawing upon powerful external forces. The emotions generated are those of strength and power. Maintain this circulation, focus, and clarity as you become inflamed with potent pneuma.	*Feel and perceive your connection to the vast network of energy and consciousness that surrounds you. Draw these powerful external energies into your body and circulate them through your etheric channels.*
26	Hold this inflamed, focused state as long as desired to gather power and maintain enhanced states of focus and perception.	*The stage of Culmination is typically held from fifteen minutes to one hour.*

| 27 | **Banishing (Optional)**
Typically, the closing step of banishing is not performed during energy cultivation. | *The closing step of banishing is typically not performed during the practice of Energy Cultivation due to the fact that undesired thoughts, emotions or energies are not generated. Banishing may, however, be used if the tone or potency of energies accessed or called upon are deemed to be disruptive or too powerful for normal states of being.* |
| 28 | **Circulation**
Cease drawing in energy from the external power source. Allow the internal energy circulation to become more relaxed as you begin to normalize the flow of energy within the body. Feel the powerful energies gathered and generated via this training flow freely through the body's etheric channels and centers. Continue to circulate these powerful internal energies until the flow of energy feels balanced, unblocked, and free of buildups. Feel the power gathered and generated during this training become integrated into your etheric body. | *The step of Circulation typically entails briefly moving energy through the body to establish a natural, balanced flow of energy throughout the body. Circulate energy up the dorsal channel and down the ventral channel. Alternately, any traditional paths of energy circulation may be used or energy may be circulated through the body in a manner that feels intuitive.* |

29	**Centering** Use the mind and breath to draw these powerful circulating energies down the body from the Centers of Mind and Emotion, collecting them in the Center of Power. As the energy leaves these centers, contract them sequentially. Upon the inhale, gather and circulate energy within the center. Upon the exhale, contract the center as energy is drawn down the ventral channel. As these energies reach the Center of Power, contract the center to its normal size.	*As the centers contract, shift the awareness back to material reality. Set the consciousness within the etheric centers and become aware of the moment at hand.*
30	**Cultivation** Upon contracting the Center of Power, cultivate internal energies within this center for future use. Feel the abundance of power gathered and generated during this practice become rooted within the Center of Power.	*Use the mind and breath to condense internal energies into the Center of Power. Feel this energy intensify as it is concentrated into the center.*
31	Use the mind and breath to reabsorb the protective barrier generated during the Preliminary Techniques back into the Center of Power.	*Upon inhale draw the sphere into the Center of Power. Upon exhale condense the sphere into the Center of Power.*

IMMORTALITY
Immortalitas

In the context of Vercanus magick the term immortality refers to the survival of the etheric body after death. Destruction of the material body does not necessarily destroy the etheric body. With proper training and transformation the etheric aspect of the self may remain fully functional after death. The untrained individual has little control of the spirit after death. Those with strong religious beliefs in life will typically attach to a deity centered etheric environment after death. In the case of ghosts, a spirit may become attached to a person or place that was an object of intense obsession in life. Many spirits are so stunned by death that they are unable to retain any level of control. Such spirits are aimlessly moved about by etheric currents like leaves in the wind. Spirits that are unable to maintain energy levels and focus may dissipate altogether. Through the arts of immortality the magus retains full control of consciousness, energy and volition past death.

The practice of immortality makes use of a variety of techniques which enable the spirit to thrive beyond death of the material body. This primarily consists of training to acquire familiarity with existence in a disembodied state. This is attained by frequent use of Spirit Projection. The technique of Spirit Projection is integrally similar to the death experience, familiarity with this state of being prepares the magus for existence beyond the material body. Through frequent use of Spirit Projection the magus masters the skills necessary to thrive in a non-corporeal state. Additionally, the magus learns to interact with surrounding phenomena as an entirely non-material being. Experience of existence in a disembodied state may also be gained via the practice of dream magick. Towards this end the magus endeavors to use Dream Magick frequently to explore existence in a non-corporeal form. In order to prevent dissipation of the spirit after death and to maintain consciousness, energy and volition, the magus must train to focus the awareness and retain power. The spirit body retains its cohesion by sheer force of will. In mastering Focused Awareness and Stillness the spirit gains control of the consciousness. Such control is necessary to resist dissipation and free the consciousness from the stream of random thoughts and emotions that would otherwise hinder volition in the disembodied state. In addition to abnormally powerful focus, achieving immortality also requires having an abnormally powerful spirit. The practice of energy cultivation while in the material body produces a powerful spirit and augments immortality practices. The ability to access and cultivate external power sources while in a disembodied state, however, is essential to maintain a spirit that is able to resist dissipation and retain the power to affect reality at the etheric level. Through frequent excursions in the disembodied state, the magus accesses external power sources, builds internal power, and fosters focused awareness. Such training transforms the spirit to the degree that it may survive death. Similar immortality practices may be found within the corpus of Taoist internal alchemy.

SHARED IMMORTALITY
Immortalitas Communicata

The practice of immortality may be used to join partners together in a state of eternal love. Shared Immortality entails the ongoing use of the primary Immortality technique in unison with a partner and a technique to bind the two together in eternal resonance. Using these techniques the partners learn to gather and cultivate energy together and foster familiarity in a disembodied state. Collaboration in a disembodied state creates resonance between the partners, which is further intensified by the technique of Eternal Embrace. This technique is a sensual, energetic union that prevents two spirits from drifting apart. This process creates a deep spiritual link that binds two partners together in eternal resonance. Spirits that have been bound in this fashion remain together in life and beyond death.

CONSCIOUS REINCARNATION
Reincarnatio Conscia

The sex act is extremely powerful. It generates the amount of energy necessary to create new life. This energy is a blend of energy from both the mother and father. Copulation can either create a new spirit or act as a gateway to the rebirth of an existing spirit. Couplings resulting in conception cause a powerful warping of etheric currents, time streams, and the inertial flow of causal events. Where these energetic and causal streams converge there are conception points, a nexus of energy merged together by the two lovers to create a corporeal being. These conception points may be described as myriad energy vortexes within the Universal Etheric Field terminating at the impassioned couplings of lovers. It is through these gateways that spirits may once again incarnate into material existence.

During Conscious Reincarnation, the magus identifies currents within the Universal Etheric Field that are in resonance with the desired path of reincarnation, as they are forming into conception points. In choosing a conception point, the magus controls reincarnation as opposed to randomly re-entering material existence. Unwanted aspects of the self, karmic attachments, and unwanted obsessions from the previous life are thoroughly banished. Striving to retain as much of the self as possible the newly reincarnated magus merges with the conception energies of the mother and father. As the new being grows, the consciousness and spirit of the magus becomes that of the developing child and experiences a lengthy period of gestation and transformation in a state of union with the mother. As the child matures, memories of the previous life often return. The new individual possesses qualities and characteristics of both mother and father, along with the faculties of power, perception and control of the reincarnated magus. The extent to which the magus is able to retain memory and skills is dependent upon focus and power.

A technique for Conscious Reincarnation is provided to perform after death has occurred. Conscious Reincarnation may be trained prior to death via the Immortality technique. This would entail projecting the spirit beyond the body to become familiar with cultivating external power sources while in a disembodied state and identifying Conception Points with which one is in resonance.

Symbol for Immortality

Paths of Immortality

The quest for immortality is undertaken for many reasons. The path of immortality chosen is dependent upon the basic nature and personal preference of the magus. Common paths of immortality pursued include etheric exploration, conscious reincarnation, service to humanity, continual knowledge, eternal union with a deity and eternal love.

Etheric Exploration

Etheric exploration is well suited to those with an unending fascination for the mysteries of existence. As a disembodied spirit, the magus is free to explore infinite etheric realms as well as the vast material expanse of the universe.

Conscious Reincarnation

Those fascinated with the visceral, sensual nature of corporeal existence may experience it repeatedly through conscious reincarnation.

Service to Humanity

Those with deep compassion may continue service to humanity after death. Examples of this path include immortal, ascended masters who foster the spiritual and magickal development of living humans from a disembodied state, or bodhisattvas who consciously forgo entry into nirvana in order to guide other sentient beings to a state of enlightenment.

Continual Knowledge

Others may seek to continually gain knowledge. Through unending existence, the magus may evolve, transform, and unravel the mysteries of existence for eons as a disembodied spirit.

Eternal Union with a Deity

Those with a powerful relationship with a deity in life may choose to attain eternal union with that deity after death.

Eternal Love

Those who find true love in life may seek to join each other eternally through Shared Immortality.

Whichever path is chosen, it need not be traveled alone. The journey past death may be taken with loved ones, family and friends. Training for immortality may be done in pairs or groups. Additionally, the techniques of Immortality enable the magus to reunite with loved ones who have previously passed on.

TECHNIQUE Immortality Training

	PROCEDURES	*ANNOTATION*
1	**Preliminary Techniques** Perform the Artes Praeviae.	*When performing the Artes Praeviae the sole focus is upon increasing internal energy. The feelings generated are those of strength and power.*
2	**Spirit Projection** Use the technique of Spirit Projection to leave the material body.	*Become aware of the energy gathered into the spirit during the Preliminary Techniques. Feel this energy strengthen and fortify the spirit body.*
3	**Etheric Exploration** Interact with your surroundings in the disembodied state of Spirit Projection. The focus achieved during the Preliminary Techniques is powerfully maintained throughout etheric exploration. Such focus prevents disorientation and maintains volition while in a disembodied state.	*Exploration may focus upon an etheric environment or a material location.*
4	**Locate an Etheric Energy Source** Use the technique of Spirit Projection to locate a source of etheric energy.	*Energy sources may include power from within the earth, celestial energies such as those from the moon, sun, and skies, energies drawn from the elements of nature, those from naturally occurring energy currents and power spots, and the complex web of energies present in etheric and material environments.*
5	**Connect to the Etheric Energy Source** Use the mind and energy to powerfully project streams of pneuma into the external energy source.	

6	**Draw Upon the Etheric Energy Source** Retract this extended energy back in through the etheric centers, bringing with it a current of energy from the external source. Use the mind and breath to draw this energy into the body. Circulate the external energy through energy channels and etheric centers filling the spirit with power.	*As the extended energy is retracted, feel the external energy flow into the etheric body. This energy may be absorbed through any of the etheric centers.*
7	**Return to Material Body** Travel back to the material body.	
8	**Re-integrate with the Material Body** Slowly re-integrate the etheric body with material body.	*This typically entails merging the etheric and material bodies together. Consciousness is then shifted back into the material self.*
9	**Closing Techniques** Perform the Artes Concludendi.	*When performing the closing technique of circulation, become aware of the energy accessed during the technique. During the closing stage of cultivation feel the abundance of power gathered and generated during this practice become rooted within the Center of Power.* *Use the mind and breath to condense internal energies into the Center of Power. Feel this energy intensify as it is concentrated into the center.*

Each of the following steps is intended to be performed in unison by both partners.

TECHNIQUE Shared Immortality Training

	PROCEDURES	ANNOTATION
1	**Select Power Spot** Select a power spot known to both partners.	*This may be a material location with which both partners are familiar or an etheric environment that both have visited.*
2	**Preliminary Techniques** Perform the Artes Praeviae.	*When performing the Artes Praeviae the sole focus is upon increasing internal energy. The feelings generated are those of strength and power.*
3	**Spirit Projection** Use the technique of Spirit Projection to project the etheric body four to fifty feet above the material body.	*Become aware of the energy gathered into the spirit during the Preliminary Techniques. Feel this energy strengthen and fortify the spirit body.*
4	Perceive your partner's spirit, then travel to the power spot together.	*If animal or therianthropic forms are used, it is helpful to know the form that your partner intends to assume.*
5	**Etheric Exploration** Interact with your surroundings in the disembodied state of Spirit Projection. The focus achieved during the Preliminary Techniques is powerfully maintained throughout etheric exploration. Such focus prevents disorientation and maintains volition while in a disembodied state.	*Exploration may focus upon an etheric environment or a material location.*

6	**Locate an Etheric Energy Source** Use the technique of Spirit Projection to locate a source of etheric energy.	*Energy sources may include power from within the earth, celestial energies such as those from the moon, sun, and skies, energies drawn from the elements of nature, those from naturally occurring energy currents and power spots, and the complex web of energies present in etheric and material environments.*
7	**Connect to the Etheric Energy Source** Use the mind and energy to powerfully project streams of pneuma into the external energy source.	
8	**Draw Upon the Etheric Energy Source** Retract this extended energy back in through the etheric centers, bringing with it a current of energy from the external source. Use the mind and energy to draw this pneuma into the etheric body. Circulate the external energy through the energy channels and etheric centers filling the spirit with power.	*As the extended energy is retracted, feel the external energy flow into the etheric body. This energy may be absorbed through any of the etheric centers.*
9	**Return to Material Body** Return together to your material bodies.	
10	**Re-integrate with the Material Body** Slowly re-integrate the etheric body with the material body.	*This typically entails merging the etheric and material bodies together. Consciousness is then shifted back into the material self.*

11	**Closing Techniques** Perform the Artes Concludendi.	*When performing the closing technique of circulation, become aware of the energy accessed during the technique. During the closing stage of cultivation feel the abundance of power gathered and generated during this practice become rooted within the Center of Power.* *Use the mind and breath to condense internal energies into the Center of Power. Feel this energy intensify as it is concentrated into the center.*

Each of the following steps is intended to be performed in unison by both partners.

TECHNIQUE Eternal Embrace

	PROCEDURES	*ANNOTATION*
1	**Preliminary Techniques** Perform the Artes Praeviae.	*When performing the Artes Praeviae focus upon your deep, eternal connection to your partner. The thoughts and emotions generated are those of undying love, passion, and determination.*
2	**Spirit Projection** Use the technique of Spirit Projection to project the etheric body four to fifty feet above the material body.	*Alternately, the couple may use Spirit Projection to travel to a favorite etheric environment or material location.*
4	**Eternal Embrace** Extend streams of energy from your etheric centers to gently penetrate the corresponding etheric centers of your partner. Draw your partner's spirit near.	

5	Use this closeness and energetic bond to circulate energy from your etheric body into that of your partner. Continue to circulate and blend your energy with that of your partner.	*Use the conjoined energetic streams and closeness of spirit to merge your internal energy flow with that of your partner. Enter a state of deep love and bliss as your energy and consciousness become one.* *The Eternal Embrace is a sensual, deep energetic union that prevents two spirits from drifting apart. This process creates a deep spiritual link that binds two partners together in eternal resonance. Spirits that have been bound in this fashion remain together in life and beyond death.*
6	Retract the extended energy streams from your partner's etheric body.	
7	**Return to Material Body** Return together to your material bodies.	
8	**Re-integrate with the Material Body** Slowly re-integrate the etheric body with the material body.	*This typically entails merging the etheric and material bodies together. Consciousness is then shifted back into the material self.*
9	**Closing Techniques** Perform the Artes Concludendi.	*When performing the closing technique of circulation, become aware of the energy accessed during the technique. During the closing stage of cultivation feel the abundance of power gathered and generated during this practice become rooted within the Center of Power.* *Use the mind and breath to condense internal energies into the Center of Power. Feel this energy intensify as it is concentrated into the center.*

TECHNIQUE Conscious Reincarnation

	PROCEDURES	*ANNOTATION*
1	**Banish** Use the mind and energy to move unwanted thoughts, emotions, and energies out of the etheric body. Move them away from the body and allow them to dissipate. Completely banish unwanted aspects of the self, karmic attachments, and unwanted obsessions from the previous life.	*Use the mind and breath to draw internal energy up the dorsal channel into each etheric center. Upon the inhale, circulate energy within the center. Upon exhale, radiate energy out from the center. Use this energy to push unwanted elements out of and away from the etheric body.*
2	**Locate an Etheric Energy Source** Use the technique of Spirit Projection to locate a source of etheric energy.	*External energy sources may include power from within the earth, celestial energies such as those from the moon, sun, and skies, energies drawn from the elements of nature, those from naturally occurring energy currents and power spots, and the complex web of energies present in etheric and material environments.*
3	**Connect to the Etheric Energy Source** Use the mind and energy to powerfully project streams of pneuma into the external energy source.	

4	**Draw Upon the Etheric Energy Source** Retract this extended energy back in through the etheric centers, bringing with it a current of energy from the external source. Use the mind and breath to draw this energy into the etheric body. Circulate the external energy through the etheric body's energy channels and etheric centers filling the spirit with power.	*As the extended energy is retracted, feel the external energy flow into the etheric body. This energy may be absorbed through any of the etheric centers.*
5	**Focused Awareness** As you circulate external energy, use Focused Awareness to become completely aware of your core being. Focus upon your knowledge, your path, your fascination, your experience and the sum total of all things that constitute your individuality.	
6	**Emotive Generation** Powerfully feel your deepest core emotions that drive you forward into a new life. This may be your compassion, your drive, your love or your will.	

7	**Concentrate and Condense Energy into the Etheric Body** Continue to draw in and circulate energy from the external source. Concentrate and condense this energy into the etheric body. Continue in this fashion until the etheric body is filled with potent pneuma.	
8	**Locate Conception Point** Use Expanded Perception to become aware of etheric currents, time streams, and the inertial flow of causal events with which you are in resonance. Perceive these phenomena converging into energy nexuses that merge the etheric into the material. Use Spirit Projection to follow these currents to a Conception Point that powerfully resonates with your path.	*Discernment, patience and care should be used when selecting the Conception Point to ensure a place of optimal rebirth.*
9	**Project the Spirit Into a Conception Point** Project the spirit through the selected conception point. Such conception points may be described as myriad energy vortexes within the Universal Etheric Field terminating at the impassioned couplings of lovers. Through this energetic gateway one may traverse the continuum from spirit to matter and be born again.	.

10	**Maintain Focus and Power** Maintain focus upon the core being and the power generated prior to entering the Conception Point. Hold this focus upon your essential self, power, and knowledge as you once again grow into a material being.	

SHAPE SHIFTING
Formarum Commutatio

In the context of Vercanus Magick the term shape shifting refers to the practice of altering the form and attributes of the etheric body to mirror those of another creature. Reshaping the etheric body into that of an animal is the most common type of shape shifting. This may be performed while the etheric body is within the material body or during Spirit Projection. Such transformations are performed to confer upon the magus the powers and attributes of the selected animal. This is accomplished by invoking a spirit animal and using its power to alter the etheric body.

Spirit animals, also known as totem or power animals, are an integral part of traditional shamanic magick. These forces of nature are the collective spiritual essence of an entire species. For example, the spirit of Wolf is the essence of all wolf kind, rather than the spirit of an individual wolf. Upon invoking a spirit animal the magus is imbued with its power and attributes. The mind and breath are then used to alter the etheric body in accordance with the animal essence.

Shape shifting is commonly performed when the etheric body is separated from the material body, as occurs during Spirit Projection. No longer confined to the material body, the magus may fully assume the form and attributes of the selected animal. This transformation also provides a convenient mode of etheric travel. Typically, flying, running, or swimming is used, depending upon the nature of the animal invoked. Upon invoking the essence of a power animal and shifting the spirit into a new form the magus may experience existence beyond the confines of one's native species.

When the etheric body is shifted without leaving the material body the change may be less pronounced, yet still powerful. For example, a magus invoking the Wolf Spirit may experience an enhanced sense of smell or improved agility as the etheric body is subtly shifted and imbued with the power of the spirit animal. When shifting without leaving the body, the magus typically takes the form of a therianthrope rather than a full animal form. A therianthrope is a fusion of human and animal form. Traditionally, shamans and warriors from various cultures have used ecstatic ritual and dance to invoke the power of a spirit animal while in the body. Examples of this include the fury of the Norse berserkers and the dances of indigenous peoples calling upon spirit animals of bear, eagle, raven, coyote etc. When focused and controlled, the power of such transformations may be brought into the experience of daily life.

TECHNIQUE Shape Shifting while in the Body

	PROCEDURES	ANNOTATION
1	**Resonate With the Spirit Animal** Use the technique of Expanded Perception to become aware of the spirit animal.	*Expand the etheric centers. Shift awareness into the Universal Etheric Field to become fully aware of the spirit animal's presence.*
2	Use this expanded perception to enter into a state of union with the spirit animal.	*Allow yourself to become completely immersed in the consciousness and power of the spirit animal.*
3	**Become Inflamed with the Animal's Power** Feel the animal's pneuma circulate through the energy channels and centers of your body.	*In attaining a state of union with the animal, the magus becomes saturated with its power. This experience can be quite euphoric as the body is filled with the power and attributes of the spirit animal.*
4	**Shift Consciousness** Allow the pneuma of the spirit animal to alter the way that you feel, perceive and move.	*The thoughts, feelings and energy of the magus are saturated with those of the spirit animal. This imbues the magus with the consciousness, power and attributes of the animal.*

5	**Shift the Etheric Form** Use the mind and breath to saturate the etheric form with the pneuma of the animal spirit.	*Upon inhale feel the energy intensify, upon exhale condense the energy into the etheric form.*
6	As you move this pneuma into the etheric form, feel its shape change to reflect the spirit of the animal.	*Upon exhale feel the form shift into this altered shape. The power of the spirit animal will naturally reshape the etheric form to reflect the nature of the animal. This reshaping may be further guided by the mind and breath. The form taken is typically that of a therianthrope, a fusion of human and animal form.*
7	**Maintain this State** This altered state may be maintained as needed to confer upon the magus the perception, powers and attributes of the selected animal.	
8	**Return the Consciousness and Etheric Body to Normal States** When the altered state is no longer required, use the mind and breath to move the pneuma of the spirit animal out of the body. Move it away from the body and allow it to dissipate.	*Become aware of the pneuma of the spirit animal. Upon inhale feel the etheric centers become filled with energy. Upon exhale, powerfully radiate energy out from the centers of Mind, Emotion, and Power. Use this energy to push the pneuma of the spirit animal out of and away from the body.*
9	Use the mind and breath to return the etheric form to its normal shape.	*As the energy of the spirit animal leaves the body, the form will naturally return to its normal shape. This transformation may be assisted by the mind and breath.*

TECHNIQUE Shape Shifting while Out of the Body

	PROCEDURES	ANNOTATION
1	**Preliminary Techniques** Perform the Artes Praeviae.	*When performing the Artes Praeviae, strongly envision the etheric form becoming that of the spirit animal.*
2	**Spirit Projection** Use the technique of Spirit Projection to leave the material body.	
3	**Resonate With the Spirit Animal** Use the technique of Expanded Perception to become aware of the spirit animal.	*Shift awareness into the Universal Etheric Field to become fully aware of the spirit animal's presence.*
4	Use this expanded perception to enter into a state of union with the spirit animal.	*Allow yourself to become completely immersed in the consciousness and power of the spirit animal.*
5	**Become Inflamed with the Animal's Power** Feel the animal's pneuma circulate through the energy channels and centers of your body.	*In attaining a state of union with the animal, the magus becomes saturated with its power. This experience can be quite euphoric as the body is filled with the power and attributes of the spirit animal.*
6	**Shift Consciousness** Allow the pneuma of the spirit animal to alter the way that you feel, perceive and move.	*The thoughts, feelings, and energy of the magus are saturated with those of the spirit animal. This imbues the magus with the consciousness, power and attributes of the animal.*
7	**Shift the Etheric Form** Use the mind and breath to saturate the etheric form with the pneuma of the spirit animal.	*Upon inhale feel this pneuma intensify, upon exhale condense the energy into the etheric form.*

8	As you move this pneuma into the etheric form, feel its shape change to reflect the spirit of the animal.	*Upon exhale feel the form shift into this altered shape. The power of the spirit animal will naturally reshape the etheric form to reflect the nature of the animal. This reshaping may be further guided by the mind and breath.*
9	**Become the Animal** Shape shifting while outside the body leaves the magus free to fully take on the form and attributes of the selected animal.	*This transformation allows the magus to experience existence as an animal. It also provides a convenient mode of etheric travel (i.e. flying, swimming, running).*
10	**Return to the Material Body** Return to the material body and normal consciousness.	
11	**Closing Techniques** Perform the Artes Concludendi.	*Do not banish any residual attributes of the animal that you may wish to retain.*

RECASTING THE SELF
Sui Ipsius Renovatio

Recasting the self entails using magick to add desired components to the self while removing undesirable components. For example the magus may wish to remove fear and anger from the self and replace them with courage and temperance. Etheric Perception is used to identify unwanted aspects of the self. Banishing is then used to remove these elements. Finally, Energy Casting is used to generate the cognitive and emotive pneuma associated with the desired traits. These desired traits are then permanently incorporated into the etheric body, replacing the unwanted traits. This practice may be applied to any thought, emotion, energy, trait, or habit that the magus may wish to alter. Using this process, the magus may either enhance the self or re-create the self entirely.

TECHNIQUE Recasting of the Self

	PROCEDURES	*ANNOTATION*
1	**Etheric Perception** Use Etheric Perception to perceive your etheric body.	*Center and banish, sequentially awaken and expand the centers of Power, Emotion and Mind. Enter Stillness and shift consciousness to the etheric aspect of existence. Focus inward to perceive the etheric aspect of self.*
2	**Identify Unwanted Aspects of the Self** Become fully aware of unwanted traits, emotions, and behaviors within yourself. From the clarity of Stillness, selectively allow unwanted aspects of the self to reemerge. Acknowledge the reason they exist and experience them completely.	*Typical traits include anger, fear, jealousy, hate, grief, attachment, anxiety, and insecurity.*
3	**Locate the Unwanted Trait Within the Body** Identify where the unwanted trait is located within the body.	*Psychological and emotional traits are often perceived to reside in specific parts of the body or in specific etheric centers. For example, grief is often in the chest or Center of Emotion, fear is often in the stomach or Center of Power, and pathological thoughts are often in the head or Center of Mind. These traits may however be found anywhere in the body.*

4	**Banish Unwanted Aspects of the Self**	*Use the mind and breath to draw internal energy up the dorsal channel into each etheric center. Upon the inhale, circulate energy within the center. Upon exhale, radiate energy out from the center. Use this energy to push unwanted elements out of and away from the body. Perform this process of purification upon any etheric center or area of the body where unwanted traits reside. Multiple traits may be sequentially banished in a single session, or a single trait may be banished in a single session.*
	Become aware of the internal energy raised to awaken the etheric centers. Remaining in a state of Stillness, use the mind and breath to draw this energy from the Center of Mind down the ventral channel back to the Center of Power. Beginning at the Center of Power, use the mind, breath, and energy to remove unwanted thoughts, emotions, and energies from the body. Upon inhale, circulate energy within this center. Upon exhale, radiate energy out from the center. Use this energy to push unwanted elements out of the center and away from the body. Raise internal energy from the Center of Power up the dorsal channel and repeat this process of purification for each etheric center and/ or each area of the body where unwanted traits reside. Once all unwanted traits have been banished, move energy from the Center of Mind down the ventral channel back to the Center of Power. Circulate purified undifferentiated internal energy up the dorsal channel and down the ventral channel for one to two rounds, returning it to the Center of Power.	

5	**Energy Summoning** Use the mind and breath to circulate and intensify the powerful energy stored within the Center of Power.	
6	Move this powerful internal energy through the body's etheric channels and out through one or more etheric center.	
7	Use the mind and breath to powerfully project streams of energy into an external energy source.	
8	Retract this extended energy back in through the etheric centers, bringing with it a current of energy from the external source. Use the mind and breath to draw this energy into the body.	
9	**Circulation** Circulate the external energy through the body's energy channels and etheric centers. Move energy up the dorsal/ spinal channel and down the ventral channel. With each circulation draw additional external energy into the body.	

10	**Generate Pneuma Associated with the Desired Traits** Powerfully generate the thoughts and emotions associated with the desired trait. Feel these powerful energies merge with the circulating raw energy to produce potent pneuma technikon.	*Typical traits include confidence, strength, courage, compassion, love, passion, and peace. Each trait is associated with a particular type of cognitive or emotive pneuma.* *Invocation of deity energy or that of a power animal may be used in lieu of generation. In this case the magus would invoke deities or power animals that possess the desired traits and attributes.*
11	**Set Traits into Body** Use the mind and breath to condense and concentrate this circulating pneuma technikon into its relevant place within the body. Continue to generate thoughts, emotions, as these energies are set into place.	*It may be beneficial to replace removed traits with their energetic opposites. For example, the magus may remove anger from the Center of Emotion in the chest and replace it with love. This has a balancing therapeutic effect.* *Multiple desired traits may be sequentially added in a single session, or a single desired trait may be added in a single session*
12	**Closing Techniques** Perform the Artes Concludendi. The closing step of Banishing is typically omitted. Leave all desired traits present within the body.	
13	**Repeat as Necessary** Repeat this process until each undesirable trait has been removed and each desirable characteristic has been added.	*This process may take time to complete. Typically, transformation of the self requires multiple sessions carried out over weeks or months.*

Volitional Consciousness
Conscientia Voluntaria

Volitional Consciousness is an advanced magickal discipline that permits the magus to continually control the contents of the self. Mundane life is primarily experienced on a reactive basis. As such, moment to moment thoughts and emotions are controlled by external stimuli. Using the practice of Volitional Consciousness, the magus may live intentionally. Rather than simply reacting to external situations, the magus continually creates desired states of being. Banishing is used to attain a state free from of unwanted thoughts, emotions and energies. The etheric centers are awakened and slightly expanded to provide more holistic, enhanced, and expanded perception of surrounding phenomena. The technique of Stillness is used to achieve a state of pure awareness, unobscured by mental chatter. Through this Stillness the magus may move beyond the myopia, noise, and distraction of self-generated cognitive and emotive states. Through Continual Refinement, unwanted thoughts, emotions, and energies are transmuted within the body as they arise. The magus becomes completely immersed in the moment at hand via Focused Awareness. This immersive focus engages the magus in the moment at hand and powerfully generates thoughts and emotions relevant to the moment at hand. Through Volitional Consciousness interaction with the world is a controlled yet intensely immersive experience. Via this discipline, the self is continually re-created in accordance with the will, ideals, goals, and situational needs of the magus. This technique is derived from Taoist internal alchemy and the disciplines of Stoicism. Volitional Consciousness may be performed on a continual basis while performing the activities of daily life. The practice may be initiated in the morning or called upon as needed throughout the day. This is a continual mindfulness of the contents of consciousness and the body's internal energy flow.

TECHNIQUE Volitional Consciousness

	PROCEDURES	ANNOTATION
1	**Center and Banish** Per instructions in the technique for Expanded Perception in chapter two.	

2	**Banish** Beginning at the Center of Power, use the mind, breath, and energy to remove unwanted thoughts, emotions, and energies from the body. Upon inhale, circulate energy within this center. Upon exhale, radiate energy out from the center. Use this energy to push unwanted elements out of and away from the body. Raise internal energy from the Center of Power up the dorsal channel and repeat this process of purification for all of the etheric centers. Once all centers have been purified, move energy from the Center of Mind down the ventral channel back to the Center of Power. Circulate purified undifferentiated internal energy up the dorsal channel and down the ventral channel for one to two rounds, returning it to the Center of Power.	*Use the mind and breath to draw internal energy up the dorsal channel into each etheric center. Upon the inhale, circulate energy within the center. Upon exhale, radiate energy out from the center. Use this energy to push unwanted elements out of and away from the body.*
3	**Etheric Perception** Use the mind and breath to awaken and slightly expand the Center of Power. Employ the inhalation and exhalation of the breath to circulate and intensify energy within this center. Upon the exhale gradually expand the center. This is a slight expansion of four to six inches in diameter.	*Awakening and expanding the centers may be performed using several breaths or a single deep inhalation and exhalation.*

4	Use the mind and breath to move the energy awakened at the Center of Power upward along the dorsal channel to awaken the Center of Emotion. Use the inhalation and exhalation of the breath to circulate and intensify energy within this center. Upon the exhale gradually expand the center. This is a slight expansion of four to six inches in diameter.	
5	Use the mind and breath to move energy awakened at the Center of Emotion upward along the dorsal channel to awaken the Center of Mind. Use the inhalation and exhalation of the breath to circulate and intensify energy within this center. Upon the exhale gradually expand the center. This is a slight expansion of four to six inches in diameter.	*As the center of Mind expands allow your awareness to shift to a more holistic and expanded perception of your surroundings.*
6	**Stillness** Become aware of the breath.	
7	Upon inhale, feel the mind become still.	
8	Upon exhale, use the energy within the Center of Mind to radially push emerging thoughts out of and away from the body.	*Push the thoughts away from the body until completely dissipated.*
9	Continue this process to hold the mind in a still state free of all thought.	

10	Immerse the mind in this state of Stillness.	*Become aware of your surroundings and the deeper, enhanced perception gained via the expanded etheric centers.*
11	**Circulation** Become aware of the internal energy raised to awaken the etheric centers. Remaining in a state of Stillness, use the mind and breath to draw this energy from the Center of Mind down the ventral channel back to the Center of Power.	
12	Use the mind and breath to circulate and intensify the powerful energy stored within this center.	*Use the inhalation and exhalation of the breath to circulate and inflame the energy within this center.*
13	Circulate this internal energy through the body's energy channels and etheric centers. Move internal energy back up the dorsal/spinal channel and down the ventral channel. Maintain control of the body's internal energy circulation throughout the extended use of this practice.	*Alternatively, any number of esoteric systems may be studied and implemented for the purpose of circulation. In lieu of an orthodox system, energy may also be circulated through the body in whichever manner feels intuitive and natural.*

14	**Continual Refinement** Use the mind, breath and the power of this internal circulation to refine unwanted thoughts and emotions back into stillness as they arise. Expel unwanted thoughts, emotions and energies along with the breath. From this place of stillness, use the power and bliss of this internal energy circulation to generate the desired thoughts and emotions.	
15	**Immersion** Use Focused Awareness to become completely immersed in the moment at hand.	*Become completely immersed in the current moment and activity at hand. Experience this moment to the exclusion of all else.*
16	Generate thoughts and emotions relevant to the moment at hand. Use the power of the internal energy circulation to intensify these thoughts and emotions as you become immersed in the moment.	*Elements generated may be in reaction to the situation at hand/or purely self-generated.*
17	When the moment has passed and the activity at hand is complete, return to the step of Continual Refinement. When engaging in a new interaction, return to the step of Immersion. Alternate between these states throughout the extended use of this practice.	

TRANSFORMATIO

COMMUNIO

POTENTIAM

Virium Pullus
IMMORTALITAS

Sensus Expansus
SUI IPSIUS RENOVATIO

CONSCIENTIA VOLUNTARIA
Formarum Commutatio

Sigil of Transformation

Chapter 4

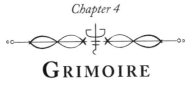

GRIMOIRE
COMPONENTS OF RITUAL

The term grimoire refers to a collection of magickal rituals, incantations and formulae. The following pages contain powerful workings designed to achieve specific magickal goals. These workings combine magickal techniques and practices with the various components of ritual. Each working provides instructions and components fundamental to the attainment of the magickal goal. To make full use of the grimoire, the magus must possess a sound understanding of ritual.

Ritual is integral to the human experience. It manifests in various forms in every culture. In the context of magick, ritual serves a variety of functions. Of primary importance is the effect of ritual upon the human mind. Performing a ritual dramatically alters consciousness. The elements of ritual direct the mind towards specific states of being. Additionally, ritual alters internal energetic states. The classic components of ritual focus the mind, inflame the emotions, and gather energy. This process naturally generates pneuma technikon while enhancing the power and efficacy of the magickal operation.

A well designed ritual guides the magickal act. The physical actions, material objects, and verbal formulae that comprise ritual augment and guide action performed at the etheric level. Ritual is the harmonious synchronization of physical action guiding the consciousness and etheric action. It is, however, important not to confuse ritual with magick itself. Ritual, although highly effective, is not necessary to perform magick. Most magi do, however, use some form of ritual to augment magickal operations. For every magickal technique and practice there exists an endless variety of corresponding rituals. The value of a ritual is judged solely by the degree to which it assists the magus in performing magick. Through trial and error, a ritual style may be developed to best suit the individual nature of the magus.

Common components of ritual include:
- ~ Gesture
- ~ Chant
- ~ Movement
- ~ Use of Magickal Tools
- ~ Materiae Magicae
- ~ Music
- ~ Sex
- ~ Recitation
- ~ Allegorical Action
- ~ Symbols

Gesture

Gestures are primarily used to direct energy through the body. When properly performed, gestures move the etheric body in perfect harmony with the material body. The material and etheric body are two aspects of a single phenomenon. Etheric energies naturally follow movement of the material body. This effect is the basis of traditional movement arts such as Tai Chi, Chi Gong, and yoga. Gestures used in ritual are shaped by the personal style of the magus and the nature of the magickal working. Such gestures range from a simple wave of the hand to a complex series of choreographed movements.

Chant

Chant is used to focus the mind and generate energy. The mind altering drone of chant serves to hold the awareness upon the magickal goal. The evocative nature of chant assists in both the generation and projection of pneuma. This effect is increased when the chant makes use of ancient magickal languages and words of power.

Movement

Ritual movement includes circumambulation, moving meditations and dance. Movement is primarily used to generate energy and induce a shift in consciousness.

Magickal Tools
Magickal tools are used to enhance specific ritual acts. Each tool performs a unique task. Common tasks include projecting and amplifying energies or transforming and consecrating substances. When used properly, magickal tools are seamlessly integrated into the physical and etheric flow of the ritual.

Materiae Magicae
The various incense, oils, candles, and potions of materiae magicae are used to transform the magus and alter the ritual space. These substances contain potent pneuma. They are skillfully incorporated into the ritual to augment magickal techniques and practices.

Music
Music profoundly alters consciousness. It is used in ritual to quickly shift thoughts, emotions, and energies into states aligned with the magickal goal. Music sets the emotive tone, ranging from meditative to frenzied states as needed. This powerful magickal tool has been used throughout human history from the earliest shamans to the present day.

Sex
Sex is used in ritual to alter consciousness and generate large amounts of potent pneuma. The ritual framework serves to harness and redirect this energy towards the magickal goal.

Recitation
In the context of ritual, recitation typically takes the form of a magickal, poetic speech. Used to exalt the emotions, it is a tool for generating emotive energy appropriate to the working at hand. It aligns the mind with the purpose of the magickal working through verbal expression. Recitation is used extensively in the invocation of deities and the evocation of spirits.

Allegorical Action
Allegorical action is a symbolic enactment of the intent of the magickal working. For example, one may tie cords around a wax image to bind an enemy, or pour water into a cauldron to bring rain. Allegorical action is a physical expression of action taken at the etheric level. This serves as a meditation to focus the mind upon the magickal goal and forms a powerful connection to the subject of the

working. When employing allegorical action, items that have been in close proximity to the subject are often included in the working, as they retain the pneuma and etheric traces of the subject. Such items greatly strengthen the connection via action of resonance and enhanced perception of the subject's etheric trace through the Universal Etheric Field.

Symbols

Symbols are typically used in ritual as a meditative focal point during the generation of pneuma. In this capacity they serve to focus the awareness while evoking specific thoughts and emotions. They may also be used as gateways to pools of energy and consciousness within the Universal Etheric Field. Examples of such symbols include yantras, mandalas, sigils, and sacred statues. Symbols of power may also be inscribed upon objects to impart them with magickal potency.

HOW TO CREATE A MAGICKAL WORKING

The creation of a magickal working is truly an art. It requires an understanding of magick, ritual, the human mind and the nature of reality. Magickal workings may consist of a single stage operation or a multiple stage magickal campaign. Single stage workings are used when the required change may be affected via a single magickal operation. Magickal campaigns are used when the goal is best served by multiple magickal operations employing various techniques and practices. The magickal working is entirely shaped by the nature of the magickal goal. The following steps may be used as a guideline for the composition of an effective working that is in line with the magickal goal.

~ Clearly define the magickal goal.
~ Meditate upon the changes that need to occur to achieve this goal.
~ Meditate upon the etheric means by which this change may be brought about.
~ Identify the magickal techniques and practices best suited to bring about this change.
~ Envision yourself using these techniques and practices to enact the magickal working.
~ Use this vision to identify ritual components that may enhance the magickal working.
~ Write out the performance of the magickal working step by step and in detail.

ABRIDGED GRIMOIRE

The following magickal workings provide step by step instructions covering the techniques, practices, and ritual components used to accomplish specific magickal goals. The workings presented may be modified, embellished, or adapted to specific situations. The chants given make use of the ancient magickal languages of Greek, Latin, and Gaelic. Also included are spoken Germanic Runes. The runes presented have been selected and combined specifically for use in Vercanus rituals. The ancient magickal languages included are by no means a comprehensive list. Additional areas of linguistic study may include Ancient Egyptian, Eastern Mantras , the languages of indigenous peoples, and the various tongues of cultures fluent in the magickal arts. The grimoire presented is not intended to be a comprehensive collection of magickal workings. Rather, the intent is to provide key magickal workings as instructional examples of the practical application of magick.

Sigil of Good Fortune

Diagram of a Magick Circle

TO CAST A CIRCLE & CALL THE QUARTERS

Brief Description	Materials for this Ritual
The Casting of the Circle is a powerful preliminary ritual used to purify, protect, bring power to, and alter the magickal space. Performed as the initial step of the banishing process, it is used in conjunction with the Artes Praeviae. This working uses the technique of Energy Casting and is supplemented by materiae magicae and the use of magickal tools. The Calling of the Quarters is a ritual used to draw the surrounding elemental powers of nature into the magickal circle.	Sanctifying Incense Censer Music (appropriate to the magickal working) Four Percipient Candles A Bell or Singing Bowl Circle Salt Purifying Water Athame, Sword, Staff or Wand

CIRCLE CHANT: By my Arts, I Consecrate this Circle

Latin Translation	Artibus meis hunc Circulum Consecro
Latin Pronunciation	**Ahr**-tee-boos **meh**-ees hoonk **keer**-koo-loom **kon**-seh-kroh
Ancient Greek Translation	Διὰ τεχνῶν ἐμῶν τοῦτον τὸν κύκλον καθιερῶ
Ancient Greek Pronunciation	Dia **tek**-nohn eh-mon **too**-tohn tohn **koo**-klohn ka-**thee**-eh-roh
Gaelic Translation	'S ann air m' eòlas a tha mi a' coisrigeadh a' chearcaill seo
Gaelic Pronunciation	Soun ehr mee-**ol**-vus eh ha mee kush-vee-**kyehk** eh kquair-**kil** shoh
Runic Formula	Fehu Elhaz Othala ᚠ ᚷ ᛟ
Rune Pronunciation	Feh-hoo Eyl-hahz Oh-thah-lah

QUARTER CHANT OF AIR: I Call Upon Air

Latin Translation	Aera Invoco
Latin Pronunciation	**Ah**-eh-rah **een**-voh-koh
Ancient Greek Translation	Ἀνακαλῶ Ἀέρα
Ancient Greek Pronunciation	Ana-**kalo ahy**-rah
Gaelic Translation	Tha mi a' gairm air an adhar
Gaelic Pronunciation	Hah mee **gehv**-em ehv em nahr
Runic Formula	Ansuz Fehu Othala ᚨ ᚠ ᚱ
Rune Pronunciation	Ahn-sooz Feh-hoo Oh-thah-lah

QUARTER CHANT OF FIRE: I Call Upon Fire

Latin Translation	Ignem Invoco
Latin Pronunciation	**Eeg**-nyehm **een**-voh-koh
Ancient Greek Translation	Ἀνακαλῶ Πῦρ
Ancient Greek Pronunciation	Ana-**kalo** pyur
Gaelic Translation	Tha mi a' gairm air an teine
Gaelic Pronunciation	Hah mee **gehv**-em ehv em **tyin**-eh
Runic Formula	Kenaz Fehu Othala ᚲ ᚠ ᚱ
Rune Pronunciation	Kay-nahz Feh-hoo Oh-thah-lah

QUARTER CHANT OF WATER: I Call Upon Water

Latin Translation	Aquam Invoco
Latin Pronunciation	**Ah**-quam **een**-voh-koh
Ancient Greek Translation	Ἀνακαλῶ Ὕδωρ
Ancient Greek Pronunciation	Ana-**kalo hyoo**-dawr
Gaelic Translation	Tha mi a' gairm air an uisge
Gaelic Pronunciation	Hah mee **gehv**-em ehv em **noosh**-ked
Runic Formula	Laguz Fehu Othala ᛚ ᚠ ᛟ
Rune Pronunciation	Lah-gooz Feh-hoo Oh-thah-lah

QUARTER CHANT OF EARTH: I Call Upon Earth

Latin Translation	Terram Invoco
Latin Pronunciation	**Teh**-rrahm **een**-voh-koh
Ancient Greek Translation	Ἀνακαλῶ Γῆν
Ancient Greek Pronunciation	Ana-**kalo** geyn
Gaelic Translation	Tha mi a' gairm air an ùir
Gaelic Pronunciation	Hah mee **gehv**-em ehv em mooth
Runic Formula	Berkano Fehu Othala ᛒ ᚠ ᛟ
Rune Pronunciation	Bair-ka-noh Feh-hoo Oh-thah-lah

The Circle

The ritual of Casting the Circle augments and enhances the standard protective barrier created during the Preliminary techniques. This ritual typically makes use of materiae magicae and magickal tools. These tools and materiae are used to create an energetically potent border surrounding the perimeter of the magickal space. The substances and energies used to create this border serve to purify, protect, bring power to, and alter the magickal space. The protective barrier formed during the Preliminary Techniques is extended to meet this boundary. This sphere of protective energy merges into the circle forming a comprehensive border encompassing the magickal space. The ritual of Casting the Circle creates a sacred space in which to perform the art of magick. Inside the circle / protective barrier, the magus is free of energies or entities that would interfere with the working. The space within the circle also serves to contain and intensify the energies accessed during the magickal working. During the Energy Summoning step of the Preliminary Techniques, the magus establishes a connection to a potent external energy source. This creates a powerful flow of energy through the magus and into the magickal space. It is within this sacred border that the magus creates an environment that is energetically conducive to the magickal goal. This barrier separates the magickal space from the mundane world creating within it a place of deep stillness and profound power. The circle should be just large enough to contain the area of working. In practice this may range from a small circle that surrounds the magus to a large circle that contains a group. The circle is typically cast moving in a clockwise direction around the magickal space. The circle chant is powerfully droned during each step of circle casting. The chant is slowly repeated, drawing out each syllable. There are various ways to cast a circle. The following ritual is specific to Vercanus Magick. The steps presented may be used in sequence, alone, or in part as needed to suit the personal style of the magus.

If practical, the boundaries of the circle may be permanently demarcated upon the floor of the magickal space. The graphic depiction of the circle typically consists of one to three concentric rings, each slightly larger than the next, forming a set of outer bands. Magickal symbols and words of power are painted within these bands. The paints used are mixed with materiae magicae to increase the potency of the circle.

Prepare for the Working

Place all items needed for the working within the magickal space. Once the circle is cast, it is not good practice to step outside the boundary.

Light a candle to be used for illumination until the percipient candles are placed and lit. This candle may also be used to light all subsequent candles.

Light the coals in the censer.
Play music appropriate to the magickal working.

Cast the Circle

Place Percipient Candles at the Four Quarters

Percipient candles greatly enhance the perception of etheric phenomena and entities. Place a percipient candle at the four cardinal points (North, South, East, and West) of the magickal space. Place the candles in such a way as to demark the outer edge of the circle. Walking clockwise, light each candle. A trimmed bamboo skewer, taper candle, or thin wooden dowel should be used to light the candles. Once the percipient candles are lit, all other candles and lights sources should be extinguished. Use candles of stable shape and size. Typically, a half pillar candle is used. Special care should be taken to keep flammable clothing and objects away from candles. Candles may be placed in glass lanterns to prevent the unintended ignition of ritual clothing. (A formula for the creation of percipient candles is listed below in the Materiae Magicae Formulae section of this chapter.)

Pour Salt to Cast the Circle

Pour a thin line of circle salt on the ground to form a border enclosing the magickal space. This salt contains a blend of herbs, oils, and pneuma technikon that exert powerful protective emanations. The use of circle salt may be omitted if it is impractical to the working space. (A formula for the creation of circle salt is listed in the Materiae Magicae Formulae section of this chapter.)

Cast the Circle using a Magickal Tool

Use a magickal tool to cast the circle. The tools most commonly used are the athame, sword, staff, and rod. Casting typically entails projecting energy from the tool while walking the circumference of the circle. This energy may also be projected from the center of the circle as the magus rotates 360 degrees. To begin this process, hold the tool in your dominant hand. Become aware of the Center of Power and the energy stored therein. Feel this center awaken and begin to radiate energy. Use the mind, breath and gestures to direct the energy through the tool and out of the body. When projecting, strongly envision a flaming ring of protective energy forming around the magickal space.

Cast the Circle with Incense
Walk the circumference of the circle while carrying a lit censer of sanctifying incense. This incense consecrates and fortifies the magickal circle. Additionally, the potent vapors expand into the magickal space, imbuing it with power. (A formula for the creation of sanctifying incense is listed below in the Materiae Magicae Formulae section of this chapter.)

Cast the Circle through Aspergation
Cast purifying wash or consecrated water along the circumference of the circle using a sprig of herb or aspergillum. This wash cleanses the magickal space. (A formula for the creation of purifying wash is listed below in the Materiae Magicae Formulae section of this chapter.)

Call the Quarters

The ritual of Calling the Quarters draws the surrounding powers of nature into the magickal space. This potentiates the space, increasing the overall energy present. To perform this ritual, walk to each quarter of the circle in succession. Use gesture, chant or recitation to draw in the surrounding powers of nature at each quarter. Depending on the preference of the magus, this may include energy within regional phenomena such as mountains, oceans, forest, the winds, etc., or the elemental forces of earth, air, water and fire, or a combination of both.

To begin this ritual, walk to the cardinal point that for you is most powerful with the element of Air. Open the arms in a welcoming gesture. Intone the Quarter Chant of Air a single time. A bell or Tibetan singing bowl, gong, or ritual bell may be rung. Use the mind and energy to draw the powers of Air into the circle. Repeat this process for the cardinal points of Fire, Water, and Earth, walking clockwise around the circle.

With the circle cast and the quarters called, the magickal space is purified, protected and filled with power. Through this ritual the magus precisely controls which energies and entities are present within the borders of the magickal space.

Artes Praeviae
Proceed to the Artes Praeviae. When performing the Artes Praeviae a powerful protective barrier is formed. Extend this barrier to meet the perimeter of the circle.

Work the Magick
Proceed to the magickal operation at hand.

Artes Concludendi
After the magickal operation is complete, perform the Closing Techniques. During the Artes Concludendi the protective barrier extended to meet the circle is reabsorbed into the Center of Power.

Dismissing the Quarters and Close the Circle
Walk to the cardinal point that for you most symbolizes the element of Air. Open the arms and bow the head in a gesture of gratitude. A bell or Tibetan singing bowl may be rung. Extinguish the candle at this quarter. Repeat this process for the cardinal points of Earth, Water, and Fire, walking counterclockwise around the circle. If a magickal tool was used to cast the circle, use this tool to reabsorb the protective ring of energy while moving counterclockwise around the circle.

Simple Sigil for Remote Viewing

FOR GENERAL DIVINATION

Brief Description	Materials for this Ritual
This general divination working makes use of a divination practice supplemented by materiae magicae.	Percipient Oil Percipient Incense Percipient Candle Meditative, trance inducing music

Play meditative, trance inducing music.
Light the percipient candle(s).

Anoint the brow, chest, and palms with percipient oil.

Burn percipient incense.

Allow the incense, oil, candle, and music to alter your consciousness.

Use one of the divination practices listed in chapter three.

Sigil of Summoning

TO SUMMON A SPIRIT

Brief Description	Materials for this Ritual	Materials for Circle Casting
The goal of this working is to evoke and interact with a spirit. Etheric Communication is used to call and communicate with the entity. Etheric Perception and materiae magicae are used to perceive the spirit. The spirit is typically evoked outside the circle.	Percipient Incense Percipient Oil Music that is in resonance with the spirit being summoned	Sanctifying Incense Censer Four Percipient Candles A Bell or Singing Bowl Circle Salt Purifying Water Athame, Sword, Staff or Wand

CHANT: Spirit, Come to Me	
Latin Translation	Spiritus, Veni ad Me
Latin Pronunciation	**Spee**-ree-toos, veh-nee ad meh
Ancient Greek Translation	Ὦ Δαίμων ἐλθὲ πρὸς ἐμέ
Ancient Greek Pronunciation	Oh **dahy**-mohn el-**teh** prohs em-**eh**
Gaelic Translation	A spioraid, thig thugam
Gaelic Pronunciation	Eh **spi**-vich heeg **hoo**-gum
Runic Formula	Fehu Raido Mannaz ᚠ ᚱ ᛗ
Rune Pronunciation	Feh-hoo Rahy-dthoh Mawn-ahz

Prepare for the Working
Play music that is in resonance with the spirit being summoned.

Cast the Circle and Call the Quarters
Perform the ritual of Casting the Circle and Calling the Quarters. During the Preliminary Techniques a powerful protective barrier is formed. Extend this barrier to meet the perimeter of the circle. When performing the Artes Praeviae, generate thoughts and emotions to summon the entity. This is typically accomplished by strongly envisioning the entity while silently intoning the summoning chant. Additional information such as the entity's name, form, abode, sigil, or evoking incantation may also be focused upon. Entities are typically summoned to manifest outside the magickal circle. Diagrams such as triangles may be used to demarcate space outside of the circle into which the spirit may be summoned. Such spaces are typically consecrated and reinforced by words of power and materiae magicae, thus providing a purified and contained space within which the spirit may manifest.

Summon the Spirit
Powerfully drone the summoning chant. The chant should be slowly repeated, drawing out each syllable.

Use Etheric Communication to call forth the spirit. Feel the potent pneuma technikon generated during the Preliminary Techniques. Project this powerful flow of thoughts and emotions across the Universal Etheric Field to call the entity. The entity may be summoned from any distance. The call is typically performed with arms held skyward when evoking upperworld spirits, arms held outwards when evoking terrestrial spirits, and arms held downwards when evoking chthonic spirits. Call the spirit by name, if known. The name may be inserted into the summoning chant.

Perceive the Spirit
Anoint the brow, chest, and palms with percipient oil. Burn percipient incense.

Use Etheric Perception to perceive the spirit. The receptive state of Etheric Perception was initiated during the Preliminary Techniques. Attune the centers of mind, visions, emotion and energy to directly perceive the entity as it manifests.

Communicate with the Spirit
Use Etheric Communication to interact with the spirit. This may be done silently or verbally. Communication is typically performed with the hands held at chest level, palms facing the spirit.

Dismiss the Spirit
Use the technique of Etheric Communication to dismiss the spirit. This may be done silently or verbally. The dismissal is typically performed with arms held skyward when dismissing upperworld spirits, arms held outwards when dismissing terrestrial spirits, and arms held downwards when dismissing chthonic spirits. In the rare instance that the spirit refuses to leave or becomes hostile, Magickal Influence or defensive techniques may be used.

Closing Techniques
Perform the Artes Concludendi. Dismiss the quarters and close the circle.

Symbol for Deity

TO INVOKE THE POWER OF A DEITY

Brief Description	Materials for this Ritual	Materials for Circle Casting
This working is used to invoke the power of a deity. Expanded Perception is used to perceive the deity. Offertory and Etheric Communication are used to call the deity. Through a state of resonance, the magus is filled with the power of the deity. Energy Casting is then used to direct the deity's power toward the magickal goal.	Altar Statue and/or Image of the Deity Offertory Incense Material Offertories Music (in resonance with the deity being invoked)	Sanctifying Incense Censer Four Percipient Candles A Bell or Singing Bowl Circle Salt Purifying Water Athame, Sword, Staff or Wand

CHANT: Hail [Deity Name] I Present this Offering	
Latin Translation	Ave [name] hanc Oblationem Praebeo
Latin Pronunciation	**Ah**-veh [*name*], hank oh-blah-tee-**oh**-nehm **prahy**-beh-oh
Ancient Greek Translation	Χαῖρε ... δίδωμι τοῦτο τὸ ἀνάθημα
Ancient Greek Pronunciation	**Kahy**-rey... **dee**-doh-mee **too**-toh toh ana-**tey**-ma
Gaelic Translation for a Female Deity	Fàilte ort Bhan-Dia, tha mi ag ìobairt seo
Gaelic Pronunciation for a Female Deity	Foulch orsh von-**jee**-a hah mee **geel**-bers shoh

Gaelic Translation for a Male Deity	Fàilte ort a Dhia, tha mi ag ìobairt seo
Gaelic Pronunciation for a Male Deity	Foulch orsh a **dee**-a hah mee **geel**-bers shoh
Runic Formula	Gebo Wunjo Fehu ᚷ ᚹ ᚠ
Rune Pronunciation	Geh-boh Woon-yoh Feh-hoo

CHANT: Imbue Me with your Power	
Latin Translation	Infunde mihi Potentiam Tuam
Latin Pronunciation	In-**foon**-deh mee-hee poh-**tehn**-tee-ahm **too**-ahm
Ancient Greek Translation	Πλῆσόν με τῆς σῆς δυνάμεως
Ancient Greek Pronunciation	**Pley**-sohn mey teys sey doo-**nah**-mey-ohs
Gaelic Translation	Cuir do chumhachd air m' fheadh
Gaelic Pronunciation	Koud fuh **hoohk** ehv meeahk
Runic Formula	Ansuz Fehu Manaz ᚨ ᚠ ᛗ
Rune Pronunciation	Ahn-sooz Feh-hoo Mawn-ahz

Prepare Deity Altar

Set up a deity altar in the magickal working space. This typically consists of a small table covered with an altar cloth. Upon this altar place offertories, statues, images, and ritual items relevant to the deity being invoked. A simple altar may consist of offertory incense and wine.

Play music that is in resonance with the deity being invoked.

Cast the Circle and Call the Quarters

Perform the ritual of Casting the Circle and Calling the Quarters. During the Preliminary Techniques a powerful protective barrier is formed. Extend this barrier to meet the perimeter of the circle. When performing the Artes Praeviae, generate thoughts and emotions that are in resonance with those of the deity to be invoked.

Become Aware of the Deity
Use Expanded Perception to become aware of the deity. Shift awareness into the Universal Etheric Field to perceive the deity.

Call Upon the Deity
Burn the offertory incense.

Hold a material offertory in your hands and present it to the deity. The offertory is typically extended skyward when offering to upperworld deities, outwards when offering to terrestrial deities, and downwards when offering to chthonic deities. Intone the offertory chant a single time. Feel the potent pneuma within the offertory radiate out with the call. The offertory is used to draw the consciousness of the deity and initiate resonance. Replace the material offertory on the altar.

Use Etheric Communication to send a call out to the deity. This entails strongly projecting thoughts and emotions through the Universal Etheric Field. The call is typically a formal request of the deity to bestow its power. Continue to drone the invocation chant while calling the deity. Alternately, the call may be accompanied via a spoken recitation. The following format may be used as a general guideline for the spoken invocation.

"Hail mighty (insert deity name)! (Insert epithet of the deity, such as Goddess of Wisdom, or Lord of the Dead.) I ask that you grace me with your power." The invocation may be spoken in the native tongue traditionally used to invoke the deity to enhance the power of the call and the intensity of the resonance. The invocation is typically performed with arms held skywards, outwards or downwards as needed to address the deity.

If the request is granted, the magus and entity enter into a state of resonance. Typically, this resonance is experienced as an overpowering wave of the deity's power, consciousness, and emotion. If this resonance is not felt, the magus should thank the deity and cease the communication. Deities rarely interact with humans with whom they do not resonate.

Resonate With the Deity
Merge into a state of union with the deity. Become completely immersed in the consciousness and power of the deity. Continue to drone the invocation chant

while resonating with the deity.

Become filled with the Deity's Power
Feel the deity's energy flow into you and circulate through the energy channels and centers of your body.

Direct Invoked Energy toward Goal
Use Energy Casting techniques to apply this energy to the magickal goal. This energy may be used to imbue the magus with the traits and powers of the deity. The energy may also be redirected towards a specific magickal goal. Additionally, power may be directed into a talisman or some form of materia magica.

Thank the Deity
Use Etheric Communication to thank the deity. This may be done silently, or accompanied by a formal recitation.

Closing Techniques
Perform the Artes Concludendi. Dismiss the quarters and close the circle.

Symbol for Banish

TO BANISH A HOSTILE SPIRIT

Brief Description	Materials for this Ritual	Materials for Circle Casting
The goal of this working is to banish a hostile spirit. Etheric perception is used to locate the spirit. Energy Casting is then used banish the entity.	Percipient Incense Percipient Oil Music of a powerful, aggressive, or martial tone	Sanctifying Incense Censer Four Percipient Candles A Bell or Singing Bowl Circle Salt Purifying Water Athame, Sword, Staff or Wand

CHANT: Spirit, I Banish Thee	
Latin Translation	Spiritus, Te Expello
Latin Pronunciation	**Spee**-ree-toos, teh ex-**pel**-loh
Ancient Greek Translation	Ὠ δαῖμον, ἐκβάλλω σέ
Ancient Greek Pronunciation	Oh **dahy**-mohn ek-**bahl**-oh seh
Gaelic Translation	A spiorad, tha mi 'gad fhuadachadh
Gaelic Pronunciation	Eh **spi**-vich hah mee gah dood-a-huqu
Runic Formula	Fehu Thurisaz Raido ᚠ ᚦ ᚱ
Rune Pronunciation	Feh-hoo Thoo-ree-sahs Rahy-dthoh

Prepare for the Working

Play music that is of a powerful, aggressive, or martial tone.

Light percipient candles.

Burn percipient incense.

Anoint the brow, chest, and palms with percipient oil.

Perform the Preliminary Techniques

This operation typically requires that the magus be physically mobile when locating the spirit. As such, during the Preliminary Techniques, the protective barrier is initially extended just beyond the material body to merge with the outer layers of the etheric form. Through this merging, the barrier is attached to the body of the magus and moves with it. This protective barrier of pneuma is later extended to merge with the magickal circle after the spirit has been located. When performing the Artes Praeviae, generate thoughts and emotions of a martial nature. Performing the last step in the Preliminary Techniques, continue to draw in external energy while generating cognitive and emotive pneuma. Circulate these energies until the body is filled to the point of overflowing with potent pneuma technikon.

Locate the Spirit

The receptive state of Etheric Perception was initiated during the Preliminary Techniques. Attune the centers of mind, emotion and power to directly perceive the spirit. Scan your surroundings until the spirit is located.

Cast the Circle

Upon locating the spirit, perform the ritual of Casting the Circle. Quickly cast the circle using salt, incense or a magickal tool. The circle is cast in a timely fashion so that the spirit may be immediately engaged. Calling of the Quarters is omitted for this same reason. Cast the circle in such a way that its perimeter stands between you and the spirit. During the Preliminary Techniques a powerful protective barrier was formed around the self. Extend this barrier to meet the perimeter of the circle.

Banish the Spirit

Use the technique of Primary Energy Casting to bombard the spirit with martial pneuma. Continue to bombard the spirit with energy, driving it far away from your local environment. Typically, spirits retreat quickly when under such bombardment. Powerfully drone the banishing chant. Strongly project this chant in a martial tone.

Cease Bombardment

Discontinue bombardment of the spirit once it has been driven far from your local environment.

Etheric Communication (Optional)

As the spirit flees, Etheric Communication may be used to deliver a warning not to return.

Sanctify the Space

After the circle has been closed, burn sanctifying incense and waft it about the area to remove any residual energy left behind by the spirit. Aspergation may also be used to purify the area.

Closing Techniques

Perform the Artes Concludendi. Close the circle.

Sigil of Blessing

FOR BLESSING OR GENERAL PROSPERITY

Brief Description	Suggested Materials	Materials for Circle Casting
This working brings general prosperity and well-being to another person. This is done through use of Expansive Union to draw beneficent phenomena toward the subject. Energy casting is then used to direct various beneficial energies into a material basis for consumption by the subject. This working may also be adapted to bring prosperity to oneself.	Blessing Oil A Goblet of Wine Music of a blissful, meditative tone	Sanctifying Incense Censer Four Percipient Candles A Bell or Singing Bowl Circle Salt Purifying Water Athame, Sword, Staff or Wand

CHANT: Blessing be Upon You	
Latin Translation	Benedictio sit Super Te
Latin Pronunciation	Beh-neh-**deek**-tee-oh seet soo-**per** teh
Ancient Greek Translation	Μακαρισμός σοι
Ancient Greek Pronunciation	Mah-kah-rees-**mohs** soi
Gaelic Translation	Beannachd ort
Gaelic Pronunciation	**Byah**-nahk orsh
Runic Formula	Gebo Wunjo Sowilo ᚷᚹᛋ
Rune Pronunciation	Geh-boh Woon-yoh Soh-wee-loh

CHANT: I Draw Blessings and Good Fortune	
Latin Translation	Traho benedictiones et Bonam Fortunam
Latin Pronunciation	**Tra**-hoh beh-neh-**deek**-tee-oh-nehs et **boh**-nahm for-**too**-nahm
Ancient Greek Translation	Ἕλκω μακαρισμούς καὶ εὐτυχίαν
Ancient Greek Pronunciation	**El**-koh mah-kah-rees-**moos** kahy euh-too-**kee**-an
Gaelic Translation	Tha mi a' tàladh bheannachdan is deagh fhortan
Gaelic Pronunciation	Hah mee **tawl**-a **byah**-nahk-un is **tyorsh**-stan
Runic Formula	Gebo Wunjo Sowilo ᚷᛈᛋ
Rune Pronunciation	Geh-boh Woon-yoh Soh-wee-loh

Play blissful, meditative music.

Cast the Circle and Call the Quarters
Perform the ritual of Casting the Circle and Calling the Quarters. Cast the circle around yourself and the subject. During the Preliminary Techniques a powerful protective barrier is formed. Extend this barrier to meet the perimeter of the circle. When performing the Artes Praeviae, intensely focus upon the desired beneficent effect upon the subject. Hold this focus throughout the working. Typically blessings are bestowed to attract prosperity or induce general happiness and well-being.

Anoint the subject's brow and chest with blessing oil.

Powerfully drone the blessing chant. The chant should be slowly repeated, drawing out each syllable. The chant may be continued throughout the working or used intermittently as needed.

Expansive Union
Stand facing the subject. Use the technique of Expansive Union to expand into a state of union with the region surrounding the subject. Expansion into a local

region, such as a city, is typically sufficient for most workings. The talented magus may however expand further to effect change on a global scale. Typically this is done with the arms extended sideways and palms facing outwards.

Draw Beneficent Phenomena

Use the technique of Expansive Union to draw beneficent phenomena towards the subject.

Become aware of beneficent phenomena surrounding the subject. This typically includes beneficent energy currents, harmonious individuals, and the fortuitous flow of events. Use the expanded mind and energies to draw these phenomena towards the subject. Blessing may also entail shifting these phenomena into configurations that bring good fortune to the subject.

Return the Etheric Body to a Normal State

Condense the etheric body back into the material body. As the etheric body condenses, draw all beneficent phenomena to the subject. Draw the arms from an open position to rest upon the subject's shoulders.

Saturate the Wine with Pneuma

During the Preliminary Techniques the body was filled with beneficent pneuma technikon. During Expansive Union the spirit was unified with various beneficent energies. Feel these energies flowing through your body. Direct this energy through the hands and into the wine. Hold the bottle aloft with both hands while intoning the blessing chant. Use the mind and breath to emit pneuma from the palms and fingertips into the wine. Concentrate and condense this pneuma into the wine. When saturating the wine envision this life force powerfully drawing beneficent phenomena to the subject. Offer the wine to the subject. In consuming these beneficent energies, the subject becomes saturated with the pneuma technikon of the magickal working and is linked to beneficent energies within the surrounding region. (If necessary, a non-alcoholic drink may be substituted for wine.)

Closing Techniques

Perform the Artes Concludendi. Dismiss the quarters and close the circle.

Sigil to Draw Love

TO ATTRACT A LOVER

Brief Description	Suggested Materials	Materials for Circle Casting
This working consists of a three stage magickal campaign designed to recreate the self and attract a lover. This is accomplished by first Recasting the Self using Transformation techniques. Expansive Union is then used to draw potential partners within a large region. Energy Casting is used to condense relevant energies into a material basis that is also used to attract lovers. In the final stage of this campaign, Etheric Communication is used to draw potential partners in the vicinity of the magus. The three stages of this working are performed over a three day period.	Love Oil Percipient Oil Purifying Wash Shallow Bowl Music of a meditative, trance inducing tone for stage 1 Music of a blissful, meditative tone for stage 2	Sanctifying Incense Censer Four Percipient Candles A Bell or Singing Bowl Circle Salt Purifying Water Athame, Sword, Staff or Wand

CHANT: Draw Closer, my Love	
Latin Translation	Accede, mi Amor
Latin Pronunciation	Ah-**keh**-deh, mee ah-**mohr**
Ancient Greek Translation (spoken to a man)	Πέλαζε ἐγγύτερον, ὦ φίλτατε
Ancient Greek Pronunciation (spoken to a man)	Peh-**lah**-dzeh ehn-**goo**-teh-rohn oh **peel**-ta-teh
Ancient Greek Translation (spoken to a woman)	Πέλαζε ἐγγύτερον, ὦ φιλτάτη
Ancient Greek Pronunciation (spoken to a woman)	Peh-**lah**-dzeh ehn-**goo**-teh-rohn oh peel-**ta**-teh
Gaelic Translation	Thig nas teinne orm, a ghaoil
Gaelic Pronunciation	Heegh nuth tjang **or**-um eh ghul
Runic Formula	Nauthiz Gebo Kenaz ᚾ ᚷ ᚲ
Rune Pronunciation	Nou-dtheez Geh-boh Kay-nahz

Stage One - Day One

Play meditative, trance inducing music.

Cast the Circle and Call the Quarters
Perform the ritual of Casting the Circle and Calling the Quarters. During the Preliminary Techniques a powerful protective barrier is formed. Extend this barrier to meet the perimeter of the circle. When performing the Artes Praeviae, generate thoughts and emotions of love and passion.

Recasting of the Self
Anoint the brow, chest and palms with percipient oil.
Follow the steps given in chapter three under Love Magick to recast the self to attract a lover.

Cleanse with Purifying Wash

Pour purifying wash into a shallow dish. Dip the hands into the water. Use a small amount of the water to cleanse the head, neck, chest, and lower abdomen.

Closing Techniques

Perform the Artes Concludendi. Dismiss the quarters and close the circle.

Stage Two - Day Two

Play blissful, meditative music.

Cast the Circle and Call the Quarters

Perform the ritual of Casting the Circle and Calling the Quarters. During the Preliminary Techniques a powerful protective barrier is formed. Extend this barrier to meet the perimeter of the circle. When performing the Artes Praeviae, generate thoughts and emotions of love and passion.

Prepare for the Working

Powerfully drone the love chant while anointing the brow, chest, and lower abdomen with love oil. The chant should be slowly repeated, drawing out each syllable. The chant may be continued throughout the working or used intermittently as needed.

Expansive Union

Follow the steps given in chapter three under Love Magick to attract a lover via Expansive Union. Typically this is done with the arms extended sideways and palms facing outwards.

Return the Etheric Body to a Normal State

Condense the etheric body back into the material body. As the etheric body condenses, draw the potential lovers to you. Draw the arms from an open position to rest upon the chest one palm atop the other.

Saturate the Oil with Pneuma

During the Preliminary Techniques the body was filled with loving, passionate pneuma technikon. During Expansive Union the spirit was unified with the energies of potential lovers. Feel these energies flowing through your body. Direct this energy through the hands and into the oil. This creates an oil that is powerfully linked to lovers within the surrounding region and saturated with the pneuma technikon of the magickal working. Hold the bottle aloft with both hands while intoning the love chant. Use the mind and breath to emit pneuma from the palms and fingertips into the oil. Concentrate and condense this pneuma into the oil. When saturating the oil envision this life force powerfully drawing lovers with whom you are in resonance.

Closing Techniques

Perform the Artes Concludendi. Dismiss the quarters and close the circle.

Stage Three - Day 3

Anoint the brow, chest, and lower abdomen with the love oil saturated during the previous stage.

Etheric Communication

Follow the steps given in chapter three under Love Magick to attract a lover via Etheric Communication. Use this communication and the power of the love oil to attract potential lovers while going about your daily life.

Sigil of Protection

FOR PROTECTION

Brief Description	Suggested Materials	Materials for Circle Casting
This working consists of a two stage magickal campaign designed to protect another person from harm. This is done using Energy Casting to create a protective talisman and Expansive Union to perceive and deflect potentially harmful phenomena. The working may also be adapted to protect oneself from harm. The two stages are performed over a two day period.	Protection Oil Protection Incense Music of a powerful, aggressive, or martial tone	Sanctifying Incense Censer Four Percipient Candles A Bell or Singing Bowl Circle Salt Purifying Water Athame, Sword, Staff or Wand

CHANT: Nothing Shall Harm You	
Latin Translation	Nihil Te Laedet
Latin Pronunciation	**Nee**-hil teh **lahy**-det
Ancient Greek Translation	Οὐδέν σε βλάψει
Ancient Greek Pronunciation	Oo-**den** seh **blahp**-sey
Gaelic Translation	Cha dèan nì sam bith cron ort
Gaelic Pronunciation	Ha tjin nee sim bee krohn orsh
Runic Formula	Thurisaz Elhaz Hagalaz ᚦᚣ ᚾ
Rune Pronunciation	Thoo-ree-sahs Eyl-hahz Hah-gah-lahz

CHANT: Nothing Shall Harm Me	
Latin Translation	Nihil Me Laedet
Latin Pronunciation	**Nee**-hil meh **lahy**-det
Ancient Greek Translation	Οὐδέν με βλάψει
Ancient Greek Pronunciation	Oo-**den** meh **blahp**-sey
Gaelic Translation	Cha dèan nì sam bith cron orm
Gaelic Pronunciation	Ha tjin nee sim bee krohn **or**-um
Runic Formula	Thurisaz Elhaz Hagalaz ᚦ ᚣ ᚺ
Rune Pronunciation	Thoo-ree-sahs Eyl-hahz Hah-gah-lahz

Stage One - Day One

Procure or create a small object that is suitable for use as a talisman. Talismanic objects are typically made from gem stones, crystals, wood, roots, metal or clay. The talisman should be small enough to be worn or carried on the body. Talismans intended for protection are typically fashioned into a pendant, ring, bracelet, or charm. Symbols may be carved or painted onto the talisman to increase its power. If the history of the object is unknown, it may be banished to remove unwanted energies. (See chapter three for specific instructions regarding the creation of a talisman.)

Play music that is of a powerful, aggressive, or martial tone.

Cast the Circle and Call the Quarters
Perform the ritual of Casting the Circle and Calling the Quarters. During the Preliminary Techniques a powerful protective barrier is formed. Extend this barrier to meet the perimeter of the circle. When performing the Artes Praeviae, generate thoughts and emotions focused upon protecting the subject. Performing the last step in the Preliminary Techniques, continue to draw in

external energy while generating cognitive and emotive pneuma. Circulate these energies until the body is filled to the point of overflowing with potent pneuma technikon.

Protection Chant
Powerfully drone the protection chant. The chant should be slowly repeated, drawing out each syllable. The chant may be continued throughout the working or used intermittently as needed.

Saturate the Talisman with Pneuma
Use the technique of Primary Energy Casting to saturate the talisman with this pneuma. Hold the talisman with both hands. Use the mind and breath to emit pneuma from the palms and into the talisman. Concentrate and condense this pneuma into the talisman. Continue to pour your thoughts, emotions, and energies into the talisman until it is completely saturated. This pneuma technikon is an extension of the self. When saturating the talisman envision this life force powerfully deflecting harmful phenomena away from the subject.

Anoint and Infuse the Talisman.
Burn protection incense.
Move the talisman through the incense smoke.
Anoint the talisman with protection oil.

Closing Techniques
Perform the Artes Concludendi. During the closing techniques banish only yourself, do not banish the talisman. Dismiss the quarters and close the circle.

Stage Two - Day Two

Play music that is of a powerful, aggressive, or martial tone.

Cast the Circle and Call the Quarters
Perform the ritual of Casting the Circle and Calling the Quarters. During the Preliminary Techniques a powerful protective barrier is formed. Extend this barrier to meet the perimeter of the circle. When performing the Artes Praeviae, generate thoughts and emotions of a defensive, martial nature.

Prepare for the Working
Anoint the subject's brow and chest with protection oil. Intone the banishing chant a single time while anointing the subject.

Burn protection incense.

Expansive Union
Stand facing the subject. Use the technique of Expansive Union to expand into a state of union with the larger region surrounding the subject. Expansion into a local region, such as a city, is typically sufficient for most workings. The experienced magus may however expand further to deflect harmful phenomena on a global scale. Typically this is done with the arms extended sideways and palms facing outwards. (See chapter three for full instructions regarding the Deflection of Harmful Phenomena via Expansive Union.)

Deflect Harmful Phenomena
Use the technique of Expansive Union to deflect harmful phenomena away from the subject. Become aware of all potentially harmful phenomena surrounding the subject. This typically includes malign energy currents, harmful individuals, and the inertial flow of potentially harmful events. Use the expanded mind and energies to deflect these phenomena away from the subject. Protection may also entail shifting these phenomena into configurations that prevent harm from occurring.

Return the Etheric Body to a Normal State
Condense the etheric body back into the material body. As the etheric body condenses, draw the arms from an open position into a closed position with the hands at the Center of Power one palm atop the other.

Shielding
Use the defense practice of Shielding to create a protective shield around the subject. Powerfully drone the protection chant. The chant should be slowly repeated, drawing out each syllable. The chant may be continued throughout the remainder of the working or used intermittently as needed. Feel the pneuma generated in the Preliminary Techniques flowing through your body. Use the mind and breath to expand a powerful sphere of this pneuma out from the palms

to encompass the outer layers of the subject's etheric form. (See chapter three for full instructions regarding the creation of a defensive shield.)

Place the Protection Talisman Upon the Subject

Closing Techniques

Perform the Artes Concludendi. During the closing techniques banish only yourself, do not banish the subject or the talisman. Dismiss the quarters and close the circle.

Simple Funerary Sigil

FUNERARY RITE

Brief Description	Suggested Materials	Materials for Circle Casting
In this two stage working, recitation and group Energy Casting are used to aid the deceased in transitioning to the next phase of existence. The first stage involves direct communication with the dying or deceased, the second is a group ritual and forum for mourning.	Percipient Oil Music selected by the friends and family of the deceased	Sanctifying Incense Censer Four Percipient Candles A Bell or Singing Bowl Circle Salt Purifying Water Athame, Sword, Staff or Wand

CHANT: Your Spirit is Free

Latin Translation	Spiritus Tuus Liber est
Latin Pronunciation	**Spee**-ree-toos too-oos **lee**-behr ehst
Ancient Greek Translation	Ἡ σὴ ψυχὴ ἐστὶν ἐλευθέρα
Ancient Greek Pronunciation	Hey sey psoo-**kay** es-**teen** el-oh-**tehr**-ah
Gaelic Translation	Tha do spiorad saor
Gaelic Pronunciation	Ha duh **spi**-did souhd
Runic Formula	Mannaz Raidho Eihwaz ᛗ ᚱ ᛃ
Rune Pronunciation	Mawn-ahz Rahyd-oh Eye-wahz

It is important to determine the afterlife preferences and expectations of the deceased. Ideally, friends and loved ones would have learned of these preferences prior to death. If the deceased's wishes are in question, the magus should obtain this information via etheric communication with the spirit of the deceased. Commonly selected afterlife paths include reincarnation, remaining a disembodied spirit, entering a blissful etheric environment or that of a specific deity, or expanding into union with the cosmos at large. (Review the section "Work of the Psychopomp" in chapter three.)

Prepare for the Working
Play music that is in resonance with the spirit being summoned.

Give the attendees a brief overview of the working.

Seat the Attendees
If possible, seat the attendees in a circle or semi-circle around the deceased or memorial.

Call the Spirit
Perform the ritual to Summon a Spirit listed earlier in this section. The Preliminary Techniques are performed from a location at the center of the magickal circle. Cast the circle large enough to include all attendees present. Intone the summoning chant upon calling the spirit. The spirit is summoned to manifest within the circle, typically at the location of the memorial. Inform the attendees when the spirit has arrived.

Communicate with the Spirit
Use Etheric Communication to interact with the spirit. Communicate your intention to assist in the transition to the next phase of existence. Confirm the spirit's afterlife preference firsthand. This communication may be performed verbally or silently.

Eulogy
The Eulogy may be performed by the magus alone or by a group of selected friends and family.

Joining of Participants

Invite the participants to encircle the deceased or memorial. The participants are a select group of family members and friends who will actively participate in the ritual. The magus remains near the deceased/memorial and all non-participant attendees remain in the audience.

Anointing of Attendees

Anoint the attendees with percipient oil. First anoint the brows of the participants, then move through the attendees, offering to anoint the brows of all attendees. Lastly, anoint the self at the brow. Upon anointing, inform each attendee of the percipient oil's effect.

Recitation (Example):

"May this oil open your perception."

Recitation (Example):

"John Smith, your loved ones, friends and family have gathered around you to assist in your transition to the next stage of existence. Your physical body can no longer hold you. The time has come for your spirit to be free, free from the limitations of material existence, free from the boundaries of the physical world, free to stay or go as you please. Feel the energy of this group strengthen you. May this gift help you on your journey into your new path."

Direct Energy into the Spirit of the Deceased

Signal the participants to begin directing energy towards the spirit of the deceased. This is typically done through gestures. The participants focus upon their thoughts and feelings for the deceased. This generates an abundance of affectionate energy which may be directed through the extended hands to the spirit.

Offerings

The participant to the right of the magus approaches the body of the deceased or memorial, then lays down a personal offering or gives a brief recitation. That participant then continues clockwise around the deceased or memorial to exit into the audience.

Each subsequent participant follows suit.

Once all of the participants have exited, gesture to the attendees to approach the deceased or memorial.

The attendees may then approach the deceased or memorial, one by one, with personal offerings.

Recitation (Example):
> *"We will now assist John's spirit to embark upon a new path. The path John has chosen is…(see examples below). Please direct your thoughts and energies with us as I escort the spirit of John Smith to his new path."*
> *"We know that John wishes to join Odhin in death. I will now escort him to the spirit realm of his deity."*
> *"We know that John wishes to incarnate into material existence. I will now guide his spirit towards an auspicious reincarnation."*
> *"We know that John wishes to remain among us as a spirit. I will now guide him to remain a vital part of our lives."*

Guide the Spirit
Guide the spirit to its desired afterlife path. Use Spirit Projection and Etheric Communication to guide the deceased to the desired etheric environment or describe the process of Conscious Reincarnation and locating resonant conception points. Such guidance may also entail helping the spirit stay present with loved ones by communicating with them via dreams and the semiconscious mind.

Various Ritual Elements
At this point, music may be played, incense burned, poetry recited or any other ritual elements requested by the family or deceased may be incorporated.

Closing Techniques
The magus performs the Artes Concludendi. Dismiss the quarters and close the circle.

Symbol for Magick

SEX MAGICK

Brief Description	Suggested Materials	Materials for Circle Casting
In this ritual, the magickal goal is achieved through saturation of an entire region with pneuma technikon. This saturation shifts all phenomena within the area into alignment with the goal. This is accomplished by using the sex act to generate energy. Energy Casting is then used to saturate the area at the moment of orgasm. (See chapter three for full instructions regarding Sex Magick.)	Love Oil, both Male and Female Sensual, trance inducing music	Sanctifying Incense Censer Four Percipient Candles A Bell or Singing Bowl Circle Salt Purifying Water Athame, Sword, Staff or Wand

Prepare for the Working
Play sensual, trance inducing music.

Cast the Circle and Call the Quarters
Perform the ritual of Casting the Circle and Calling the Quarters.

Center, Banish, and Expand Protective Barrier
Center, banish, and expand a sphere of protective energy to encompass the entire magickal space. Each partner should center and banish individually. It is only necessary for one partner to create a barrier. Extend this barrier to meet

the perimeter of the circle.

Anoint Partner

Anoint your partner with love oil. The male anoints the female with female love oil and vice versa. Typically the oils are applied to the forehead, throat, chest, solar plexus, abdomen just below the navel and wrist. Female love oil contains materiae magicae of a feminine, erotic nature. The same is true of male love oil. During sex, these two oils blend, creating potent, sexually charged energies. In same sex couples, partners should select the oil of the gender with which they identify. If same gender oils are blended, the result is an intensification of the power of that particular gender. The power of sex magick is not affected by sexual preference.

Begin Sex

Initiate the sex act.

Circulate with Partner

Become aware of the Center of Power and the energy stored therein. Use the mind and breath to circulate and intensify the energy stored within this center. Move energy from the Center of Power down to the Sex Center. Use the mind and breath to emit energy from the Sex Center into your partner. Draw your partner's energy back into your body along with your partner's breath. Circulate this energy through your partner's body and back through your own body.

Generate Cognitive and Emotive Pneuma

Focus upon the magickal goal while maintaining circulation with your partner. Circulate cognitive, emotive, and raw sexual pneuma until both partners are inflamed with potent pneuma technikon.

Saturate the Area

At the moment of orgasm, each partner explosively expands this pneuma from the Sex Center. Allow the force of orgasm to expand a radial pulse of pneuma technikon outward from the Sex Center to encompass the entire area of enchantment. The area may include immediate surroundings or an entire geographic region.

Banishing

Beginning at the Center of Power, use the mind, breath, and energy to remove unwanted thoughts, emotions, and energies from the body. Upon inhale, circulate energy within this center. Upon exhale, radiate energy out from the center. Use this energy to push unwanted elements out of and away from the body. Raise internal energy from the Center of Power up the dorsal channel and repeat this process of purification for all of the etheric centers. Once all centers have been purified, move energy from the Center of Mind down the ventral channel back to the Center of Power. Circulate purified undifferentiated internal energy up the dorsal channel and down the ventral channel for one to two rounds, returning it to the Center of Power.

Dismiss the quarters and close the circle.

Symbol for Bless

TO BLESS VIA IMPROMPTU CASTING

Brief Description	
This working is used to quickly bless a subject encountered in daily life. The magus uses the mental and emotive reaction to the situation at hand to produce harmonious, beneficent pneuma technikon. The subject is then saturated with this pneuma using Impromptu Casting, gesture and chant.	
CHANT: Blessing be Upon You	
Latin Translation	Benedictio sit Super Te
Latin Pronunciation	Beh-neh-**deek**-tee-oh seet **soo**-per teh
Ancient Greek Translation	Μακαρισμός σοι
Ancient Greek Pronunciation	Mah-kah-rees-**mohs** soi
Gaelic Translation	Beannachd ort
Gaelic Pronunciation	**Byah**-nahk orsh
Runic Formula	Gebo Wunjo Sowilo ᚷᛈᛋ
Rune Pronunciation	Geh-boh Woon-yoh Soh-wee-loh

Powerfully drone the blessing chant. The chant may be continued throughout the working or used intermittently as needed.

Use the technique of Impromptu Casting to quickly generate beneficent pneuma technikon. When generating pneuma, intensely focus upon drawing beneficent phenomena to the subject. Such phenomena typically include beneficent energy currents, harmonious individuals, and the fortuitous flow of events.

Use the mind, breath, and gesture to project this pneuma into the subject. Feel the power of the chant intensify this projection. Typically the gesture entails extending one or both arms in a fluid movement. The arms are extended towards the subject, palms facing outward.

Saturate the subject with pneuma. Use the mind and breath to concentrate and condense pneuma into the subject. Continue to pour your thoughts, emotions, and energies into the subject until it is completely saturated. This pneuma technikon is an extension of the self. When saturating, envision this life force powerfully drawing beneficent phenomena to the subject.

This technique may be performed with minimal gestures and whispered or internalized chants if discretion is preferred.

Symbol for Protect

TO PROTECT VIA IMPROMPTU CASTING

Brief Description

This working is used to quickly protect a person encountered in daily life. The magus uses the mental and emotive reaction to the situation at hand to produce protective pneuma technikon. The subject is then saturated with this pneuma using Impromptu Casting, gesture and chant.

CHANT: Nothing Shall Harm You	
Latin Translation	Nihil Te Leadet
Latin Pronunciation	**Nee**-hil teh **lahy**-det
Ancient Greek Translation	Οὐδέν σε βλάψει
Ancient Greek Pronunciation	Oo-**den** seh **blahp**-sey
Gaelic Translation	Cha dèan nì sam bith cron ort
Gaelic Pronunciation	Ha tjin nee sim bee krohn orsh
Runic Formula	Elhaz Tiwaz Thurisaz ᛉ ᛏ ᚦ
Rune Pronunciation	Eyl-hahz Tee-wahz Thoo-ree-sahs

Powerfully drone the protection chant. The chant may be continued throughout the working or used intermittently as needed.

Use the technique of Impromptu Casting to quickly generate protective pneuma technikon. When generating pneuma, intensely focus upon deflecting harmful phenomena away from the subject. Such phenomena typically include malign energy currents, harmful individuals, and the inertial flow of potentially harmful events.

Use the mind, breath, and gesture to project this pneuma into the subject. Feel the power of the chant intensify this projection. Typically the gesture entails extending one or both arms in a fluid movement. The arms are extended towards the subject, palms facing outward.

Saturate the subject with pneuma. Use the mind and breath to concentrate and condense pneuma into the subject. Continue to pour your thoughts, emotions, and energies into the subject until it is completely saturated. This pneuma technikon is an extension of the self. When saturating, envision this life force powerfully deflecting harmful phenomena away from the subject.

This technique may be performed with minimal gestures and whispered or internalized chants if discretion is preferred.

Simple Sigil for Binding

TO BIND VIA IMPROMPTU CASTING

Brief Description
This working is used to dissuade an individual from taking a specific action. The magus uses the mental and emotive reaction to the situation at hand to produce binding pneuma technikon. The subject is then saturated with this pneuma using Impromptu Casting, gesture and chant. This technique is typically used to prevent an individual from harming another in situations that preclude the use of a lengthy technique.

CHANT: I Shall Bind You	
Latin Translation	Te Vinciam
Latin Pronunciation	Teh **veen**-kee-ahm
Ancient Greek Translation	Καταδήσω σέ
Ancient Greek Pronunciation	Kah-tah-**dey**-soh seh
Gaelic Translation	Ceanglaidh mi thu
Gaelic Pronunciation	Kqueel-vee mee-oo
Runic Formula	Fehu Isa Nauthiz ᚠ ᛁ ᚾ
Rune Pronunciation	Feh-hoo Ee-sah Nou-dtheez

Powerfully drone the binding chant. The chant may be continued throughout the working or used intermittently as needed.

Use the technique of Impromptu Casting to quickly generate pneuma technikon. When generating pneuma, intensely focus upon preventing the subject from enacting the specific behavior. This focus typically consists of commanding thoughts and emotions such as "you will not harm x" or "you will treat x well".

Use the mind, breath, and gesture to project this pneuma into the subject . Feel the power of the chant intensify this projection. Typically the gesture entails extending one or both arms in a fluid movement. The arms are extended towards the subject, palms facing outward.

Saturate the subject with pneuma. Use the mind and breath to concentrate and condense pneuma into the subject's etheric centers of Mind, Emotion, and Power.

Continue to pour your thoughts, emotions, and energies into the subject until completely saturated. This pneuma technikon is an extension of the self. When saturating, envision this life force powerfully binding the subject in accordance with the desired behavior.

This technique may be performed with minimal gestures and whispered or internalized chants if discretion is preferred.

Mandrake

MATERIAE MAGICAE FORMULAE

PERCIPIENT OIL - *Oleum Percipiens*

Brief Description	
Percipient oil facilitates etheric perception by inducing the expanding of the etheric centers. It contains a blend of trance inducing herbs, essential oils and pneuma technikon.	
CHANT: Awaken and Perceive	
Latin Translation	Expergiscere et Percipe
Latin Pronunciation	Ex-per-**gee**-sheh-reh et **per**-kee-peh
Ancient Greek Translation	Ἐγείρου καὶ αἰσθάνου
Ancient Greek Pronunciation	Eh-geh-**ee**-roo kahy **ayhs**-kah-noo
Gaelic Translation	Dùisg is amhairc
Gaelic Pronunciation	Doosh-kis **ah**-vehk
Runic Formula	Ansuz Kenaz Mannaz ᚠ ᚲ ᛗ
Rune Pronunciation	Ahn-sooz Kay-nahz Mawn-ahz

Instructions: Use the Creation of a Magickal Oil technique delineated in chapter three. During the Preliminary Techniques, generate thoughts and emotions of a receptive, clairvoyant nature. Use the mind and breath to concentrate and condense this pneuma into the oil. Continue to pour your thoughts, emotions, and energies into the oil until it is completely saturated. This pneuma technikon is an extension of the self. When saturating the oil strongly envision this life force causing the etheric centers to awaken and expand, facilitating perception of etheric reality. The ritual chants provided may be droned during the generation of pneuma and the saturation of the incense.

Formula:

Essential oils: Sandalwood (*Santalum album / Santalum spicatum*), Myrrh (*Commiphora myrrha*), Frankincense (*Boswellia*), Cedar (*Cedrus atlantica*).

MATERIAE MAGICAE FORMULAE

PERCIPIENT OIL - *Oleum Percipiens*

Brief Description	
Percipient oil facilitates etheric perception by inducing the expanding of the etheric centers. It contains a blend of trance inducing herbs, essential oils and pneuma technikon.	
CHANT: Awaken and Perceive	
Latin Translation	Expergiscere et Percipe
Latin Pronunciation	Ex-per-**gee**-sheh-reh et **per**-kee-peh
Ancient Greek Translation	Ἐγείρου καὶ αἰσθάνου
Ancient Greek Pronunciation	Eh-geh-**ee**-roo kahy **ayhs**-kah-noo
Gaelic Translation	Dùisg is amhairc
Gaelic Pronunciation	Doosh-kis **ah**-vehk
Runic Formula	Ansuz Kenaz Mannaz ᚠ ᚲ ᛗ
Rune Pronunciation	Ahn-sooz Kay-nahz Mawn-ahz

Instructions: Use the Creation of a Magickal Oil technique delineated in chapter three. During the Preliminary Techniques, generate thoughts and emotions of a receptive, clairvoyant nature. Use the mind and breath to concentrate and condense this pneuma into the oil. Continue to pour your thoughts, emotions, and energies into the oil until it is completely saturated. This pneuma technikon is an extension of the self. When saturating the oil strongly envision this life force causing the etheric centers to awaken and expand, facilitating perception of etheric reality. The ritual chants provided may be droned during the generation of pneuma and the saturation of the incense.

Formula:

Essential oils: Sandalwood (*Santalum album / Santalum spicatum*), Myrrh (*Commiphora myrrha*), Frankincense (*Boswellia*), Cedar (*Cedrus atlantica*).

Ratio: Equal parts Sandalwood and Myrrh, with a lesser amount of Cedar and Frankincense.

Dried herbs: Mugwort (*Artemisia vulgaris*), Wormwood (*Artemisia absinthium*), Gotu Kola (*Centella asiatica*), Cinquefoil (*Potentilla*), Bay Laurel (*Laurus nobilis*)*, Frankincense tears (*Boswellia*).

Ratio: Mix dried herbs in equal amounts. Use only enough to fill the lower quarter of the bottle.

Powdered plant materiae should be avoided as these will create an oil with a muddy texture. Cut leaf, and resin pieces should be used.

* Bay Laurel is typically labeled as Bay Leaf.

PERCIPIENT INCENSE - *Tus Percipiens*

Brief Description	
Percipient incense facilitates etheric perception by inducing the expanding of the etheric centers. It contains a blend of trance inducing herbs and pneuma technikon.	
CHANT: Awaken and Perceive	
Latin Translation	Expergiscere et Percipe
Latin Pronunciation	Ex-per-**gee**-sheh-reh et **per**-kee-peh
Ancient Greek Translation	Ἐγείρου καὶ αἰσθάνου
Ancient Greek Pronunciation	Eh-geh-**ee**-roo kahy **ayhs**-kah-noo
Gaelic Translation	Dùisg is amhairc
Gaelic Pronunciation	Doosh-kis **ah**-vehk
Runic Formula	Ansuz Kenaz Mannaz ᚠ ᚲ ᛗ
Rune Pronunciation	Ahn-sooz Kay-nahz Mawn-ahz

Instructions: Use the Creation of a Magickal Incense technique delineated in chapter three. During the Preliminary Techniques, generate thoughts and emotions of a receptive, clairvoyant nature. Use the mind and breath to concentrate and condense this pneuma into the incense. Continue to pour your thoughts, emotions, and energies into the incense until it is completely saturated. This pneuma technikon is an extension of the self. When saturating the incense strongly envision this life force causing the etheric centers to awaken and expand, facilitating perception of etheric reality. The ritual chants provided may be droned during the generation of pneuma and the saturation of the incense.

Formula:

High Grade Frankincense (*Boswellia*), White Sandalwood (*Santalum album / Santalum spicatum*), Mugwort (*Artemisia vulgaris*), Bay Laurel (*Laurus nobilis*)*.

Ratio: Seventy percent Frankincense, thirty percent Sandalwood, a pinch of Mugwort and Bay Laurel (Mugwort and Bay are potent somewhat toxic herbs, only a small amount is needed to be effective).

* Bay Laurel may be purchased in the spice section of any market. It is typically labeled as Bay Leaf.

PERCIPIENT CANDLE - *Candela Percipiens*

Brief Description

The percipient candle illuminates etheric phenomena. This candle is created using substances that possess particularly powerful etheric emanations. To this is added pneuma technikon crafted to intensify the emanations of surrounding etheric phenomena. The magickal flame produced by this candle radiates potent energies that greatly intensify the emanations of surrounding etheric phenomena rendering them more perceptible to the magus or clairvoyant.

CHANT: Illuminate the Unseen	
Latin Translation	Illumina Invisibilia
Latin Pronunciation	Ee-**loo**-mee-nah een-vee-see-**bee**-lee-ah
Ancient Greek Translation	Φώτιζε τὸ ἀφανές
Ancient Greek Pronunciation	**Poh**-ti-dzeh toh ah-pah-**ness**
Gaelic Translation	Soillsich an rud nach fhaicear
Gaelic Pronunciation	Seh-**yeesh**-ee eh rood nah hahy-skyehd
Runic Formula	Kenaz Ansuz Dagaz ᚲ ᚨ ᛞ
Rune Pronunciation	Kay-nahz Ahn-sooz Dah-gahz

A percipient candle enhances the visual perception of etheric phenomena. The emanations from this magickal flame serve to illuminate etheric phenomena much in the same way that visible light serves to illuminate material phenomena, the effect however is much more subtle. The candle is comprised of a blend of materiae magicae that possess particularly powerful etheric emanations. To this is added a large amount of pneuma technikon crafted to intensify the emanations of surrounding etheric phenomena. Such a candle produces a magickal flame that powerfully radiates energy along with candle light. This magickal tool is a potent energy source that intensifies the emanations of surrounding etheric phenomena, rendering them more perceptible to the Magus. Additionally, the candle contains substances that expand the etheric centers, inducing etheric perception.

Instructions: Use the Creation of a Magickal Candle technique delineated in chapter three. During the Preliminary Techniques, summon powerful external energy. Strongly envision this pneuma illuminating and intensifying the emanations of surrounding phenomena. Use the mind and breath to concentrate and condense this pneuma technikon into the candle. This pneuma technikon is an extension of the self. When saturating the candle, strongly envision this pneuma radiating out with the candle light to powerfully intensify the emanations of surrounding etheric phenomena. To be effective, the percipient candle must be saturated with a large amount of pneuma. Continue to pour pneuma into the candle until it is completely saturated. The ritual chants provided may be droned during the generation of pneuma and the saturation of the candle. Emotive pneuma is not produced during the creation of this candle. As such, the step of emotive generation is omitted during the Preliminary Techniques.

A percipient candle is typically shades of ivory or light tan.

Formula:
Essential oils: Sandalwood (*Santalum album / Santalum spicatum*), Myrrh (*Commiphora myrrha*), Frankincense (*Boswellia*), Cedar (*Cedrus atlantica*).

Ratio: Equal parts Sandalwood and Myrrh, with a lesser amount of Cedar and Frankincense.

Dried herbs: Mugwort (*Artemisia vulgaris*), Wormwood (*Artemisia absinthium*), Gotu Kola (*Centella asiatica*), Vervain (*Verbena officinalis*), Cinquefoil (*Potentilla*).

Ratio: Mix dried herbs in equal amounts.

SANCTIFYING INCENSE - *Tus Sanctificans*

Brief Description

Sanctifying incense is used to prepare a space for magickal use. It contains herbs, woods, and resins that radiate unusually powerful etheric emanations. These particular substances have been uses for millennia to purify and imbue the magickal space with power. Pneuma technikon is then added to this blend.

CHANT: Purify and Imbue with Power

Latin Translation	Purifica et Infunde Potentiam
Latin Pronunciation	Poo-**ree**-fee-kah et een-**foon**-deh poh-**tehn**-tee-ahm
Ancient Greek Translation	Ἁγνίζε καὶ κράτυνε
Ancient Greek Pronunciation	**Hahg**-nee-dzeh kahy **krah**-toon-eh
Gaelic Translation	Sgùr is thoir comas
Gaelic Pronunciation	Skood is huv **kohm**-ehs
Runic Formula	Ansuz Fehu Uruz ᚨ ᚠ ᚢ
Rune Pronunciation	Ahn-sooz Feh-hoo Oor-rooz

Instructions: Use the Creation of a Magickal Incense technique delineated in chapter three. During the Preliminary Techniques, generate thoughts and emotions of a purifying, sanctifying nature. Use the mind and breath to concentrate and condense this pneuma into the incense. Continue to pour your thoughts, emotions, and energies into the incense until it is completely saturated. This pneuma technikon is an extension of the self. When saturating the incense, strongly envision the pneuma driving away unwanted energies as it fills the space with power. The ritual chants provided may be droned during the generation of pneuma and the saturation of the incense.

Formula:

Dried herbs: High grade Frankincense (*Boswellia*), White Sandalwood (*Santalum album / Santalum spicatum*), White Sage* (*Salvia apiana*), high grade Myrrh (*Commiphora myrrha*).

Ratio: Sixty percent Frankincense, twenty five percent Sandalwood, ten percent White Sage, five percent Myrrh.

*White Sage is typically purchased as a "smudge" sage bundle.

CIRCLE SALT - *Sal Circularis*

Brief Description	
Circle salt is used to purify and strengthen the magickal circle. This salt contains a blend of herbs and essential oils used to greatly enhance the potency of the magickal circle. Pneuma technikon is then added to this blend.	

CHANT: Protect from Harm	
Latin Translation	Protege a Malo
Latin Pronunciation	**Proh**-teh-geh ah **mah**-loh
Ancient Greek Translation	Φύλαττε ἀπὸ βλάβης
Ancient Greek Pronunciation	Phu-**lah**-tah ah-poh **blah**-beys
Gaelic Translation	Dìon bho chron
Gaelic Pronunciation	**Jee**-an voh kquron
Runic Formula	Thurisaz Elhaz Hagalaz ᚦᚤᚾ
Rune Pronunciation	Thoo-ree-sahs Eyl-hahz Hah-gah-lahz

Instructions: Use the Creation of a Magickal Powder technique delineated in chapter three. During the Preliminary Techniques, generate thoughts and emotions of a purifying, defensive nature. Use the mind and breath to concentrate and condense this pneuma into the salt. Continue to pour your thoughts, emotions, and energies into the salt until it is completely saturated. This pneuma technikon is an extension of the self. When saturating the salt, strongly envision this life force powerfully sanctifying the magickal space and deflecting harmful phenomena. The ritual chants provided may be droned during the generation of pneuma and the saturation of the salt.

Formula:

Essential oils: Myrrh (*Commiphora myrrha*), Vetiver Root (*Chrysopogon zizanioides*).

Ratio: Primarily Myrrh with a relatively small amount of Vetiver Root.

Add just enough essential oil to strongly scent the herb and salt blend (using too much oil will result in a muddy powder). When creating circle salt, use only pure essential oils. Using essential oils mixed with a carrier oil will prevent the powder from pouring properly.

Dried herbs: Angelica Root (*Angelica archangelica*), Rue (*Ruta graveolens*), Vervain (*Verbena officinalis*), Solomon's Seal (*Polygonatum multiflorum / biflorum*).

Ratio: Mix dried herbs in equal amounts.

Salt to Herb Ratio: Ninety-five percent salt, five percent dried herbs. Use only coarse salt. This may typically be purchased as Kosher salt or sea salt. Do not grind the salt as this will produce too fine a powder. Grind the herbs in a mortar and pestle prior to mixing with the salt. The herbs should be ground into a coarse powder*. Add the essential oils to the herbs prior to mixing with the salt.

*If the material is too difficult to grind by hand, an electric grinder may be used. Some herbs may also be purchased pre-powdered for convenience. Angelica Root is commonly available in powdered form.

Note: White sand may be substituted for salt if the circle is cast in a location where salt may harm the local environment.

OFFERTORY INCENSE - *Tus Offertorium*

Brief Description	
Offertory incense is presented as a gift to etheric entities. Etheric entities greatly value such offertories, as they nourish and make them powerful. Offertory incense is comprised of materiae naturally rich in pneuma. This materiae is enhanced through the addition of pneuma technikon that is in resonance with the specific entity. A general purpose offertory may be produced by adding pneuma of a blissful, pleasurable nature.	

CHANT: Nourish and Bring Bliss	
Latin Translation	Nutri et Beatifica
Latin Pronunciation	**Noo**-tree et beh-ah-**tee**-fee-kah
Ancient Greek Translation	Τρέφε καὶ μακάριζε
Ancient Greek Pronunciation	Ter-**eh**-teh kayh mahk-ah-**ree**-dzeh
Gaelic Translation	Àraich's thoir sonas
Gaelic Pronunciation	**Aah**-ree his hohr **soh**-nus
Runic Formula	Fehu Uruz Wunjo ᚠ ᚢ ᛈ
Rune Pronunciation	Feh-hoo Oor-rooz Woon-yoh

Instructions: Procure Frankincense, Myrrh, White Sandalwood, and Deer's Tongue. They may be purchased in powdered form or ground into a rough powder. Combine the ingredients according to the ratio listed in the formula. Then follow the steps in chapter three to create a Material Offertory. When creating pneuma for use as an offertory, generate thoughts and emotions in resonance with those of the entity. A general purpose offertory may be produced by generating thoughts, emotions, and energies of bliss and pleasure. The incense is then saturated with this powerful pneuma technikon. The ritual chants provided may be droned during the generation of pneuma and the saturation of the incense.

Formula:

Dried herbs: High grade Frankincense (*Boswellia*), White Sandalwood (*Santalum album / Santalum spicatum*), high grade Myrrh (*Commiphora myrrha*), Deer's Tongue Leaves (*Liatris odoratissima*).

Ratio: Sixty percent Frankincense, twenty five percent Sandalwood, ten percent Myrrh, five percent Deer's Tongue.

PROTECTION INCENSE – *Tus Protogens*

Brief Description	
Protection incense is used to protect a subject or location. It contains an herb and resin blend that exerts powerful defensive emanations. The pneuma technikon added is specifically crafted to deflect harmful phenomena.	

CHANT: Protect from Harm	
Latin Translation	Protege a Malo
Latin Pronunciation	**Proh**-teh-geh ah **mah**-loh
Ancient Greek Translation	Φύλαττε ἀπὸ βλάβης
Ancient Greek Pronunciation	Phu-**lah**-tah ah-poh **blah**-beys
Gaelic Translation	Dìon bho chron
Gaelic Pronunciation	**Jee**-an voh kquron
Runic Formula	Thurisaz Elhaz Hagalaz ᚦ ᛉ ᚺ
Rune Pronunciation	Thoo-ree-sahs Eyl-hahz Hah-gah-lahz

Instructions: Use the Creation of a Magickal Incense technique delineated in chapter three. During the Preliminary Techniques, generate thoughts and emotions of a defensive nature. Use the mind and breath to concentrate and condense this pneuma into the incense. Continue to pour your thoughts, emotions, and energies into the incense until it is completely saturated. This pneuma technikon is an extension of the self. When saturating the incense, strongly envision the pneuma deflecting all harmful phenomena. The ritual chants provided may be droned during the generation of pneuma and the saturation of the incense.

Formula:

Dried herbs: Dragon's Blood (*Daemonorops draco*), White Sage (*Salvia apiana*).

Ratio: Eighty percent Dragon's Blood, twenty percent White Sage.

PROTECTION OIL - *Oleum Protegens*

Brief Description	
Protection oil is used to protect an object or subject. It contains an essential oil, root, herb, and resin blend that exerts powerful defensive emanations. The pneuma technikon added is specifically crafted to deflect harmful phenomena.	

CHANT: Protect from Harm	
Latin Translation	Protege a Malo
Latin Pronunciation	**Proh**-teh-geh ah **mah**-loh
Ancient Greek Translation	Φύλαττε ἀπὸ βλάβης
Ancient Greek Pronunciation	Phu-**lah**-tah ah-poh **blah**-beys
Gaelic Translation	Dìon bho chron
Gaelic Pronunciation	**Jee**-an voh kquron
Runic Formula	Thurisaz Elhaz Hagalaz ᚦ ᛉ ᚺ
Rune Pronunciation	Thoo-ree-sahs Eyl-hahz Hah-gah-lahz

Instructions: Use the Creation of a Magickal Oil technique delineated in chapter three. During the Preliminary Techniques, generate thoughts and emotions of a defensive nature. Use the mind and breath to concentrate and condense this pneuma into the oil. Continue to pour your thoughts, emotions, and energies into the oil until it is completely saturated. This pneuma technikon is an extension of the self. When saturating the oil, strongly envision the pneuma deflecting all harmful phenomena. The ritual chants provided may be droned during the generation of pneuma and the saturation of the oil.

Formula:

Essential oils: Rosemary (*Rosmarinus officinalis*), Cypress (*Cupressus sempervirens*), Myrrh (*Commiphora myrrha*).

Ratio: Primarily Rosemary, with a lesser amount of Cypress, and a relatively small amount of Myrrh.

Dried herbs: Small pieces of Angelica Root (*Angelica archangelica*), Small pieces of Dragon's Blood Resin (*Daemonorops draco*), Vervain (*Verbena officinalis*).

Ratio: Mix roots, resins and dried herbs in equal amounts.

Powdered plant materiae should be avoided as these will create an oil with a muddy texture. Cut root, and resin pieces should be used.

PURIFYING WASH - *Lavatio Purgans*

Brief Description
Purifying wash is used to remove unwanted thoughts, emotions, and energies. It contains a blend of essential oils possessing cleansing and purifying properties. The pneuma technikon added is specifically crafted to remove unwanted phenomena.

CHANT: Cleanse and Purify	
Latin Translation	Purga et Purifica
Latin Pronunciation	**Poor**-gah et poo-**ree**-fee-kah
Ancient Greek Translation	Καθαίρε καὶ ἁγνίζε
Ancient Greek Pronunciation	Kah-**tahy**-rey kahy hahg-**nee**-dzeh
Gaelic Translation	Glan is sgùr
Gaelic Pronunciation	Glawn i sgoodh
Runic Formula	Laguz Fehu Uruz ᛚ ᚠ ᚢ
Rune Pronunciation	Lah-gooz Feh-hoo Oor-rooz

Instructions: Use the Creation of a Magickal Wash technique delineated in chapter three. This particular wash does not contain plant materia. The formula is simply a blend of pure essential oils in Vodka. Omit all steps referring to the processing of plant materia. During the Preliminary Techniques, generate thoughts and emotions of a purifying, cleansing nature. Use the mind and breath to concentrate and condense this pneuma into the wash. Continue to pour your thoughts, emotions, and energies into the wash until it is completely saturated. This pneuma technikon is an extension of the self. When saturating the wash, strongly envision the pneuma removing all unwanted thoughts, emotions, and energies. The ritual chants provided may be droned during the generation of pneuma and the saturation of the wash.

Formula:

Essential oils: Bergamot (*Citrus bergamia*), Neroli (*Citrus aurantium*), Lavender (*Lavandula angustifolia*).

Ratio: Equal amounts Bergamot and Neroli with a very small amount of Lavender.

*Use only pure essential oils in this formula. Using essential oils that are mixed with a carrier oil will produce an unpleasant, greasy wash.

BLESSING OIL - *Oleum Benedictionis*

Brief Description Blessing oil is used to bless a subject. It contains a blend of essential oils and roots that are beneficent and harmonious in nature. The pneuma technikon added is specifically crafted to attract beneficent phenomena.	
CHANT: Draw Blessings and Good Fortune	
Latin Translation	Trahe Benedictiones et Bonam Fortunam
Latin Pronunciation	**Tra**-heh beh-neh-**deek**-tee-oh-nehs et **boh**-nahm for-**too**-nahm
Ancient Greek Translation	Ἕλκε μακαρισμούς καὶ εὐτυχίαν
Ancient Greek Pronunciation	**El**-keh mah-kah-rees-**moos** kahy euh-too-**kee**-an
Gaelic Translation	Tàlaidh beannachdan is deagh fhortan
Gaelic Pronunciation	Tawl-lee **byah**-nahk-un is **tyorsh**-stan
Runic Formula	Gebo Wunjo Sowilo ᚷ ᚹ ᛋ
Rune Pronunciation	Geh-boh Woon-yoh Soh-wee-loh

Instructions: Use the Creation of a Magickal Oil technique delineated in chapter three. During the Preliminary Techniques, generate harmonious, beneficent thoughts and emotions. Use the mind and breath to concentrate and condense this pneuma into the oil. Continue to pour your thoughts, emotions, and energies into the oil until it is completely saturated. This pneuma technikon is an extension of the self. When saturating the oil, strongly envision the pneuma attracting beneficent phenomena. The ritual chants provided may be droned during the generation of pneuma and the saturation of the oil.

Formula:
Essential oils: Neroli (*Citrus aurantium*), Sandalwood (*Santalum album / Santalum spicatum*).

Ratio: Primarily Neroli, with a lesser amount of Sandalwood.

Dried herbs: Small pieces of Angelica Root (*Angelica archangelica*), Small pieces of High John The Conqueror Root (*Ipomoea jalapa*).

Ratio: Mix dried roots in equal amounts.
Powdered plant materiae should be avoided as these will create an oil with a muddy texture. Cut root pieces should be used.

LOVE OIL, MALE - *Oleum Amoris Masculini*

Brief Description	
This oil is worn by a man to attract a lover. It contains a blend of essential oils and herbs that emanate loving and passionate energies. The pneuma technikon added is specifically crafted to draw potential partners.	

CHANT: Draw Closer, my Love	
Latin Translation	Accede, mi Amor
Latin Pronunciation	Ah-**keh**-deh, mee ah-**mohr**
Ancient Greek Translation	Πέλαζε ἐγγύτερον, ὦ φιλτάτη
Ancient Greek Pronunciation	Peh-**lah**-dzeh ehn-**goo**-teh-rohn oh peel-**ta**-teh
Gaelic Translation	Thig nas teinne orm, a ghaoil
Gaelic Pronunciation	Heegh nuth tjang **or**-um eh ghul
Runic Formula	Nauthiz Gebo Kenaz ᚾ ᚷ ᚲ
Rune Pronunciation	Nou-dtheez Geh-boh Kay-nahz

Instructions: Use the Creation of a Magickal Oil technique delineated in chapter three. During the Preliminary Techniques, generate thoughts and emotions of love and passion. Use the mind and breath to concentrate and condense this pneuma into the oil. Continue to pour your thoughts, emotions, and energies into the oil until it is completely saturated. This pneuma technikon is an extension of the self. When saturating the oil, strongly envision the pneuma attracting a lover with whom you are in resonance. The ritual chants provided may be droned during the generation of pneuma and the saturation of the oil.

Formula:
Essential oils: Rosewood (*Aniba roseodora*), Sandalwood (*Santalum album / Santalum spicatum*).

Ratio: Equal amounts of Rosewood and Sandalwood.

Dried herbs: Small pieces of High John The Conqueror Root (*Ipomoea jalapa*), Deer's Tongue Leaves (*Liatris odoratissima*), Small pieces of Dragon's Blood Resin (*Daemonorops draco*).
Ratio: Mix dried herbs in equal amounts.

Powdered plant materiae should be avoided as these will create an oil with a muddy texture. Cut leaf, root, and resin pieces should be used.

LOVE OIL, FEMALE - *Oleum Amoris Feminini*

Brief Description

This oil is worn by a woman to attract a lover. It contains a blend of essential oils, herbs that emanate loving and passionate energies. The pneuma technikon added is specifically crafted to draw potential partners.

CHANT: Draw Closer, my Love	
Latin Translation	Accede, mi Amor
Latin Pronunciation	Ah-**keh**-deh, mee ah-**mohr**
Ancient Greek Translation	Πέλαζε ἐγγύτερον, ὦ φίλτατε
Ancient Greek Pronunciation	Peh-**lah**-dzeh ehn-**goo**-teh-rohn oh **peel**-ta-teh
Gaelic Translation	Thig nas teinne orm, a ghaoil
Gaelic Pronunciation	Heegh nuth tjang **or**-um eh ghul
Runic Formula	Nauthiz Gebo Kenaz ᚾ ᚷ ᚲ
Rune Pronunciation	Nou-dtheez Geh-boh Kay-nahz

Instructions: Use the Creation of a Magickal Oil technique delineated in chapter three. During the Preliminary Techniques, generate thoughts and emotions of love and passion. Use the mind and breath to concentrate and condense this pneuma into the oil. Continue to pour your thoughts, emotions, and energies into the oil until it is completely saturated. This pneuma technikon is an extension of the self. When saturating the oil, strongly envision the pneuma attracting a lover with whom you are in resonance. The ritual chants provided may be droned during the generation of pneuma and the saturation of the oil.

Formula:

Essential oils: Neroli (*Citrus aurantium*), Sandalwood (*Santalum album / Santalum spicatum*), Lavender (*Lavandula angustifolia*).

Ratio: Primarily Neroli, with a lesser amount of Sandalwood, and a very small amount of Lavender.

Dried herbs: Lavender(*Lavandula angustifolia*), Rose (*Rosa spp*), Damiana (*Turnera aphrodisiaca*), Small pieces of Dragon's Blood Resin (*Daemonorops draco*).

GRIMOIRE

HEALING OIL - *Oleum Curans*

Brief Description	
Healing oil contains a blend of essential oils and herbs that emanate harmonious, healing energies. The pneuma technikon added is specifically crafted to heal.	

CHANT: Heal and Make Well	
Latin Translation	Cura et Fac Bonum
Latin Pronunciation	**Koo**-rah et fak **boh**-noom
Ancient Greek Translation	Θεράπευε καὶ ἀποσῶσον
Ancient Greek Pronunciation	Tehr-**ah**-pah-wey kahy ahp-oh-**soh**-sohn
Gaelic Translation	Thoir slàinte 's math
Gaelic Pronunciation	Hoh **slaun**-ches mah
Runic Formula	Fehu Uruz Laguz ᚠ ᚢ ᛚ
Rune Pronunciation	Feh-hoo Oor-rooz Lah-gooz

Instructions: Use the Creation of a Magickal Oil technique delineated in chapter three. During the Preliminary Techniques, generate thoughts and emotions of healing and compassion. Use the mind and breath to concentrate and condense this pneuma into the oil. Continue to pour your thoughts, emotions, and energies into the oil until it is completely saturated. This pneuma technikon is an extension of the self. When saturating the oil, strongly envision these healing energies moving into the patient's body to relieve illness, injury, or imbalance. If the oil is created for use with a specific patient, envision the pneuma healing the subject's specific medical issue. The ritual chants provided may be droned during the generation of pneuma and the saturation of the oil.

Formula:

Essential oils: Bergamot (*Citrus bergamia*), Lavender (*Lavandula angustifolia*), Basil (*Ocimum basilicum*).

Ratio: Primarily Bergamot, with a lesser amount of Lavender, and a relatively small amount of Basil.

Dried herbs: Small pieces of Angelica Root (*Angelica archangelica*), Lavender (*Lavandula angustifolia*), Basil (*Ocimum basilicum*).

Ratio: Mix dried herbs in equal amounts.

Powdered plant materiae should be avoided as these will create an oil with a muddy texture. Cut leaf, bud, and root pieces should be used.

Select Bibliography

Agrippa, Henry Cornelius. *Three Books of Occult Philosophy or Magic.* Translated by Willis F. Whitehead. Chicago, IL: Hahn & Whitehead, 1898.

Algra, Keimpe. *The Cambridge History of Hellenistic Philosophy.* Cambridge,Eng.: Cambridge UP, 1999.

Amoss, Pamela. *Coast Salish Spirit Dancing: The Survival of an Ancestral Religion.* Seattle, WA: University of Washington P, 1978.

Anonymous Author. *The Chaldean Oracles.* Translated by Francesco Patrizzi and Thomas Stanley. Leiden, NL: Brill, 1989.

Anonymous Author. *The Grand Grimoire: Being a Source Book of Magical Incidents and Diabolical Pacts.* Edited by Darcy Kuntz. Edmonds, WA: Holmes , 2001.

Anonymous Author. *The Pyramid Texts.* Translated by Samuel A.B. Mercer, New York, NY: Longmans, 1952.

Anonymous Author. *The Saga of the Volsungs.* Translated by Jesse L. Byock. London,Eng. : Penguin, 2000.

Anonymous Author. *The Sagas of Icelanders.* Introduced by Robert Kellogg. London, Eng.: Penguin, 2000.

Anonymous Author. Translated and introduced by Eva Wong. *Harmonizing Yin and Yang: The Dragon-Tiger Classic.* Boston, MA: Shambhala, 1997.

Anonymous Authors. *The Yellow Emperor's Classic Of Medicine: A New Translation of the Neijing Suwen with Commentary.* Translated by Maoshing Ni. Boston, MA: Shambhala, 1995.

Atkinson, William Walker, Clint Marsh, Ed. Swami Panchadasi's *Clairvoyance & Occult Powers.* San Francisco, CA: Red Wheel/Weiser, 2011.

Aurelius, Marcus, Translated by Robin Hard. *Meditations.* Oxford, Eng.: Oxford UP, 2011.

Balikci, Asen. *The Netsilik Eskimo.* 1st ed. Garden City, NY: Natural History P, 1970.

Banerjea, Akshaya Kumar. *Philosophy of Gorakhnath.* [Reprint.] ed. Delhi etc.: Motilal Banarsidass, 1983.

Bardon, Franz, and Gerhard Hanswille. *The Practice of Magical Evocation.* New American ed. Salt Lake City, UT: Merkur, 2001.

Barrett, Francis, and Johannes Trithemius. *The Magus.* London, Eng.: Lackington, Allen & Co., 1801.

Bean, Lowell John. *California Indian Shamanism.* Menlo Park, CA: Ballena P, 1992.

Betz, Hans Dieter. *The Greek Magical Papyri in Translation, Including the Demotic Spells.* Chicago, IL: University of Chicago P, 1986.

Blavatsky, H. P. *Isis Unveiled: A Master-key to the Mysteries of Ancient and Modern Science and Theology.* Pasadena, CA: Theosophical University P, 1976.

Bogoras, Waldemar. *The Chukchee.* New York, NY: Johnson Reprint Corp., 1966.

Brown, Joseph Epes, and Michael F. Steltenkamp. *The Sacred Pipe: Black Elk's Account of the Seven Rites of the Oglala Sioux.* New York, NY: MJF Books, 1996.

Budge, E. A. Wallis. *Egyptian Magic.* New York, NY: Dover, 1971.

Budge, E. A. Wallis. *The Book of the Dead: The Papyrus of Ani in the British Museum.* New York, NY: Dover, 1967.

Budge, E. A. Wallis. *The Liturgy of Funerary Offerings.* London, Eng.: Kegan Paul, 1909.

Burkert, Walter. *Ancient Mystery Cults (Carl Newell Jackson Lectures).* Cambridge, MA.: Harvard University Press, 1989.

Caesar, Julius. *The Conquest of Gaul.* Translated by S. A. Handford. Edited by Jane F. Gardner. London, Eng.: Penguin, 1982.

Chawdhri, L. R. *Practicals of Mantras and Tantras.* New Delhi, Ind.: Sagar, 1990.

Chawdhri, L. R. *Secrets of Yantra, Mantra and Tantra.* New Delhi Ind.: Sterling, 1992.

Chi, Chang Chen. Translated by C. A. MUSES. *Esoteric Teachings of the Tibetan Tantra.* York Beach, ME: Weiser, 1982.

Chungli Ch'uan and Lü Tung-pin. Translated and introduced by Eva Wong. *The Tao of Health, Longevity, and Immortality: The Teachings of Immortals Chung and Lu.* Boston, MA: Shambhala, 2000.

Cleary, Thomas F. *The Secret of the Golden Flower.* San Francisco, CA: Harper, 1991.

Collins, Derek. *Magic In The Ancient Greek World.* Malden, MA: Blackwell, 2008.

Cooper, J. C. Chinese *Alchemy: the Taoist Quest for Immortality.* New York, NY: Sterling, 1984.

Crowley, Aleister, and Israel Regardie. *Magick Without Tears.* Tempe, AZ: New Falcon Publications, 1991.

Crowley, Aleister, Mary Desti, Leila Waddell, and Hymenaeus Beta. *Magick: Liber ABA, Book Four, Parts I-IV.* 2nd rev. ed. York Beach, ME: Weiser, 1997.

Crowley, Aleister. *Eight Lectures On Yoga.* Dallas, TX: Sangreal Foundation, 1939.

Crowley, Aleister. *Magick In Theory And Practice.* New York, NY: Dover, 1976.

Crowley, Aleister. *The Book of the Law.* 100th anniversary ed. York Beach, ME: Weiser, 2004.

Czaplicka, Marie Antoinette. *Shamanism in Siberia.* Whitefish, MT: Kessinger, 2004.

Dawa-Samdup, Lama Kazi. *The Tibetan Book of the Dead; Or, the After-Death Experiences on the Bardo Plane.* Translated by W. Y. Wentz. 3rd ed. London, Eng.: Oxford UP, 1960.

Descartes, Rene, John Cottingham, Robert Stoothoff, and Dugald Murdoch. *The Philosophical Writings of Descartes.* Cambridge, Eng: Cambridge UP, 1984.

Dickie, Matthew W. *Magic and Magicians in the Greco-Roman World.* London, New York, NY: Routledge, 2001.

Eliade, Mircea, and Willard R. Trask. *Shamanism: Archaic Techniques of Ecstasy.* Princeton, NJ: Princeton UP, 1970.

Eliade, Mircea. *Yoga: Immortality And Freedom.* 2009 ed. Princeton, NJ: Princeton UP, 2009.

Elkin, A. P. *Aboriginal Men of High Degree: Initiation and Sorcery in the World's Oldest Tradition.* Rochester, VT: Inner Traditions, 1994.

Elliott, Ralph Warren Victor. *Runes, An Introduction.* Reprint of the ed. Westport, CT. Greenwood , 1981.

Ellis, Peter Berresford. *The Druids.* Grand Rapids, MI: Eerdmans, 1995.

Faraone, Christopher A. *Ancient Greek Love Magic.* Cambridge, MA: Harvard UP, 1999.

Faraone, Christopher A., and Dirk Obbink. *Magika Hiera: Ancient Greek Magic and Religion.* New York, NY: Oxford UP, 1997.

Feuerstein, Georg. *Tantra: The Path of Ecstasy.* Boston, MA: Shambhala, 1998.

Frazer, James George. *The Golden Bough.* New York, NY: Macmillan, 1963.

Gager, John G. *Curse Tablets and Binding Spells from the Ancient World.* New York, NY: Oxford UP, 1992.

Galenus, Claudius. *The Passions and Errors of the Soul.* Translated by Paul W. Harkins. Columbus, OH: Ohio State UP, 1963.

Goswami, Shyam Sundar. *Layayoga.* London, Eng.: Routledge & Kegan Paul, 1980.

Graf, Fritz. *Magic In The Ancient World.* Cambridge, MA: Harvard UP, 1997.

Guthrie, William K. C. *A History Of Greek Philosophy*. Reprint. ed. Cambridge, Eng.: Cambridge UP, 1979.

Gyatso, Geshe Kelsang. *Clear Light of Bliss*. London, Eng.: Tharpa, 1995.

Gyatso, Geshe Kelsang. *Guide to Dakini Land*. London, Eng.: Tharpa, 1991.

Halliday, W. R. *Greek Divination; A Study of its Methods and Principles*. Whitefish, MO: Kessinger, 2003.

Hegel, Georg Wilhelm Friedrich. *Hegel, The Essential Writings*. New York, NY: Harper & Row, 1974.

Hollander, Lee M. *The Poetic Edda*. Austin, TX: University of Texas P, 1928.

Hughes, John. *Self Realization in Kashmir Shaivism the Oral Teachings of Swami Lakshmanjoo*. Albany, NY: SUNY, 1994.

Iamblichos. *Theurgia*. Translated by Alexander Wilder. New York, NY: Metaphysical Publishing, 1911.

Inwood, Brad. *The Cambridge Companion to The Stoics*. Cambridge, Eng.: Cambridge UP, 2003.

Kalweit, Holger. *Dreamtime & Inner Space: the World of the Shaman*. Boston, MA: Shambhala, 1988.

Kalweit, Holger. *Shamans, Healers, and Medicine Men*. Boston, MA: Shambhala, 1992.

Kant, Immanuel, and Ernest Belfort Bax. *Kant's Prolegomena, and Metaphysical Foundations of Natural Science*. 2d ed. London, Eng: Bell, 1891.

Kant, Immanuel, and F. Max Muller. *Immanuel Kant's Critique of Pure Reason*. 2d ed. New York, NY: Macmillan, 1902.

Katz, Richard, Megan Biesele, and Verna Denis. *Healing Makes Our Hearts Happy: Spirituality & Cultural Transformation Among the Kalahari Ju/'Hoansi*. Rochester, VT: Inner Traditions, 1997.

Katz, Richard. *Boiling Energy: Community Healing Among the Kalahari Kung*. Cambridge, MA: Harvard UP, 1982.

King, L. W. *Babylonian Magic and Sorcery: Being "The Prayers of the Lifting of the Hand"*. London, Eng.:Luzac and Co., 1896.

Kingsley, Peter. *Ancient Philosophy, Mystery, and Magic: Empedocles and Pythagorean Tradition*. Oxford, Eng.: Oxford UP, 1996.

Kingsley, Peter. *In the Dark Places of Wisdom*. Inverness, CA: Golden Sufi Center, 1999.

Kluckhohn, Clyde. *Navaho Witchcraft*. Boston, MA: Beacon, 1944.

Kohn, Livia. *The Taoist Experience an Anthology*. Albany,NY: SUNY, 1993.

Kroeber, A. L. *The Religion of the Indians of California*. Berkeley, CA: University of California Publications in American Archaeology and Ethnology, 1907.

Lakshanjoo, Swami. *Kashmir Shaivism: The Secret Supreme*. Culver City, CA: Universal Shaiva Fellowship, 2007.

Lakshmanjoo, Swami. *Shiva Sutras: "The Supreme Awakening": with the Commentary of Kshemaraja*. 2nd ed. Culver City, CA: Universal Shaiva Fellowship, 2007.

Lao-tzu. *Cultivating Stillness: A Taoist Manual for Transforming Body and Mind*. Translated and introduced by Eva Wong. Boston, MA: Shambhala, 1992.

Lawson, J. C. *Modern Greek Folklore And Ancient Greek Religion: A Study in Survivals*. New York NY: University Books, 1964.

Leadbeater, C. W. *Clairvoyance*. Adyar, Madras, Ind.: Theosophical Pub., 1903.

Leadbeater, C. W. *The Chakras*. Wheaton, IL: Theosophical Pub., 1927.

Levi, Eliphas. *Transcendental Magic: Its Doctrine and Ritual (1910)*. Translated by Arthur Edward Waite. Kila, MT: Kessinger, 1942.

Lewis-Williams, J.D. *Ethnographic Evidence Relating to 'Trance' And 'Shamans' Among Northern and Southern Bushmen*. Vlaeberg: South African Archaeological Society, 1992.

Liu Hua-Yang. *Cultivating the Energy of Life*. Translated by Eva Wong. Boston, MA: Shambhala, 1998.

Long, A. A. *Hellenistic Philosophy; Stoics, Epicureans, Sceptics*. New York, NY: Scribner, 1974.

Long, A. A., and D. N. Sedley. *The Hellenistic Philosophers*. Cambridge, Eng: Cambridge University Press, 1987.

Lu Xixing and Li Xiyue. Translated and introduced by Eva Wong. *Three Taoist Classics on Meditation, Breath Regulation, Sexual Yoga, and the Circulation of Internal Energy*. Boston, MA: Shambhala, 2005.

Maloney, Clarence. *The Evil Eye*. New York, NY: Columbia UP, 1976.

Martin, Emily, and Arthur P. Wolf. *Religion and Ritual In Chinese Society*. Stanford, CA: Stanford UP, 1974.

Mathers, S. L. MacGregor, Aleister Crowley, and Hymenaeus Beta. *The Goetia: The Lesser Key Of Solomon the King*. York Beach, ME: Weiser, 1995.

Mathers, S. L. MacGregor. *The Book of the Sacred Magic of Abramelin the Mage*. London, Eng.: John M. Watkins, 1900.

Mathers, S. Liddell MacGregor. *The Key of Solomon the King*. London, Eng.: G. Redway, 1889.

Mirecki, Paul Allan, and Marvin W. Meyer. *Magic and Ritual in the Ancient World*. Leiden, NL: Brill, 2002.

Mooney, James, and Frans M. Olbrechts. *Cherokee Sacred Formulas and Medicinal Prescriptions*. Washington DC: U. S. Govt. Print. Off., 1932.

Naropa. *Tsongkhapa's Six Yogas of Naropa*. Translated by Glenn H. Mullin. Ithaca, NY: Snow Lion, 1996.

Neihardt, John Gneisenau. *Black Elk Speaks: Being the Life Story of a Holy Man of the Oglala Sioux*. Lincoln, NE: University of Nebraska P, 1932.

Nicholson, Shirley J. *Shamanism*. Wheaton, IL: Theosophical Pub., 1987.

Ogden, Daniel. *Magic, Witchcraft, and Ghosts in the Greek and Roman Worlds: a Sourcebook*. New York, NY: Oxford UP, 2002.

Ogden, Daniel. *Night's Black Agents: Witches, Wizards and the Dead in the Ancient World*. London, Eng.: Hambledon Continuum, 2008.

Page, Raymond Ian. *An introduction to English Runes*. 2. ed. London, Eng.: Boydell, 1999.

Patanjali. *Yoga Sutras of Patanjali*. Translated by Mukunda Stiles. 2nd ed. Pune, Ind.: International Academy of Ayurveda, 2001.

Peters, Larry. *Tamang Shamans: An Ethnopsychiatric Study of Ecstasy and Healing in Nepal*. New Delhi, Ind.: Nirala, 1998.

Peterson, Joseph H. *Grimorium Verum: A Handbook of Black Magic*. Scotts Valley, CA: CreateSpace, 2007.

Plotinus. *The Six Enneads*. Translated by Stephen MacKenna, B. S. Page, Chicago, IL: Encyclopedia Britannica, 1952.

Plotkin, Mark J. *Tales Of A Shaman's Apprentice: An Ethnobotanist Searches for New Medicines in the Amazon Rain Forest*. New York, NY: Viking, 1993.

Ramacharaka, Yogi. *A Series of Lessons in Raja Yoga*. Another ed. Pp. 281. London, Eng.: L.N. Fowler, 1917.

Ramacharaka, Yogi. *Fourteen Lessons in Yogi Philosophy and Oriental Occultism*. London, Eng.: L. N. Fowler, 1917.

Ramacharaka, Yogi. *The Science of Psychic Healing*. Chicago,IL: Yogi Publication Society, 1906.

Randolph, Paschal Beverly, and Maria de Naglowska. *Magia Sexualis*. Rochester, VT.: Inner Traditions, 2012.

Regardie, Israel, Cris Monnastre, and Carl Llewellyn Weschcke. T*he Golden Dawn: A Complete Course in Practical Ceremonial Magic: The Original Account of the Teachings, Rites, and Ceremonies of the Hermetic Order of the Golden Dawn (Stella Matutina)*. 6th ed. St. Paul, MN: Llewellyn, 1989.

Russell, Bertrand. *A History of Western Philosophy.* New York, NY: Simon and Schuster, 1972.

Saraswati, Swami Satyananda. *Kundalini Tantra.* 2nd ed. Munder, Bihar: Bihar School of Yoga, 1996.

Sellars, John. *Stoicism.* Berkeley, CA: University of California P, 2006.

Shastri, Mahamahopadhyaya Lakshmana. *Tantraraja Tantra.* Translated by Sir John Woodroffe. Delhi: Motilal Banarsidass, 1981.

Singh, Jaideva. *Pratyabhijnahrdayam: The Secret of Self-Recognition.* Delhi: Motilal Banarsidass, 2008.

Singh, Jaideva. *Siva Sutras: The Yoga of Supreme Identity.* Delhi: Motilal Banarsidass, 1979.

Singh, Jaideva. *Spanda-Karikas: The Divine Creative Pulsation.* Delhi: Motilal Banarsidass, 2001

Singh, Jaideva. *Vijnanabhairava or Divine Consciousness: A Treasury of 112 Types of Yoga.* Reprint. ed. Delhi u.a.: Motilal Banarsidass, 1981.

Sivananda, Swami. *Kundalini Yoga.* 7th ed. Sivanandanagar, UP: Divine Life Society, 1980.

Sivananda, Swami. *Raja Yoga.* Whitefish, MT: Kessinger, 1950.

Smith, Steven R. *Wylundt's Book of Incense.* York Beach, ME: Weiser, 1989.

Spinoza, Benedictus de. *Ethics.* Translated by Edwin Curley. London, Eng.: Penguin, 1996.

Sturluson, Snorri. *King Harald's Saga: Harald Hardradi of Norway: From Snorri Sturluson's Heimskringla.* Translated by Magnus Magnusson and Hermann Palsson. London, Eng.: Penguin, 1976.

Sturluson, Snorri. *Prose Edda Tales from Norse Mythology.* Mineola, NY: Dover, 2012.

Swatmarama. *The Hatha Yoga Pradipika.* Translated by Pancham Sinh. New York, NY: AMS, 1974.

Tacitus, Cornelius. *Germania.* Translated by J. G. C Anderson, Bristol: Bristol Classical Press, 1997.

Trismegistus, Hermes. *Corpus Hermeticum.* Translated by G.R.S. Mead. West Yorkshire: Jeremy Mills, 2007.

Trismegistus, Hermes. *The Emerald Tablet of Hermes.* Translated by Dr. Jane Ma'ati Smith. Whitefish, MT: Kessinger, 2004.

Upanisad-Brahma-Yogin, S'ri. *The Yoga Upanishads.* Translated by T.R. S'rinvasa Ayyangar. Adyar, Madras: The Vasanta Press, 1938.

Vasu, Srisa Chandra. *The Gheranda Samhita.* Delhi: Sri Satguru Pub, 1979.

Vasu, Srisa Chandra. *The Siva Samhita.* 2nd ed. New Delhi: Oriental Books Reprint Corp, 1975.

Waite, Arthur Edward. *The Book of Ceremonial Magic.* Pbk. ed. Maple Shade, NJ: Lethe, 2002.

Walker, Phillip L., and Travis Hudson. *Chumash Healing: Changing Health and Medical Practices in an American Indian Society.* Banning, CA (Morongo Indian Reservation): Malki Museum Press, 1993.

Wang Tao, Chang Po-tuan, Yang Xiong. Translated and introduced by Eva Wong. *Nourishing the Essence of Life: The Outer, Inner, and Secret Teachings of Taoism.* Boston, MA: Shambhala, 2004.

Wangyal, Rinpoche Tenzin, and Mark Dahlby. *Healing with Form, Energy and Light: The Five Elements in Tibetan Shamanism, Tantra, and Dzogchen.* Ithaca, NY: Snow Lion, 2002.

White, David Gordon. *Tantra in Practice.* Princeton, NJ: Princeton UP, 2000.

Wile, Douglas. *Art of the Bedchamber: The Chinese Sexual Yoga Classics Including Women's Solo Meditation Texts.* Albany, NY: SUNY, 1992.

Wojkowitz, Rene de. *Oracles and Demons of Tibet: The Cult and Iconography of the Tibetan Protective Deities.* Kathmandu, Nepal: Book Faith India, 1996.

Wong Eva. *Taoism.* Boston, MA: Shambhala, 1997.

Woodroffe, John George. *Mahanirvana Tantra (Tantra of the Great Liberation)*. Whitefish, MT: Kessinger, 2006.

Woodroffe, John George. *The Serpent Power: The Secrets of Tantric and Shaktic Yoga*. Reproduction ed. New York, NY: Dover, 1974.

Woodroffe, John. *Kularnava Tantra*. Delhi: Motila Banarsidass, 1965.

Yeshe, Lama Thubten. *The Bliss of Inner Fire: Heart Practice of the Six Yogas of Naropa*. Translated by Robina Courtin. Boston, MA: Wisdom Pub, 1998.

Yronwode, Catherine. *Hoodoo Herb and Root Magic: A Materia Magica of African-American Conjure and Traditional Formulary, Giving the Spiritual Uses of Natural Herbs, Roots, Minerals, and Zoological Curios*. Forestville, CA: Lucky Mojo Curio Co., 2002.

Yu Lu K'uan. *Taoist Yoga: Alchemy and Immortality*. San Francisco, CA: Red Wheel/Weiser LLC, 1973.

Znamenski, Andrei A. *Shamanism in Siberia: Russian Records of Indigenous Spirituality*. Dordrecht, NL: Kluwer Academic Pub, 2003.